Lecture Notes in Computer Science 12793

More information about this subseries at http://www.springer.com/series/7409

Robert A. Sottilare · Jessica Schwarz (Eds.)

Adaptive Instructional Systems

Adaptation Strategies and Methods

Third International Conference, AIS 2021
Held as Part of the 23rd HCI International Conference, HCII 2021
Virtual Event, July 24–29, 2021
Proceedings, Part II

 Springer

Editors
Robert A. Sottilare
Soar Technology, Inc.
Orlando, FL, USA

Jessica Schwarz
Fraunhofer FKIE
Wachtberg, Germany

ISSN 0302-9743   ISSN 1611-3349 (electronic)
Lecture Notes in Computer Science
ISBN 978-3-030-77872-9   ISBN 978-3-030-77873-6 (eBook)
https://doi.org/10.1007/978-3-030-77873-6

LNCS Sublibrary: SL3 – Information Systems and Applications, incl. Internet/Web, and HCI

This Springer imprint is published by the registered company Springer Nature Switzerland AG
The registered company address is: Gewerbestrasse 11, 6330 Cham, Switzerland

Foreword

Human-Computer Interaction (HCI) is acquiring an ever-increasing scientific and industrial importance, and having more impact on people's everyday life, as an ever-growing number of human activities are progressively moving from the physical to the digital world. This process, which has been ongoing for some time now, has been dramatically accelerated by the COVID-19 pandemic. The HCI International (HCII) conference series, held yearly, aims to respond to the compelling need to advance the exchange of knowledge and research and development efforts on the human aspects of design and use of computing systems.

The 23rd International Conference on Human-Computer Interaction, HCI International 2021 (HCII 2021), was planned to be held at the Washington Hilton Hotel, Washington DC, USA, during July 24–29, 2021. Due to the COVID-19 pandemic and with everyone's health and safety in mind, HCII 2021 was organized and run as a virtual conference. It incorporated the 21 thematic areas and affiliated conferences listed on the following page.

A total of 5222 individuals from academia, research institutes, industry, and governmental agencies from 81 countries submitted contributions, and 1276 papers and 241 posters were included in the proceedings to appear just before the start of the conference. The contributions thoroughly cover the entire field of HCI, addressing major advances in knowledge and effective use of computers in a variety of application areas. These papers provide academics, researchers, engineers, scientists, practitioners, and students with state-of-the-art information on the most recent advances in HCI. The volumes constituting the set of proceedings to appear before the start of the conference are listed in the following pages.

The HCI International (HCII) conference also offers the option of 'Late Breaking Work' which applies both for papers and posters, and the corresponding volume(s) of the proceedings will appear after the conference. Full papers will be included in the 'HCII 2021 - Late Breaking Papers' volumes of the proceedings to be published in the Springer LNCS series, while 'Poster Extended Abstracts' will be included as short research papers in the 'HCII 2021 - Late Breaking Posters' volumes to be published in the Springer CCIS series.

The present volume contains papers submitted and presented in the context of the 3rd International Conference on Adaptive Instructional Systems (AIS 2021) affiliated conference to HCII 2021. I would like to thank the Co-chairs, Robert A. Sottilare and Jessica Schwarz, for their invaluable contribution in its organization and the preparation of the Proceedings, as well as the members of the program board for their contributions and support. This year, the AIS affiliated conference has focused on topics related to conceptual models and instructional approaches, design, development and evaluation of AIS systems, learner modelling and state assessment, as well as adaptation strategies and methods.

I would also like to thank the Program Board Chairs and the members of the Program Boards of all thematic areas and affiliated conferences for their contribution towards the highest scientific quality and overall success of the HCI International 2021 conference.

This conference would not have been possible without the continuous and unwavering support and advice of Gavriel Salvendy, founder, General Chair Emeritus, and Scientific Advisor. For his outstanding efforts, I would like to express my appreciation to Abbas Moallem, Communications Chair and Editor of HCI International News.

July 2021   Constantine Stephanidis

HCI International 2021 Thematic Areas
and Affiliated Conferences

Thematic Areas

- HCI: Human-Computer Interaction
- HIMI: Human Interface and the Management of Information

Affiliated Conferences

- EPCE: 18th International Conference on Engineering Psychology and Cognitive Ergonomics
- UAHCI: 15th International Conference on Universal Access in Human-Computer Interaction
- VAMR: 13th International Conference on Virtual, Augmented and Mixed Reality
- CCD: 13th International Conference on Cross-Cultural Design
- SCSM: 13th International Conference on Social Computing and Social Media
- AC: 15th International Conference on Augmented Cognition
- DHM: 12th International Conference on Digital Human Modeling and Applications in Health, Safety, Ergonomics and Risk Management
- DUXU: 10th International Conference on Design, User Experience, and Usability
- DAPI: 9th International Conference on Distributed, Ambient and Pervasive Interactions
- HCIBGO: 8th International Conference on HCI in Business, Government and Organizations
- LCT: 8th International Conference on Learning and Collaboration Technologies
- ITAP: 7th International Conference on Human Aspects of IT for the Aged Population
- HCI-CPT: 3rd International Conference on HCI for Cybersecurity, Privacy and Trust
- HCI-Games: 3rd International Conference on HCI in Games
- MobiTAS: 3rd International Conference on HCI in Mobility, Transport and Automotive Systems
- AIS: 3rd International Conference on Adaptive Instructional Systems
- C&C: 9th International Conference on Culture and Computing
- MOBILE: 2nd International Conference on Design, Operation and Evaluation of Mobile Communications
- AI-HCI: 2nd International Conference on Artificial Intelligence in HCI

List of Conference Proceedings Volumes Appearing Before the Conference

1. LNCS 12762, Human-Computer Interaction: Theory, Methods and Tools (Part I), edited by Masaaki Kurosu
2. LNCS 12763, Human-Computer Interaction: Interaction Techniques and Novel Applications (Part II), edited by Masaaki Kurosu
3. LNCS 12764, Human-Computer Interaction: Design and User Experience Case Studies (Part III), edited by Masaaki Kurosu
4. LNCS 12765, Human Interface and the Management of Information: Information Presentation and Visualization (Part I), edited by Sakae Yamamoto and Hirohiko Mori
5. LNCS 12766, Human Interface and the Management of Information: Information-rich and Intelligent Environments (Part II), edited by Sakae Yamamoto and Hirohiko Mori
6. LNAI 12767, Engineering Psychology and Cognitive Ergonomics, edited by Don Harris and Wen-Chin Li
7. LNCS 12768, Universal Access in Human-Computer Interaction: Design Methods and User Experience (Part I), edited by Margherita Antona and Constantine Stephanidis
8. LNCS 12769, Universal Access in Human-Computer Interaction: Access to Media, Learning and Assistive Environments (Part II), edited by Margherita Antona and Constantine Stephanidis
9. LNCS 12770, Virtual, Augmented and Mixed Reality, edited by Jessie Y. C. Chen and Gino Fragomeni
10. LNCS 12771, Cross-Cultural Design: Experience and Product Design Across Cultures (Part I), edited by P. L. Patrick Rau
11. LNCS 12772, Cross-Cultural Design: Applications in Arts, Learning, Well-being, and Social Development (Part II), edited by P. L. Patrick Rau
12. LNCS 12773, Cross-Cultural Design: Applications in Cultural Heritage, Tourism, Autonomous Vehicles, and Intelligent Agents (Part III), edited by P. L. Patrick Rau
13. LNCS 12774, Social Computing and Social Media: Experience Design and Social Network Analysis (Part I), edited by Gabriele Meiselwitz
14. LNCS 12775, Social Computing and Social Media: Applications in Marketing, Learning, and Health (Part II), edited by Gabriele Meiselwitz
15. LNAI 12776, Augmented Cognition, edited by Dylan D. Schmorrow and Cali M. Fidopiastis
16. LNCS 12777, Digital Human Modeling and Applications in Health, Safety, Ergonomics and Risk Management: Human Body, Motion and Behavior (Part I), edited by Vincent G. Duffy
17. LNCS 12778, Digital Human Modeling and Applications in Health, Safety, Ergonomics and Risk Management: AI, Product and Service (Part II), edited by Vincent G. Duffy

http://2021.hci.international/proceedings

3rd International Conference on Adaptive Instructional Systems (AIS 2021)

Program Board Chairs: **Robert A. Sottilare,** *Soar Technology, Inc., USA*, **and Jessica Schwarz,** *Fraunhofer FKIE, Germany*

- Roger Azevedo, USA
- Brenda Bannan, USA
- Avron Barr, USA
- Michelle D. Barrett, USA
- Benjamin Bell, USA
- Shelly Blake-Plock, USA
- Barbara Buck, USA
- Jody Cockroft, USA
- Jeanine Defalco, USA
- Jim Goodell, USA
- Ani Grubisic, Croatia
- Andrew Hampton, USA
- Xiangen Hu, USA
- Cheryl Johnson, USA
- Benny Johnson, USA
- Mercedes T. Rodrigo, Philippines
- Vasile Rus, USA
- Jordan Richard Schoenherr, Canada
- K. P. Thai, USA
- Richard Tong, USA
- Rachel Van Campenhout, USA
- Joost Van Oijen, Netherlands
- Elizabeth Veinott, USA
- Elizabeth Whitaker, USA
- Thomas E. F. Witte, Germany

The full list with the Program Board Chairs and the members of the Program Boards of all thematic areas and affiliated conferences is available online at:

http://www.hci.international/board-members-2021.php

HCI International 2022

The 24th International Conference on Human-Computer Interaction, HCI International 2022, will be held jointly with the affiliated conferences at the Gothia Towers Hotel and Swedish Exhibition & Congress Centre, Gothenburg, Sweden, June 26 – July 1, 2022. It will cover a broad spectrum of themes related to Human-Computer Interaction, including theoretical issues, methods, tools, processes, and case studies in HCI design, as well as novel interaction techniques, interfaces, and applications. The proceedings will be published by Springer. More information will be available on the conference website: http://2022.hci.international/:

General Chair
Prof. Constantine Stephanidis
University of Crete and ICS-FORTH
Heraklion, Crete, Greece
Email: general_chair@hcii2022.org

http://2022.hci.international/

Contents – Part II

Learner Modelling and State Assessment in AIS

Contents – Part I

Evaluation of AIS

Learner Modelling and State Assessment in AIS

Helping Instructor Pilots Detect and Respond to Engagement Lapses in Simulations

Benjamin Bell[1](✉), Winston Wink Bennett[2], Benjamin Nye[3], and Elaine Kelsey[1]

[1] Eduworks Corporation, Corvallis, OR, USA
{benjamin.bell,elaine.kelsey}@eduworks.com
[2] Warfighter Readiness Research Division, Wright Patterson AFB, 711 HPW/RHA,
Wright-Patterson AFB, OH, USA
winston.bennett@us.af.mil
[3] USC Institute for Creative Technologies, Playa Vista, CA, USA
nye@ict.usc.edu

Abstract. Adapting training in real time can be challenging for instructors. Real-time simulation can present rapid sequences of events, making it difficult for an instructor to attribute errors or omissions to specific underling gaps in skills and knowledge. Monitoring multiple students simultaneously imposes additional attentional workload on an instructor. This challenge can be further exacerbated when an instructor's view of the student is obscured by virtual reality (VR) equipment. To support instructors' ability to adapt training, Eduworks and USC's Institute for Creative Technologies are developing machine learning (ML) models that can measure user engagement during training simulations and offer recommendations for restoring lapses in engagement. We have created a system, called the Observational Motivation and Engagement Generalized Appliance (OMEGA), which we tested in the context of a new U.S. Air Force approach to Specialized Undergraduate Pilot Training (SUPT) called Pilot Training Next (PTN). PTN integrates traditional flying sorties with VR-enabled ground-based training devices to achieve training efficiencies, improve readiness, and increase throughput. The virtual environment provides a rich source of raw data that machine learning models can use to associate user activity with user engagement. We created a testbed for data capture to construct the ML models, based on theoretical foundations we developed previously. Our research explores OMEGA's potential to help alert an instructor pilot (IP) to student distraction by flagging attention and engagement lapses. Our hypothesis is that OMEGA could help an IP adapt learning, and potentially manage multiple students at the same time, with alerts of lapsed attention and recommendations for restoring engagement. To test this hypothesis, we ran pilots through multiple PTN scenarios to create data for training the model. In this paper, we report on work to create machine learning models using three different techniques, and present model performance data using standard machine learning metrics. We discuss the modeling approach used to generate instructor recommendations. Future work will present results from a formative evaluation using instructor pilots. These early findings provide preliminary validation for the use of ML models for learning to detect engagement from the rich data sources characteristic of virtual environments. These findings will be applicable across a broad range of conventional and VR training applications.

© Springer Nature Switzerland AG 2021
R. A. Sottilare and J. Schwarz (Eds.): HCII 2021, LNCS 12793, pp. 3–14, 2021.
https://doi.org/10.1007/978-3-030-77873-6_1

Keywords: Adaptive training · Machine learning · Virtual reality

1 Introduction

1.1 Supporting Instructors with Adaptive Learning

Adaptive learning can accelerate skill mastery and retention in intelligent tutoring systems [1]. For training with live instructors, however, adapting training in real time can be challenging. Real-time simulation of tactical scenarios can present rapid sequences of events, making it difficult for an instructor to attribute errors or omissions to specific underling gaps in skills and knowledge. A key factor in adapting training is a learner's level of engagement, which is widely accepted as a critical mediating factor in both learning retention [2] and learning outcomes [3]. Assessing engagement adds to an instructor's challenge because engagement is not a directly measurable attribute. Indirect measures that instructors can use to infer engagement levels can be complicated when an instructor is monitoring multiple students simultaneously, which imposes additional attentional workload. Finally, this challenge can be further exacerbated when an instructor's view of the student is obscured by virtual reality (VR) equipment.

To support instructors' ability to adapt training, Eduworks and USC's Institute for Creative Technologies are developing machine learning (ML) models that can measure user engagement during training simulations and offer recommendations for restoring lapses in engagement. We have created a system, called the Observational Motivation and Engagement Generalized Appliance (OMEGA). A particular focus of our work is training in VR simulations. The virtual environment provides a rich source of raw data that machine learning models can use to associate user activity with user engagement.

We created a testbed for data capture in order to construct the ML models, based on theoretical foundations we developed previously. Our current research explores OMEGA's potential to help alert an instructor pilot (IP) to student distraction by flagging attention and engagement lapses. Our hypothesis is that OMEGA could help an IP adapt learning, and potentially manage multiple students at the same time, with alerts of lapsed attention and recommendations for restoring engagement.

To test this hypothesis, we ran pilots through representative scenarios to create data for training different variants of machine learning models and analyzed the performance of each using standard machine learning metrics. We next describe the example test environment.

1.2 Exemplar Use Case: Pilot Training Next

Our research is being conducted in the context of a new U.S. Air Force approach to Specialized Undergraduate Pilot Training (SUPT) called Pilot Training Next (PTN). PTN integrates traditional flying sorties with VR-enabled ground-based training devices to achieve training efficiencies, improve readiness, and increase throughput. While PTN student pilots fly the same hours and sorties in the T-6 as do their legacy pilot training counterparts, the ground-based training is done using an immersive PC-based flight

Fig. 1. PTN station: VR headset, controls, displays. (U.S. Air Force photo by Sean M. Worrell)

simulator (Lockheed Martin's Prepar3D®), VR headset (HTC's VIVE™ Pro), stick, throttle and rudder pedals, and a syllabus of PTN scenarios (Fig. 1).

During scenarios flown in the simulator, objective data is readily captured for every time interval, such as aircraft state (position, attitude, airspeed) and configuration (aileron, rudder and elevator deflections; flap and gear positions). Instructors can also monitor how the scenario is progressing and can provide verbal feedback in real-time.

Some important metrics though are less directly observable or measurable. Student engagement is widely accepted as a critical mediating factor in both learning retention [2] and learning outcomes [3]. The importance of engagement is not lost on instructors (though labels like attention and focus are more common in pilot training), and is often the basis for, or at least an element of, scoring situational awareness (SA).

Two additional factors make engagement even more salient for PTN. First, instructors have less visibility into student engagement (due to the VR headset) than in conventional simulators. Second, a vision for PTN is for one instructor to be monitoring multiple students simultaneously. Indirectly-observable measures such as engagement will thus require some level of automation support to cue instructors when lapses are detected.

2   Models of Engagement

2.1   General Model of Engagement

Several theoretical frameworks for characterizing engagement informed our general model of engagement. We created an inventory of nine relevant engagement and disengagement models from the literature that emphasize behavioral indicators (e.g., data from log files or from direct queries to the user) [4]. These included Intrinsic vs. Extrinsic [5]; Two Factor Hygiene-Motivator Theory [6]; Motivators from Maslow's Hierarchy (Ibid); Achievement Goal Theory [7]; D'Mello and Graesser's Engagement model [8]; and Baker's indicators of passive vs. active disengagement [9]. From this we synthesized a multi-timescale engagement and motivation model [10].

More recently, we refined the model to reflect the aviation focus of this project, preferring metrics associated with *event response* tasks (e.g., maneuvering to avoid a new hazard) and *monitoring* tasks (e.g., maintaining straight and level attitude). These characteristics are better aligned with how instructors monitor student pilot performance in training sorties. Maneuvers are evaluated by observing air speed, vertical speed, attitude, angle of attack, and so on. Instructors are also interested in situational awareness (SA), which they can assess by observing the student's ability to "stay ahead of the airplane": anticipating upcoming changes in heading, airspeed, or altitude; applying smooth control inputs to adjust bank angle, pitch and power; and maintaining proper scan of the flight instruments.

We incorporated significant research conducted to identify indicators of distraction and disengagement for accidents attributed to loss of control and airplane state awareness [11, 12]. A subset of these states is relevant to flight tasks performed in simulated environments: attention versus distraction [11]; boredom and distraction [13]; attentional tunneling [12]; and vigilance [14].

Composite Measure of Engagement: Inverse weighted average of Performance, Efficiency, and Responsiveness			
Weight	**Category**	**Metric**	**Calculation**
15%	Performance (Over/Under)	Metric 1: Conf(Expected)	Conf(Expected) * % Tasks Missed (z-score) / Expected (z-score)
		Metric 2: % Tasks Missed (z-score)	
		Metric 3: % Expected (z-score)	
35%	Efficiency	Metric 4: Deviation from an ideal path (max(0, |z-score| -1) of closest distance	Normalized, weighted composite
		Metric 5: Time to complete each segment (z-score)	
		Metric 6: % Resources (Fuel) Remaining (z-score)	
50%	Responsiveness (Reaction Time)	Metric 7: Reaction Time: How long after an 'event' does a detectable change occur? - Normalized by expertise level (% Expected) - Rapid response discounted (if incorrect)	Normalized, weighted composite
		Metric 8: Corrections - How long to correct after going off-course	

Fig. 2. Engagement model

The model resulting from this additional analysis is shown in Fig. 2. This general model is based on eight input metrics, used to compute three mid-level features: Performance, Efficiency, and Responsiveness. An overall composite measure of current engagement within a given window is derived from these mid-level features. The relative weights and derivation methods shown in Fig. 2 represent initial trial conditions.

2.2 VR Influences on Engagement Metrics

A desktop flight simulator generates a rich set of data, including aircraft position, attitude and configuration. From such data, objective performance metrics can be calculated with some reliability. For instance, detecting when a student pilot lowers the gear while the airspeed exceeds the maximum gear-down speed is straightforward. To monitor engagement, however, requires aggregating observable measures to generate an indirect estimate of engagement. Our model, for instance, specifies eight such indirect measures.

The addition of a VR head-mounted display (HMD) adds additional data points that could be incorporated as part of a suite of metrics to monitor engagement levels. Typical VR headset and sensors can capture head position and movement; higher-end devices, such as the VIVE Pro Eye, can capture eye tracking data. The VR environment thus adds to the already rich data stream available from the simulator. This apparent abundance of data, however, does not solve the problem of developing reliable measures of engagement. Several challenges for interpreting the data remain, including, non-exhaustively: (1) Understanding which data points are relevant to engagement; (2) Setting proper coefficients representing how each data point should be weighted; (3) Distinguishing between and properly applying a single data point x observed at time t compared with a trend of how x behaves over some interval (*e.g.*, from $t - 5$ s to $t + 5$ s); and (4) Incorporating the velocity of the change in a data point, for instance, how abrupt an aileron deflection or throttle movement the student applied.

A principal emphasis of this work is to explore the role that machine learning models could play in interpreting simulator and VR device data in order to develop measures to drive our conceptual model of engagement. This machine learning approach is summarized in the next section.

3 Machine Learning Model Design and Training

3.1 Machine Learning Models

We employ machine learning to allow OMEGA to develop more accurate predictive associations between raw data inputs and higher-level aggregated engagement metrics. This section describes the techniques and architecture of the OMEGA machine learning component. Our design leverages the underlying data streams available from Prepar3D to provide better predictive power in situations where there is limited access to interpreted data (e.g. when interpreted metrics of event occurrence, event success/failure, and efficiency are not available). To achieve this, we employ three methods: The *general model*, a conceptual, research-based model described previously; Support Vector Machines (SVM), a standard machine learning technique; and Hidden Markov Models (HMM), a machine learning approach based on the statistical Markov model.

We use *Support Vector Machines* to attempt to accurately predict engagement and disengagement in input metric sequences. This approach is attractive because it enjoys fast estimation methods with low run-time, and therefore can provide near-instant feedback to instructors. SVM techniques are most powerful in cases where sequence classification is not strongly context-dependent. For OMEGA, however, we expect some context-dependence in the data. For example, rapid adjustments of heading, altitude and airspeed may represent recovery from a period of inattention if these maneuvers occur between waypoints, but may represent an attentive reaction if observed during an event requiring active response (e.g. a heading change when passing a waypoint). To mitigate this risk and to improve the model, we explored an additional layer of machine learning more robust to sequence classification in context-dependent data.

Hidden Markov Models are one of the most efficient methods for modeling shorter-term dependencies between adjacent time intervals, including sensor and metric-based time series modeling. We used a function to transform the continuous stream of metric input data into a discrete sequence of values, based on a range of time intervals from 0.16 s to 20 s. As in the other modeling approaches, an interval of 10 s consistently produced the best results and was compatible with the requirements of the instructor dashboard.

We used the standard Viterbi algorithm for decoding, as well as the Expectation Maximization method (specifically the Baulm-Welch Learner) to train the model using the training set time series. Convergence was checked using a measure of change relative to the previous iteration. As expected, the HMM approach produced superior results, as compared to both the General Model alone, and the SVM model. However, we were not able to achieve convergence in all training scenarios, within a reasonable time, under all time intervals. Specifically, time intervals of less than 1.2 s usually failed to converge under most modeling scenarios.

3.2 Model Training

Data for training the machine learning components derives from experimental subjects who fly a pre-selected set of PTN scenarios in a data collection station that mirrors most of a PTN simulator, namely, the simulation software, stick and throttle, and VIVE Pro HMD and sensors. The data collection station also includes a dedicated application for the experimenter to monitor each scenario, interact with the subject, and time-stamp relevant events. Figure 3 shows an experimenter and subject during a data collection session.

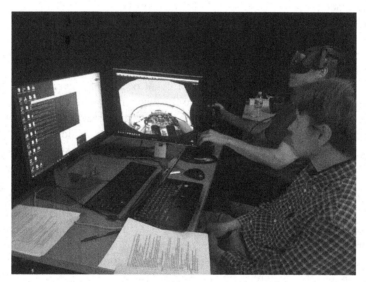

Fig. 3. Data collection (background), experimenter (foreground) stations. Photo by the authors.

For purposes of creating training data for the machine learning models, experimenters are trained in a protocol to (1) time-stamp lower-intensity and higher-intensity segments of a scenario, to help the models account for workload in processing measures of user activity; and (2) engage the subject in conversation at specific points during a scenario. Conversing with the subject acts as a surrogate for disengagement. We posit that loss of attention, or distraction, will be statistically detectable in the simulation log files. Specifically, we anticipate three possible types of deviations:

1) Response Time: Most dominantly, we anticipate that subjects' time to respond to changes in the environment will be slower and/or less precise when engaging in conversation. Specifically, we anticipate a longer duration with no response after an event that requires a maneuver *(e.g.* heading change), followed in some cases by an initial control input that is more abrupt, more prone to overcorrect, or may even be in the wrong direction.

2) Performance: We anticipate more likely failure to accomplish scenario goals (e.g., missing required waypoints).

3) Efficiency: We anticipate that periods of distraction will tend to be less efficient, due to the above issues and due to less precise control over the aircraft (e.g., slower damping of over-correcting heading changes).

Subjects were recruited from flying clubs in the Corvallis, OR and Los Angeles regions. Subjects qualified for the study through meeting either flying hour criteria or flight simulator experience criteria. Each subject was given a practice period with the PTN station and then asked to complete six PTN scenarios. The collected data were used to train the machine learning models, comparing both the predictive power and the latency and resource requirements for each of our learning modeling techniques.

4 Supporting Instructors: Adaptive Recommendations

4.1 Adaptive Recommendations Model

OMEGA processes detect engagement levels to generate adaptive recommendations to help an instructor restore lapsed engagement. During a scenario, based on combinations of different state signals, OMEGA will generate a set of intermediate inferences. These inferences include, for example, whether poor performance is due to consistently bad results versus irregular behaviour or inconsistency (e.g., carelessness). The model employs both the basic state model and the aggregated inferences as inputs to calculate a scoring ranking for different adaptive interventions.

Our model considers three levels of outcomes: performance, responsiveness, and efficiency, each representing a distinct dimension of quality. Performance represents the basic ability to complete the assigned tasks, based on the performance criteria for those tasks (e.g., following a set of waypoints). Responsiveness represents the speed and effectiveness for a learner to adjust to new tasks or requirements (e.g., if a waypoint is moved, how quickly does the user adjust heading). Efficiency represents lean and strategic use of resources to complete a scenario (e.g., faster completion times).

These quality criteria can each be thought of as building upon each other: a learner must adjust heading to a new waypoint or else there is no way to determine responsiveness. Likewise, efficiency is impossible if the user is not responsive enough to stay on course. This means that only some factors should be addressed with certain types of learners (e.g., high vs. low expertise). For example, if a user is failing to master proper take-off procedures, critiquing fuel efficiency would add no training value. On the other hand, an otherwise high-performing student pilot who is drifting off-course or leaving assigned altitudes may benefit from noting a need for improved in-flight checks.

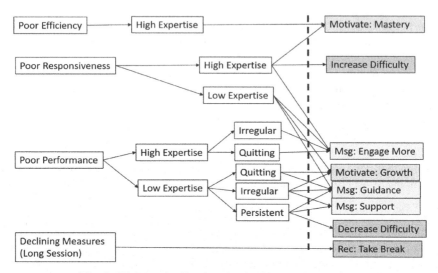

Fig. 4. High-level policy for adaptive interventions in PTN

The policy for adaptive interventions is depicted schematically in Fig. 4. The right-hand side of Fig. 4 shows the interventions used for PTN. These include three distinct types of interventions: Messaging (Information about the task), Motivation (Context about the task and learning goals), and Recommendations (Suggestions on different tasks or breaks to improve learning). The left-hand side of Fig. 4 outlines a high-level policy for when specific interventions are expected to be appropriate for users with different skill levels and in different states. These connections between intervention types and student states do not represent the actual model. Instead, they represent key dynamics that the model will produce. However, since the actual state space to calculate an effective intervention policy is too large to easily convert into a short graph, this model captures the key behaviours that the intervention model will be tested against, to ensure it behaves reasonably versus what would align to theoretical frameworks for engagement and responding to disengagement. The intervention types are outlined in Table 1.

4.2 Adaptive Recommendation Methods

We investigated two distinct methods for generating adaptation recommendations based on the internal state of the models used to detect disengagement in the sensor data stream from Prepar3D. The first approach is much less computationally-intensive and produces recommendations with lower latency. However, given the highly contextualized nature of the input data stream, we explored a second approach to produce more accurate results, and tested the trade-offs between timeliness and quality under different simulation conditions.

Table 1. Intervention types for PTN

Category	Type	Description
Messaging	Engage More	A suggestion or warning that signs of decreased engagement were noticed, with a suggestion on how to improve
	Guidance	A useful hint about how to do better on the specific scenario or skills
	Support	Affective feedback to help a learner who is struggling
Motivate	Mastery	Information about how better training can improve later real-life performance
	Growth Mindset	Feedback about how sustained effort leads to improved skills and outcomes
Recommend	Increase Difficulty	Suggest that the user might need more challenging scenarios to engage with
	Decrease Difficulty	Suggest user might benefit from trying some easier scenarios before this one
	Take Break	Suggest that user returns after taking a break, due to decreasing performance

In the first approach, we use the calculated values from the general model of engagement (performance, efficiency, and responsiveness) and its sub-component features, as inputs into a machine learning classification model. Using the labeled data set produced during the data collection trials with licensed pilots, we applied a traditional machine learning modeling technique (SVM) to the classification task, where the outputs are the available set of adaptations available in the PTN training environment.

This technique however does not account for the contextual nature of the data stream, instead analyzing each time slice as a separate case. However, as was the case for detecting engagement levels, the determination of an appropriate adaptation depends highly on the context in which the disengagement event occurs, as well as on the environmental conditions being simulated. Here we define context as the data stream of pilot behaviors and actions preceding and following the time slice of interest, and environment as the set of conditions that obtain for that particular segment of the simulation (e.g. aircraft attitude, airspeed, vertical speed, status of systems, to name a few). To fully account for the contextual nature of both the disengagement event detection and the recommendation of an appropriate adaptation, we employed the HMM approach discussed previously.

5 Model Performance

To assess the performance of each of our models, we conducted analyses based both on the engagement/distraction/boredom labels, and on collapsing distraction and boredom into a single proxy measure for disengagement. The datastream provided data from Prepar3D at intervals of 0.16 s. We experimented with a range of time intervals for analysis, ranging from 0.16 s to 20 s. All results reported here are for a time interval of 10 s, as shown in Fig. 5.

Accuracy is the ratio of correctly predicted observations (boredom or distraction) to the total observations. It can be a useful measure for symmetric datasets where values of false positive and false negatives are equivalent. Since that is not the case here, we employ additional parameters to evaluate the model. *Precision* is the ratio of correctly predicted positive observations to the total predicted positive observations. In our case, this metric answers the question "of all instances of boredom the model identified, what percentage were actual instances of boredom". High precision indicates a low false positive rate. *Recall* refers to the ratio of correctly predicted positive observations to all positive observations. In this instance, Recall answers the question "of all actual instances of boredom, what percentage did the model notice?". High recall indicates a low false negative rate. The *F1 Score* is the weighted average of Precision and Recall,

Boredom

	Accuracy	Precision	Recall	F_1
General Model	0.744	0.497	0.550	0.522
SVM	0.759	0.523	0.580	0.550
HMM	0.825	0.630	0.750	0.685

Distraction

	Accuracy	Precision	Recall	F_1
General Model	0.760	0.382	0.530	0.444
SVM	0.770	0.404	0.550	0.466
HMM	0.823	0.508	0.700	0.589

Boredom and Distraction Combined

	Accuracy	Precision	Recall	F_1
General Model	0.714	0.616	0.542	0.577
SVM	0.729	0.640	0.568	0.602
HMM	0.807	0.732	0.730	0.731

Fig. 5. Results of three modeling approaches.

which takes both false positives and false negatives into account. F1 is more relevant than Accuracy in our case, because of the uneven class distribution.

HMM models consistently out-performed the other approaches we tested. Precision was higher than recall for the combined (Boredom + Distraction) model. This suggests that the model is usually correct when it detects an incident of disengagement but suffers from false negatives. In the context of OMEGA, this is a preferred balance, as we expect that instructors are more likely to trust the system if the percentage of false positives is minimized. The size of the data sets and the process for dividing the labeled data suggest that we cannot rule out overfitting as a contributing factor to the high scores. The presence of data from the same users in both the training and test sets may have produced a model that is well-tuned to the specific set of users from this trial. Collecting additional data to conduct further testing of the model on a larger range of users and scenarios would mitigate the potential influences of overfitting.

6 Conclusions and Future Work

This work will help advance learning outcomes and retention for training using simulations and VR. A key factor in achieving positive outcomes is learner engagement, which is more challenging to assess than directly observable or objectively measurable factors. In some instances, the VR environment itself can obscure cues relevant to learning engagement from instructor view. OMEGA addresses this gap by using machine learning models to develop predictive associations between simulation events and learner actions on the one hand, and learner engagement on the other. OMEGA also incorporates a model of adaptive interventions to remedy engagement lapses, and employs machine learning to develop associations between the context and environment of the engagement lapse and the optimal intervention to recommend.

The data presented above provide early validation of the machine learning models as a viable approach to detecting engagement lapses. The next phase of this work will include data collection for a formative evaluation using instructor pilots to provide feedback on OMEGA's recommendations.

Our results will provide concept validation to establish more general-purpose, service-oriented appliance that client learning applications can employ for detecting lapses in engagement and motivation, and for recommending adaptive interventions. OMEGA can thus address a need, across a diversity of applications, to ensure that simulation-based training, and training incorporating VR, results in engaged and motivated warriors, using adaptive instruction and providing data to help training managers track the efficacy of new technologies and paradigms.

References

1. Sottilare, R.A., Goodwin, G.A.: Adaptive instructional methods to accelerate learning and enhance learning capacity. In: International Defense & Homeland Security Simulation Workshop of the I3M Conference (2017)
2. Hu, P.J.H., Hui, W.: Examining the role of learning engagement in technology-mediated learning and its effects on learning effectiveness and satisfaction. Decis. Support Syst. **53**(4), 782–792 (2012)

3. Chi, M.T., Wylie, R.: The ICAP framework: linking cognitive engagement to active learning outcomes. Educ. Psychol. **49**(4), 219–243 (2014)
4. Core, M.G., Georgila, K., Nye, B.D., Auerbach, D., Liu, Z.F., DiNinni, R.: Learning, adaptive support, student traits, and engagement in scenario-based learning. In: I/ITSEC (2016)
5. Porter, L.W., Lawler, E.E.: Managerial attitudes and performance. R.D. Irwin, Homewood (1968)
6. Gawel, J.E.: Herzberg's theory of motivation and Maslow's hierarchy of needs. Pract. Assess. Res. Eval. **5**(11), 3 (1997)
7. Pintrich, P.R.: Multiple goals, multiple pathways: the role of goal orientation in learning & achievement. J. Educ. Psych. **92**(3), 544 (2000)
8. D'Mello, S., Graesser, A.: Dynamics of affective states during complex learning. Learn. Instr. **22**(2), 145–157 (2012)
9. Baker, R.S., Corbett, A.T., Roll, I., Koedinger, K.R.: Developing a generalizable detector of when students game the system. User Model. User-Adap. Inter. **18**(3), 287–314 (2008)
10. Bell, B., Kelsey, E., Nye, B. Monitoring engagement and motivation across learning environments. In: Proceedings of the 2019 MODSIM World Conference, Norfolk, VA (2019)
11. Harrivel, A.R., et al.: Prediction of cognitive states during flight simulation using multimodal psychophysiological sensing. In: AIAA Information Systems-AIAA Infotech, p. 1135 (2017)
12. Wickens, C.D.: Attentional tunneling and task management. In: 2005 International Symposium on Aviation Psychology, p. 812 (2005)
13. Cummings, M.L., Mastracchio, C., Thornburg, K.M., Mkrtchyan, A.: Boredom and distraction in multiple unmanned vehicle supervisory control. Interact. Comput. **25**(1), 34–47 (2013)
14. Casner, S.M., Schooler, J.W.: Vigilance impossible: diligence, distraction, and daydreaming all lead to failures in a practical monitoring task. Conscious. Cogn. **35**, 33–41 (2015)

Dynamic Analytics for the Detection of Quality and Alignment Issues in an Online Hybrid Adaptive Instructional and Assessment System

Jinah Choi$^{(\boxtimes)}$ (ID) and Michelle D. Barrett (ID)

Edmentum, Bloomington, MN 55437, USA
jinah.choi@edmentum.com
https://www.edmentum.com

Abstract. In a system that combines elements of adaptive instruction and assessment, misalignment at the intersection of instruction and assessment and assessment quality issues can result in poor learner experience and faulty system recommendations and prescriptions. This paper contains elements relevant for the detection and remediation of such issues in an online hybrid instructional and assessment system. The first section presents motivation of this research, and the advantage we can expect when we address misalignment and quality issues. The second section describes an exemplar hybrid adaptive instruction and assessment system which includes the following components: adaptive instruction, practice, mastery quiz, progress check, and adaptive diagnostic assessments. The potential for and impact of alignment and quality issues in the progress check, which measures students' skill mastery for an adaptive loop, is described. The third section proposes psychometric methods that may be appropriate for the detection of misalignment and quality. The fourth section includes an empirical example of the proposed method with data from a production hybrid system, comments on the perceived utility of the procedure to date, outlines a workflow used to implement the processes from data analysis to dynamic result reporting, and presents a view of a dashboard used to increase collaboration among psychometric and content experts.

Keywords: Adaptive instruction · Assessment · Psychometric analysis · Content alignment

1 Introduction

Education delivered through online platforms has become a common and essential mode of education for contemporary times. Thus, a variety of online education programs have been utilized with their own distinct characteristics. Educational systems using methods that closely integrate instruction and assessment

© Springer Nature Switzerland AG 2021
R. A. Sottilare and J. Schwarz (Eds.): HCII 2021, LNCS 12793, pp. 15–31, 2021.
https://doi.org/10.1007/978-3-030-77873-6_2

are referred to in this paper as hybrid systems. Such a system includes instructional content as well as assessments that gather evidence of learning and diagnose the students' learning achievement obtained from the content. It is obvious that a well designed hybrid system has the potential to be much more effective and efficient than other programs that focus on either instructional contents or assessments alone, because the hybrid program can directly reflect organic and sequential relationship between learning and evaluation in the system.

Within a hybrid educational system, different kinds of assessments can be equipped to serve its purpose. Some assessments can diagnose students' levels of learning achievement and load different starting points on the learning journey depending on previous achievement. Another assessments attached as parts of instructional modules can monitor if the students are approaching to the learning objective defined in the instruction, and they can also verify if the students achieve the goal when one unit of learning instruction finishes. By extension, summative assessments which measure wider range of learning contents can be used for reviewing what they learned within a certain period of time, for example, for one semester or one school year. Also, such assessments can give the information on the students are ready to move on the next stage of learning. For these influential assessment components of hybrid education system, alignment of instruction and assessment and the quality of the assessment are key factors in the program's ability to drive positive student outcomes.

To maximize the benefits of this hybrid system, connections between instruction and assessment should be thoroughly and systematically aligned. Yet, in systems of substantial scale, often instructional content and assessment content are developed by different people, departments, or even companies. Misalignment at the intersection of instruction and assessment and assessment quality issues can result in poor learner experience and faulty system recommendations and prescriptions. For example, if assessments are too difficult compared to the level of instructional content, the system might require students to take the instruction repeatably and without opportunity to progress to subsequent levels of instruction. This might lead to decrease students' motivation or learning volition. On the other hand, if assessments are too easy, they are less likely give any meaningful information to students, students are less likely to take the instruction zealously, and the system is more likely to lead to overestimation of student ability level, advancing students to subsequent levels of instruction that are too difficult. Thereby making faulty recommendations when adapting to the next instructional content. In addition, this kind of alignments and quality check need to be appropriate to assessments with different scopes and purposes within the system, considering the stakes associated with each layer of assessment. For example, compared to short quizzes per instructional topic or skill-level assessments for checking progress, in which the consequences may result in less efficient use of learning time, misalignment of end of unit or end of semester assessments may result in additional consequences for learners.

This paper introduces the instructional architecture of a hybrid adaptive instructional and assessment system, proposes statistical indices that may be used to identify the possibility of misalignment or quality issues, and shares an empirical example in which these indices were computed and used to correct misalignment issues. Through investigation of misalignment between instruction and assessment and quality issues in assessment items, the hybrid education system can be expected that not only will learning and assessment components become more relevant to one another, but also the program will provide more qualified and helpful content recommendations and feedback with ultimately better learner outcomes.

2   Hybrid Adaptive Instruction and Assessment System

Hybrid adaptive instruction and assessment systems can greatly facilitate individualized learning. Unlike an older tradition that presumed teaching to the average in a uniform fashion would be the most cost-effective method, the concept of mastery learning was introduced by scholars such as Bloom [1], Bruner [3] and Carroll [4]. Mastery learning maintains that students must achieve a level of mastery in prerequisite knowledge before proceeding to a more advanced learning task. The ability to understand instruction is assumed to vary significantly among students, and environmental conditions, such as time allowed for learning, are modified to fit the needs of different students. Therefore, in mastery learning, students are given enough time and instruction until they succeed [1]. Later and related concepts of differentiated and individualized instruction, with computer-facilitated scale, can introduce flexibility to instruction based on students' particular learning needs. In individualized instruction, the academic goals remain the same for a group of students, but individual students can progress through the curriculum at different speeds or along different paths. This approach serves students who need to proceed through the curriculum more slowly or immerse themselves in a certain topic or principle to really "get" it. It can also be used to accelerate students. When the system includes a learning model that allows a differentiated curriculum prescribed for each student and recognizes and accommodates differentiated rates of learning for each student, learning outcomes such as scores on district and school standardized interim assessments have been shown to improve with positive and statistically significant effect sizes averaging 0.29 (reading) and 0.41 (mathematics) [9,12].

Adaptive instructional systems tend to primarily focus on instruction and immediate formative feedback, a tight inner loop [8]. The hybrid adaptive instructional and assessment system introduces additional layers of assessment based on evidence of learning in the system that can service wider adaptive loops and the interim assessment needs of a balanced assessment system, which are horizontal-coherently aligned among curriculum, instruction, and assessment regarding a common vision of learning and how students develop the content's proficiency [11].

Figure 1 illustrates components of an exemplar hybrid adaptive system. Figure 1 on the left top shows that educational intervention starts with a diagnosis through a screener diagnostic assessment; then moves to instruction aimed

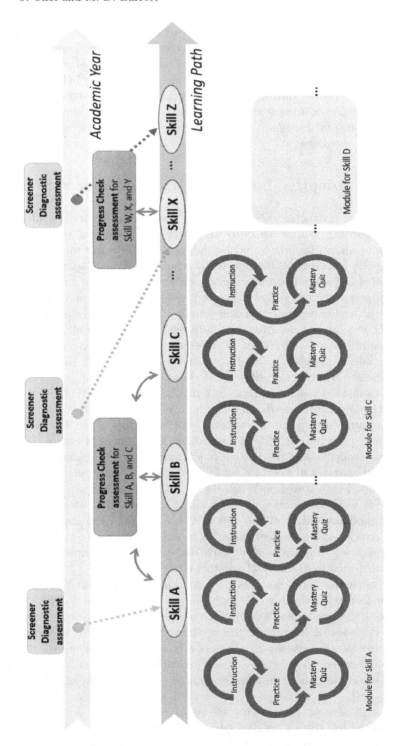

Fig. 1. Components of hybrid adaptive instruction and assessment system

to meet the student; then assigns practice to apply what has been taught; and wraps up with a suitable method of checking, or testing, whether the student has learned the lesson. The process is rendered as circular process to suggest that the student takes immediate assessment to confirm that he/she has or has not advanced to the expected level of achievement. The learning path of a subject is designed according to the progression of cognitive components of development (or advancement) in the content area [2]. The cognitive components are specified into skills and topics as the backbone of instruction.

Within this exemplar hybrid system, in addition to instruction and practice, there are three levels of assessments, each with different formats, purposes, and specifications, in addition to evidence gathered from the student while learning: mastery quiz assessment, progress check assessment, and screener adaptive diagnostic assessment. The following descriptions will start in the inner loop, where adaptive instructional loops occur, and extend through the additional levels of assessment available in the system.

2.1 Instructional Module

Instruction in this hybrid system consists of modules comprised of an instructional lesson with scaffolded interactions and practice. An instructional module will address a portion of a skill in the system, i.e., there is a many to one relationship between instructional modules and skills. For example, a skill named "Context Clues" for grade 2 of the reading subject area has three modules named "Word Detectives", "The Big City", and "Using Context Clues", the contents of which are each determined a learning objective. The lesson delivers content appropriately chunked for the age level, skill, and time expectations, and creates excitement through using various properties, such as high-quality animation and other audio-visual presentation with effective character-driven dialog. The primary role of "practice" component involved in the instruction's topic is to reinforce the lesson by eliciting direct physical engagement, such as drawing, reciting, calculating, and other activities with decreasing scaffolds. Learning activities through this practice in computer-assisted instruction forges implicit learning of the concepts and skills to strengthen explicit learning [5].

2.2 Mastery Quiz Assessment

At the conclusion of the lesson and practice in each instructional module, the student is presented a short quiz to establish whether they can demonstrate independent (i.e., non-scaffolded) mastery of the lesson, with content narrowly focused on the lesson and at a level of difficulty intentionally targeted to inform a mastery decision. Should the student not demonstrate mastery upon first attempt, the student is free to revisit the lesson and attempt variants of this quiz multiple times. Students who demonstrate mastery on the mastery quiz on multiple modules are then allowed to proceed to progress check.

2.3 Progress Check Assessment

To master a skill, students are typically required to complete more than one instructional module. Once a student has completed a set of modules (typically two or three modules in the exemplar system), a progress check assessment is administered. Importantly, because the modules are determined specific to an individual's location in the learning path and learning pace, the skills measured and items selected for each the progress check depends on the learner. The progress check confirms the learner's competency of the skill(s) learned in the last set of modules. Thus, the progress check assessments are an important mechanism in monitoring students' achievement at the skill level. If a learner scores lower than the mastery cut score, the system recommends the learner return and review the content of the module of the skill not passed. In addition, the student will also receive recommendations for new (more advanced) modules for those skills passed. The next progress check will include items from both the previous (not passed) skill and the new skills. The construction of the progress check is therefore dynamic and depends heavily on metadata in the system to select the appropriate items.

2.4 Screener Adaptive Diagnostic Assessment

The screener adaptive diagnostic assessment is designed for repeated administration as an efficient computerized adaptive testing. Within a subject area, it assesses students against several domains. It is used to measure the student's academic growth over the course of an academic year by administering during up to four testing windows (e.g., fall, winter, early spring, and end of year). In addition, it helps educators understand the grade level proficiency of a student: allows for precise measurement below- and above-grade level in addition to on-grade level. Furthermore, this assessment can be also linked to state assessment results that enable to predict state-specific grade level proficiency. Importantly, it is also used to place a student in the hybrid system's learning path best suited that individual student's skill profile.

3 Psychometric Methods for Detecting Misalignment of Instruction and Assessment and Checking Item Quality

In previous section, the components of an exemplar hybrid online adaptive education system were described. It is evident that the strong link between learning progression on learning path and assessment is a key feature of this hybrid adaptive education system. Because of the interconnected nature of instruction and assessment, and the influence of the assessment results on the learner's instructional path, the quality of alignment of the instructional content and the assessment content and the quality of instructional interactions and assessment items is paramount to an effective hybrid system. As shown in Fig. 2, when misalignment occurs, the instruction teaches something the assessment doesn't assess or vice versa. In an ideal world, aligning each component to the standards or competency framework would be sufficient for ensuring alignment and separate content authors would be able to work independent of one another; however, in reality, the framework often includes a larger set of concepts than an individual instructional module would deliver and a short assessment can assess. In addition, understandings regarding the performance level required to demonstrate mastery can vary among content writers. Therefore, even when alignment between instruction and assessment is believed to exist, post-hoc analysis of the assessment data is warranted as it can provide insights as to areas of potential misalignment.

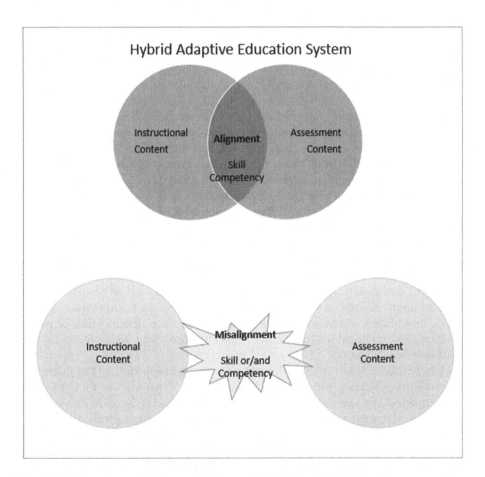

Fig. 2. Alignment vs. misalignment between instructional content and assessment content in hybrid adaptive education system

Although all assessments components are essential, the remainder of this paper will turn focus to the progress check assessment because of its location in the exemplar system at the intersection of instruction and assessment and the consequences associated with low scores on this assessment. Recall that the progress check is utilized for checking skill mastery and determining the next set of instructional modules for a learner to receive. Therefore, depending on the results of the progress check test, the student's unique journey on learning path is determined. A learner may be asked to study the non-mastered skills again if their score points for a skill are lower than mastery threshold score. On the other hand, if the progress check test confirms that the students mastered the skill the test are measuring, the program guides the students to more advanced (next) skills on the learning path defined based on theories of cognitive components in subjects [6, 13]. The efficiency of the system for the learner hinges on the ability of the progress check assessment to correctly determine mastery of the skill. That said, the techniques presented below are likely suitable for evaluation of mastery quiz assessments in the exemplar system, as well as alignment checks in other hybrid system implementations. They are also a subset of the set of analyses required for establishing the validity and reliability of the screener adaptive diagnostic assessment.

Psychometric theories and methodologies can be used for verifying whether the difficulty levels of progress check tests are appropriate to the level of instructional content of the skills, or whether progress check tests can discriminate students who mastered from those who did not master the skills. The results from analysis can provide quantitative evidence for improving items which will be used continuously in the system or eliminating ambiguous/misleading items. For the purposes of identifying misalignment and quality issues, we propose using a few methods from classical test theory, namely classical item analysis [7, 10]. Although the results of the proposed methods are dependent on the specific sample of examinees for which the method is applied, they can be conducted with a reasonably low number of examinee responses, tend to be simple for assessment and content designers to understand, and are very often used as quality control indices on more rigorously validated assessments (e.g., state summative assessments). In addition, there are minimal penalties of over-identification of items for review, and no penalties to examinees, so thresholds can be set to err on the side of over-identification.

We hypothesize that misaligned items will exhibit one or both of the following characteristics: (1) they will be more difficult than expected for students who have completed the associated instruction to answer correctly and (2) a correct response on the item will have a low correlation with the overall assessment score, thereby poorly discriminating between students who have and have not mastered the skill. The reader will note that these can also be indicators of items of low quality (e.g., items with no correct or multiple correct responses, mis-keys, items that do not render properly, etc.), and will also note that an item that is too easy may also indicate problems (e.g., correct response is obvious given the prompt; the item measures a previous skill that students have already learned but isn't related to the current skill) and lower the reliability of the progress check. Several types of indices of item difficulty and item discrimination can be estimated as statistics commonly used in the field of educational measurement.

For the purpose of detecting misalignment, as the item difficulty index, we propose using p-value. P-value, or p_i, is calculated as the mean score on item i

$$p_i = \frac{\Sigma X_{ij}}{N},$$ (1)

when X_{ij} for represents the score of examinee j on item i, N is the total number of examinees, and X is restricted to 0 or 1. Therefore, the p-value is the proportion of students that answered the item correctly, and ranges from 0 to 1. For example, a p-value of .48 indicates that 48% of students answered the item correctly. As is evident, this index highly depends on the students in the sample. A higher ability sample will yield a higher p-value than a lower ability sample. Our empirical example later in the paper will demonstrate ways in which the analysis may be run and interpreted to reduce risk of mis-interpretation.

Items that perform well psychometrically are able to differentiate between students of low and high ability on the construct of interest. In other words, if the item is performing well measuring the intended content, students with high ability on the skill should answer the item correctly and students with low ability on the skill should answer the item incorrectly. Tests with high internal consistency typically consist of item with mostly positive relationships with total test score. Various calculation procedures have been used to compare item response to total test scores using high and low scoring groups of students (need to add reference).

For the purpose of detecting misalignment, as the item discrimination index, we propose using an adjusted point-biserial coefficient, which measures the correlation of a correct response on the item i with the total test score X minus item i. The adjusted point-biserial correlation, or $\rho_{i(X-i)}$, is calculated as

$$\rho_{i(X-i)} = \frac{\rho_{Xi}\sigma_X - \sigma_i}{(\sigma_i^2 + \sigma_X^2 - 2\rho_{Xi}\sigma_X\sigma_i)^{1/2}},$$ (2)

where

$$\rho_{i(X-i)}$$

is the correlation between and item score and the total score with that item removed and

$$\sigma_X$$

and

$$\sigma_i$$

are the total and item standard deviations respectively. The adjustment of removing the item from the total score calculation is necessary due to the low number of items typically used in the progress check assessment.

4   Empirical Example

4.1   Data and Cleaning Rules

Based on the psychometric methods described in the previous section, this section illustrates an empirical application result as an example. Item level student response data were collected from the progress check assessment for reading, mathematics, and language arts subject areas administered during academic year 2019–2020 for skills at the K-2 grade levels. The number of items to check for quality and alignment were 1,535, 817, and 812 for reading, mathematics, and language arts, respectively. The total numbers of students' responses collected for the item analysis were approximately 7M, 8M, and 3.5M for reading, mathematics, and language arts, respectively.

Several data cleaning steps were followed prior to calculation of difficulty and discrimination indices. First, as students are allowed to take the variants of the progress check multiple times, only item responses corresponded to the test in the first attempt are included into analysis. Second, the period for collecting the response data covers the whole academic year to offset any influence on the time of studying. Finally, to increase the stability of the statistics, only items with at least 200 student responses were targeted for analysis. As a result of the data cleaning process, the final sample sizes for analysis slightly decreased and two items (one for reading and one for mathematics) were excluded due to the lack of sample size. Though the sample size for each item is all different by subject and skill grade level, a majority of items had numbers of student responses ranging from 2,000 through 3,500.

4.2 Application Procedure

For the purpose of detecting misalignment, p-value and the adjusted point-biserial coefficient for each item were calculated as specified in Eqs. 1 and 2. Because of the dependence of these statistics on the sample, calculations were conducted first with all cleaned student responses, then with student responses grouped by student grade spans. To be specific, the "overall" group included any students in grades K-12 responding to the item; the "on-grade" group included students in the same grade as the item's skill grade; the "below-grade" group included students one or two grade levels below the item's skill grade; and the "above-grade" group included students up to two grade levels above the item's skill grade. Because the items used for this application study are limited to K-2 grade skill levels, the "overall group" includes students across K-12 grades, while other subgroups includes at most up to grade 4 in "above-grade" group.

Distributions of both indices were examined to investigate how the items performed as components of the progress check assessment. On average, for the items developed for progress check test, above 70% of students answered correctly to items, the discrimination index values were above .25 (Table 1).

Next, thresholds were set for referring items for review of potential alignment and quality issues by learning and assessment designers, and named categories were assigned to assist those reviewing the items with a more intuitive grasp of the items' performance. It is important to consider the threshold based on the context of the assessment, therefore these thresholds may seem different than those psychometric might recognize as rule of thumb for standardized summative assessment. It should be noted that poor item indices values do not necessarily mean that the item itself is low quality, but they are provided as a starting

Table 1. Descriptive statistics for item index by student group

Index	Student group	Statistics	Language arts	Math	Reading
N	Overall	Min	854	25	47
		Max	14739	17569	11072
		Average	3252	7415	3549
		SD	1793	3024	1475
	On-grade	Min	119	8	30
		Max	2172	3264	1771
		Average	391	1136	362
		SD	268	577	216
	Below-grade	Min	25	6	18
		Max	690	1208	340
		Average	108	354	83
		SD	92	240	52
	Above-grade	Min	353	11	16
		Max	7202	7675	5651
		Average	1441	3530	1640
		SD	856	1329	750
Difficulty	Overall	Min	0.20	0.19	0.09
		Max	0.96	0.98	0.98
		Average	0.66	0.75	0.69
		SD	0.17	0.16	0.15
	On-grade	Min	0.17	0.19	0.10
		Max	0.95	0.98	0.98
		Average	0.60	0.69	0.64
		SD	0.16	0.17	0.15
	Below-grade	Min	0.19	0.22	0.17
		Max	0.93	0.97	0.98
		Average	0.61	0.70	0.66
		SD	0.15	0.14	0.15
	Above-grade	Min	0.19	0.18	0.09
		Max	0.97	0.99	0.98
		Average	0.65	0.75	0.68
		SD	0.17	0.16	0.16
Discrimination	Overall	Min	−0.05	−0.10	−0.22
		Max	0.60	0.62	0.64
		Average	0.31	0.36	0.33
		SD	0.12	0.11	0.11
	On-grade	Min	−0.02	−0.01	−0.22
		Max	0.59	0.64	0.64
		Average	0.30	0.35	0.33
		SD	0.12	0.10	0.12
	Below-grade	Min	−0.30	−0.24	−0.21
		Max	0.80	0.68	0.80
		Average	0.37	0.43	0.38
		SD	0.15	0.11	0.16
	Above-grade	Min	−0.12	−0.35	−0.25
		Max	0.57	0.63	0.61
		Average	0.28	0.34	0.31
		SD	0.12	0.11	0.11

guideline to identify the most egregious cases of poor item performance; content experts will use their judgement that considers the indices values alongside the holistic view of the item and the instructional component from the perspective of a subject matter expertise.

Recall that the item difficulty represents the proportion of students responding correctly to the item. Therefore, the statistic may range from 0 to 1. In addition, the progress check is placed in the system subsequent to instruction the student receives and is intended to measure master of that delivered instruction. In this system, it is expected that students can pass the progress check by correctly answering 4 or 5 of 5 items per skill because they have already opportunities to practice the concept and pass mastery quizzes for the skill. The reader should note that this is not a general recommendation for determining mastery and that different thresholds may be appropriate in other systems. The items for progress check test should have a p-value of .8 or higher to be consistent with the progress check passing criteria. To be specific, the p-value is categorized into four difficulty levels according to its range: "very hard" category ranges equal or less than .25; "hard" category ranges .25 to .5; "medium" category ranges .5 to .8; and "reasonably easy" category ranges greater than .8.

Recall that the item discrimination represents the correlation between a correct response on the item and the total test score (minus the item). Therefore, the statistic may range from -1 to 1 although the reader may note that due to the discrete variable, the actual range may be more highly restricted. The item discrimination index is also categorized into four levels according to its range: "bad" category ranges equal or less than 0; "marginal" category ranges 0 to 1; "OK (fair)" category ranges .1 to .2; and "good" category ranges greater than .2. Tables 2 through 4 show the distribution of items by difficulty and discrimination categories in this application.

Finally, it is not efficient that content experts randomly audit of all items for the progress check assessment in the system. Therefore, we set priority for reviewing the items according to combinations of the two item indices' categories. For example, if the item is very hard and has bad or marginal discrimination index, it was given immediate priority for review. The second priority set the case that point-biserial coefficient is lower than 0.2, and the third priority set the case that the discrimination index is okay but difficulty value is somewhat low. Table 5 shows the distribution of items by priority for review category.

Once the statistics were calculated, thresholds set, and items were categorized into review categories, the data was shared with learning and assessment designers following a training session to describe the statistics and appropriate interpretations. While formal analysis of the consistency of the item flagging with findings of misalignment from the subsequent the content expert review of the item, false positive and false negative rates associated with the established thresholds, and extensions of analysis that may improve the recommendations remains as future research, the content experts have to date indicated that the statistics have been useful in pinpointing items with issues and that they would like to extend the analysis to skills from additional grade levels without waiting

Table 2. Distribution of items by difficulty and discrimination category-language arts

		Discrimination				
		Bad	Marginal	Ok	Good	Grand total
Difficulty	Very hard	2	6	3	4	15
	Hard	3	22	55	99	179
	Medium		3	42	442	487
	Reasonably easy			7	124	131
	Grand total	5	31	107	669	812

Table 3. Distribution of items by difficulty and discrimination category-mathematics

		Discrimination				
		Bad	Marginal	Ok	Good	Grand total
Difficulty	Very hard		1			1
	Hard	1	3	26	40	70
	Medium			18	369	387
	Reasonably easy		1	13	344	358
	Grand total	1	5	57	753	816

Table 4. Distribution of items by difficulty and discrimination category-reading

		Discrimination				
		Bad	Marginal	Ok	Good	Grand total
Difficulty	Very hard	7	6	1		14
	Hard	3	27	59	80	169
	Medium		1	56	891	948
	Reasonably easy		1	4	399	404
	Grand total	10	35	120	1370	1535

Table 5. Distribution of items by priority for review category

Priority for review	Language arts	Math	Reading	Grand total
1: Immediate priority for review	8		1	11	20
2: Review as time permits	189	89	221	499
3: Item mostly ok but somewhat difficult	491	449	959	1899
4: Fine as is	124	276	343	743
5: Insufficient data		1	1	2
Grand total	812	816	1535	3163

for those formal analyses as they have found the data from the K-2 skills usable and highly valuable (Table 3 and 4).

4.3   Workflow Process from Data Analysis to Result Reporting

Given the interest and demand from content experts for these statistics for progress checks of all skills in the system, and the continuous nature of data collection as students proceed along their individualized learning paths, it makes sense to shift the analysis from a one-time analysis run by a psychometric into a dynamic dashboard that updates information as it becomes available and allows interactive and cross-functional collaboration between content experts and psychometric. Therfore, under this purpose and situation, we used tools commonly used for business intelligence analytics to shift the analysis and reporting from a single event to a dynamic dashboard.

Amazon Web Service (AWS) provides platforms that facilitate processing in big data. It may have been evident to the reader that millions of data points are available for analysis from the exemplar hybrid system, and tools appropriate for high volume data are necessary. This solution used S3 (data storage), Athena (query), and EC2 (compute) AWS services. To facilitate the work of the psychometrician, R Studio was installed on an EC2 instance to reduce data transfer needs while supporting analytic functions commonly used by researchers.

Power BI is part of the Microsoft suite and used for rapid visualization of data, most commonly for business decisions. It can help unify data from many

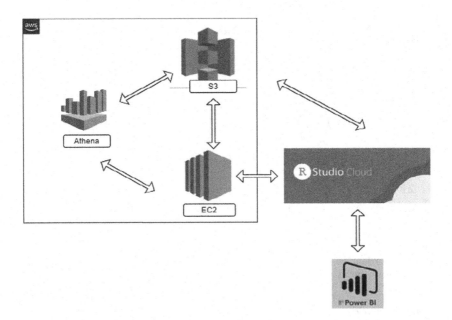

Fig. 3. Architecture diagram of workflow process

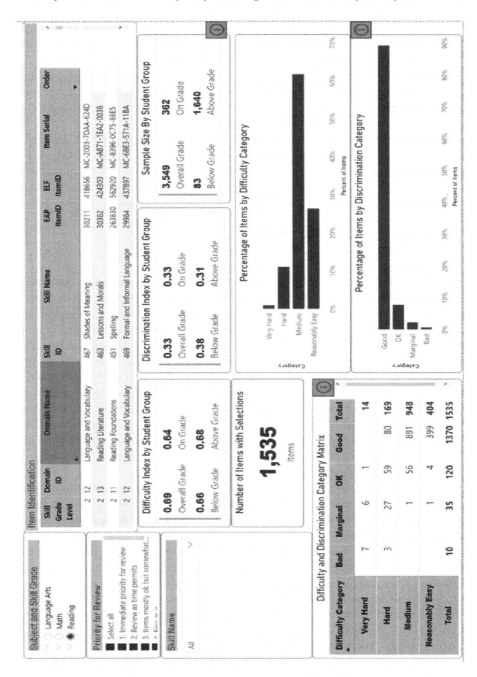

Fig. 4. Screenshot of dynamic dashboard utilizing Power BI

resources to create interface, immersive dashboards and reports that provide actionable insights. Data can be automatically refreshed as it becomes available in the system. Figure 3 shows a simplified diagram of the work flow process.

Figure 4 is a screenshot of the interactive dashboard created to share the item statistics and review recommendations with content experts. Through various filtering mechanisms built into PowerBI, the content experts are able quickly identify items for review and take subsequent review actions.

While the data used for the empirical example in this paper was compiled over the course of an academic year, with strict limits on numbers of responses required to assume statistical stability, it is possible to envision adjustments to methodology that would allow for ongoing monitoring of item performance with increasing statistical accuracy over time, as data becomes available from student use.

5   Conclusion

In this paper, we showed how traditional item analysis methods can be combined with modern dashboard tools to quickly identify low quality and misaligned assessment content in a hybrid adaptive instruction and assessment system in the interest of improving the student experience and increasing efficiency and opportunities for learning. We found that, while simple applications of psychometric analysis, the proposed indices and criteria for flagging items were useful for prioritizing items that should be reviewed by learning and content designers. These processes allow for identification and removal of poor or misaligned content and refinement of the item pools for each skill as well as lay the basis for further investigation of alignment of instructional materials and progress check tests. Further, by converting the analysis to a dynamic dashboard rather than an infrequent process, flawed or misaligned content can be identified and removed quickly, positively impacting student learning experiences.

This study has several potential limitations. While positive feedback was received by content experts, it is possible that further efforts to gather and measure consistency of classification with content expert reviews will yield areas for improvement. Therefore, further research on the impact of different threshold decisions should be conducted. Also, this study only looked at issues with assessment content and not issues with instructional content. Further research is necessary to develop methods of identifying quality issues with instructional content. Finally, it is possible that some items showed good statistical performance but measured skills students had already mastered, thereby masking alignment issues between the instructional module and the related progress check.

To maximize the benefits of hybrid adaptive instructional and assessment systems, connections between instruction and assessment should be thoroughly and systematically aligned. Misalignment at the intersection of instruction and assessment and assessment quality issues can result in poor learner experience and faulty system recommendations and prescriptions. This paper demonstrated one potential method, and advancements in machine learning and natural language processing alongside more traditional analytics such as those proposed in this paper are likely to be fruitful in further improving horizontal and vertical coherence in these systems.

Acknowledgements. The author is grateful to Dr. David King for his thoughtful review and comments during the preparation of this paper.

References

1. Bloom, B.S.: Learning for mastery. instruction and curriculum. regional education laboratory for the Carolinas and Virginia, topical papers and reprints, number 1. Eval. Comment **1**(2), n2 (1968)
2. Briggs, D.C., Diaz-Bilello, E., Peck, F., Alzen, J., Chattergoon, R., Johnson, R.: Using a learning progression framework to assess and evaluate student growth. National Center for the Improvement of Educational Assessment (2015)
3. Bruner, J.S., et al.: Toward a Theory of Instruction, vol. 59. Harvard University, Cambridge (1966, in Press)
4. Carroll, J.B.: The carroll model: a 25-year retrospective and prospective view. Educ. Researcher **18**(1), 26–31 (1989)
5. Cheung, A.C.K., Slavin, R.E.: The effectiveness of education technology for enhancing reading achievement: a meta-analysis. Center for Research and reform in Education (2011)
6. Collins, A., Brown, J.S., Newman, S.E.: Cognitive apprenticeship: teaching the craft of reading, writing and mathematics. Thinking J. Philos. Child. **8**(1), 2–10 (1988). https://doi.org/10.5840/thinking19888129
7. Crocker, L., Algina, J.: Introduction to Classical and Modern Test Theory. ERIC (1986)
8. Durlach, P.J., Spain, R.D.: Framework for instructional technology: methods of implementing adaptive training and education. Technical report, Army Research Inst for the Behavioral and Social Sciences, Fort Belvoir, VA (2014). https://doi.org/10.13140/RG.2.1.4075.8247
9. Bill & Melinda Gates Foundation. Early progress: Interim research on personalized learning (2014)
10. Livingston, S.A.: Criterion-referenced applications of classical test theory 1, 2. J. Educat. Measur. **9**(1), 13–26 (1972). https://doi.org/10.1111/j.1745-3984.1972.tb00756.x
11. Marion, S., Thompson, J., Evans, C., Martineau, J., Dadey, N.: A tricky balance: the challenges and opportunities of balanced systems of assessment. Center for Assessment. Systems of Assessment. NCME 3(13/19), 1 (2019)
12. Pane, J.F., Steiner, E.D., Baird, M.D., Hamilton, L.S.: Continued progress: promising evidence on personalized learning. Rand Corporation (2015). https://doi.org/10.7249/j.ctt19w724m
13. Pea, R.D.: The social and technological dimensions of scaffolding and related theoretical concepts for learning, education, and human activity. J. learn. Sci. **13**(3), 423–451 (2004). https://doi.org/10.1207/s15327809jls1303_6

Predicting Literacy Skills via Stealth Assessment in a Simple Vocabulary Game

Ying Fang[✉], Tong Li, Rod D. Roscoe, and Danielle S. McNamara

Arizona State University, Tempe, AZ 85281, USA
yfang61@asu.edu

Abstract. iSTART is a game-based intelligent tutoring system (ITS) designed to improve students' reading skills by providing training on reading comprehension strategies. Game-based practice in iSTART follows two main approaches: generative practice and identification practice. Generative practice games ask students to author self-explanations using one or more of the instructed strategies. Identification practice games require students to recognize or select appropriate strategies based on their analysis of example texts. This study explored the feasibility of implementing stealth assessments in iSTART using only an identification game. Specifically, this study examined the extent to which participants' performance and attitudes related to a simple vocabulary game could predict the outcomes of standardized reading assessments. MTurk participants (N = 211) played identification games in iSTART and then rated their subjective gameplay experience. Participants also completed measures of their vocabulary and reading comprehension skills. Results indicated that participants' performance in a vocabulary practice game was predictive of literacy skills. In addition, the possibility that students' attitude towards the game moderated the relation between game performance and literacy skills was ruled out. These findings argue for the feasibility of implementing stealth assessment in simple games to facilitate the adaptivity of ITSs.

Keywords: Stealth assessment · iSTART · Game-based learning environment

1 Introduction

Intelligent tutoring systems (ITSs) are computer-based instructional systems that provide adaptive instruction and timely feedback to learners with reduced intervention from a human teacher [1]. To provide this personalized instruction, ITSs must evaluate students to inform decisions regarding the specific adaptations needed by each individual student [2]. One major challenge for ITSs in the domain of reading is dynamically assessing students' reading skills. Traditional literacy assessments (e.g., standardized reading tests) are usually static, lengthy, and decontextualized, thus making it difficult (and perhaps even invalid) for ITSs to use such assessments to assess students' learning progress and personalize instruction in real time.

One innovative way to meet the requirements of dynamic assessments in ITSs is to implement *stealth assessment* [3]. Stealth assessment refers to assessments that are

© Springer Nature Switzerland AG 2021
R. A. Sottilare and J. Schwarz (Eds.): HCII 2021, LNCS 12793, pp. 32–44, 2021.
https://doi.org/10.1007/978-3-030-77873-6_3

seamlessly embedded in a computer-based or gaming environment such that learners are largely unaware of being assessed [4]. Unlike traditional assessments, testing items are replaced with learning or gaming tasks and activities; stealth assessment is unobtrusive. Prior research on stealth assessment has primarily focused on evaluating students' higher-order skills (e.g., problem solving and creativity) and knowledge in science-related domains [3, 5]. Only a few studies have examined stealth assessment in the domain of reading [6, 7]. The latter have used natural language processing (NLP) to extract linguistic and semantic features from constructed responses (e.g., essays and explanations) to predict students' literacy skills (e.g., reading skills). This study adopted a different approach by exploring stealth assessment within a simple vocabulary identification game. In such games, students do not construct responses and thus no NLP data are obtainable; yet their game performance (e.g., answer selections) may still be revealing. If successful, this approach would enable very efficient and rapid stealth literacy assessment.

1.1 iSTART

Interactive Strategy Training for Active Reading and Thinking (iSTART) is a game-based ITS designed to improve students' reading comprehension skills. iSTART originated from a successful human-led intervention named Self-Explanation Reading Training (SERT) [8, 9], which teaches students how to self-explain while reading using comprehension strategies (i.e., comprehension monitoring, paraphrasing, predicting, bridging, elaborating). iSTART also includes strategy training modules to learn and practice summarization and question asking [10–12]. iSTART uses natural language processing (NLP) algorithms to analyze students' self-explanations and provide rapid formative feedback. The feedback informs students of the quality of their self-explanations and guides them towards more effective practice [10, 11]. Students' improvement in reading comprehension after iSTART training has been shown to be comparable to the improvement with SERT [13].

1.2 iSTART Games

One distinctive feature of the current version of iSTART is game-based training. Previous research comparing game-based practice and non-game practice indicated that game-based learning environments were more enjoyable and motivating [14, 15]. In iSTART games, students can practice reading strategies by exploring game narratives, conquering game challenges, and interacting with game characters. There is also a reward system whereby students can earn points via gameplay, which in turn can be "spent" to unlock additional games or customize personal avatars.

iSTART games contribute to effective training by enabling immediate feedback during or after gameplay. Timely feedback during practice helps students to identify their strengths and weaknesses while keeping them engaged [16], and it is based on the assessment of students' performance on the in-game tasks. How such evaluations occur depend on the nature of the game. Generative games usually embed open-ended questions or prompts that elicit constructed textual responses. NLP methods and algorithms are implemented to evaluate these answers and inform real-time feedback. In contrast, identification games usually integrate multiple-choice items wherein correct and incorrect answer choices have been carefully preconstructed to diagnose students' understanding or confusion. The instant feedback based on the in-game assessments of students' performance guides their practice within the games.

iSTART incorporates both generative practice games and identification practice games [17]. Generative games allow students to practice by authoring self-explanations using one or more of the instructed strategies. For example, in Map Conquest (see Fig. 1), players (i.e., learners) earn flags and conquer the map by self-explaining target sentences in giving texts. Assessment of performance in these games requires NLP-based analyses of the constructed responses.

In contrast, identification games ask students to recognize or select appropriate strategies based on their analysis of example texts. In Dungeon Escape (see Fig. 2), players (i.e., learners) escape a dungeon by selecting the best topic sentences for a series of texts. Performance in these games is based on students' response selection--no NLP metrics or computations are necessary--which enables potentially very fast and efficient stealth assessments.

1.3   Literacy Assessment for Personalized Training

In-game assessments enable iSTART to provide real-time feedback. However, such assessments are task specific, and the results cannot be used by games with different tasks (e.g., games focus on a different strategy training). These assessments help customize training at the micro level (e.g., training within a game) instead of the macro level (e.g., training across games and modules).

Traditional literacy assessments can be used for macro-level customization, such as recommending instruction that broadly matches students' level of reading skill. However, these traditional assessments are typically time-consuming, not dynamic, and students

Fig. 1. Screenshot of a generative game - Map Conquest

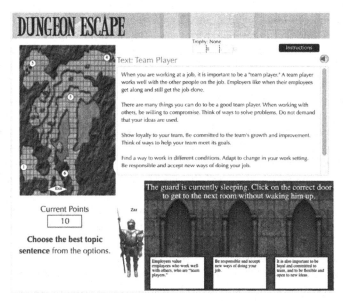

Fig. 2. Screenshot of a generative game - Dungeon Escape

may even have to pause instruction for testing purposes (i.e., students are "pulled out" of the classroom to complete the testing). Implementing this assessment approach in iSTART is likely to demotivate students, cause test anxiety, and interrupt training, all of which undermine the goals of iSTART training.

In contrast to traditional literacy assessments, stealth assessments that are seamlessly embedded in computer-based learning environments can evaluate students' literacy skills unobtrusively. For instance, students can be assessed while playing games in iSTART, which may be more authentic and not interrupting students' practice. Prior studies have explored the possibility of assessing students' literacy skills using generative games and NLP embedded within iSTART. Linguistic features such as the complexity of students' words and sentences within self-explanations are predictive of their reading test scores [6, 7]. Such an approach is promising but requires linking the games or tasks to the computer programs necessary to compute these features and NLP algorithms. This study explores an alternative approach of using metrics based entirely on game actions and selections to predict literacy skills.

1.4   Current Study

The current study explores the implementation of stealth literacy assessment in an iSTART identification game. Specifically, this study seeks to predict students' literacy skills (i.e., scores on standardized literacy measures) via their performance in a simple vocabulary game.

Over the course of a larger study, students played three identification games, including a vocabulary game and two others focusing on main ideas. For the purposes of this analysis, we focus on one of these games, Vocab Flash (see Fig. 3), in which students select a synonym for a target word, completing as many words as possible within 5 min. Albeit a simple game, it is one of the favorite games in iSTART (by teachers and students). One distinctive feature of the vocabulary game is its adaptivity (see Sect. 2.2). The words in the game are categorized based on varying levels of difficulty. Students begin at the lowest level and progress to higher levels as they answer correctly. Adaptive testing has been reported to be able to achieve a high level of precision with relatively fewer testing items [18]. Thus, we hypothesize that performance in this simple (quick) vocabulary game (i.e., accurate answers and attaining higher levels of difficulty) will be associated with (and strongly predictive of) students' performance on the Gates MacGinitie vocabulary test (H1). To test the first hypothesis, we will predict students' vocabulary test scores as a function of their game performance. In addition, we also investigate a more distal relation between game performance and reading comprehension skill (as measured by the Gates MacGinitie Reading Test; GMRT). We expect to find a moderate relation between game performance on Vocab Flash and performance on the GMRT because comprehension is strongly correlated with vocabulary knowledge [19–22]. Therefore, we also investigate the extent to which performance in the simple vocabulary game predicts comprehension skill. We expect the vocabulary game performance to be predictive of reading comprehension skill (H2). To test the second hypothesis, we will model students' reading test scores as a function of their game performance.

Fig. 3. Screenshot of Vocab Flash

At the same time, we expect most students to enjoy playing the game. Nonetheless, we also attempt to rule out the possibility that students' attitude towards the game will moderate the relation between game performance and literacy skills. If the game is not considered to be enjoyable by the participants, their game accuracy may be impacted, which in turn may reduce the ability of the game to tap into their literacy skills. As such, we assess participants' attitudes toward the game, and examine the extent to which attitudes contribute to the model.

2   Methods

2.1   Participants

Participants were 211 people (98 female, 113 male) recruited on Amazon Mechanical Turk in the winter of 2020. The sample was 77.2% Caucasian, 6.6% Hispanic, 10.9% African-American, 4.3% Asian, and 1.0% identified as other ethnicities. The average age of the participants was 37.2 years (range 17–68). The majority (81.5%) had a bachelor's or advanced degree.

2.2   Procedure, Materials, and Measures

Participants completed a demographic survey and were then provided with three links for three iSTART games: Vocab Flash, Dungeon Escape and Adventurer's Loot. The order of the three games was counterbalanced. After each game, participants completed a survey asking about their attitudes towards the game. Participants next completed the Gates-MacGinitie vocabulary and comprehension subtests. Both subtests were timed.

Gates-MacGinitie Reading Test (GMRT). Participants' reading skills were measured using Gates-MacGinitie Reading Test (GMRT) level 10/12 form S. GMRT is a well-established measure of reading comprehension ($\alpha = .85$–$.92$) [23]. It consists of two subtests: the vocabulary and the comprehension subtests. The vocabulary subtest is a 45-item multiple-choice test in which participants select the meaning of target words in the given sentences. The comprehension subtest asks participants to read short passages and then answer two to six questions about the content of each passage. There are 48 multiple-choice questions in total.

Literacy skills were operationalized as the raw scores (i.e., number of correct answers) on GMRT subtests. Specifically, vocabulary skill was measured by the raw score of vocabulary subtest, and reading comprehension skill was measured by the raw score of reading comprehension subtest.

Vocab Flash. Vocab Flash (see Fig. 3) is a 5-min iSTART game in which students are given a target word and must select a synonym from four alternatives (i.e., one correct term and three incorrect foils). Students are encouraged to complete as many words as possible within 5 min. Success is defined by choosing accurate synonyms. Importantly, the target words vary in difficulty, as operationalized by their frequency in Corpus of Contemporary American English (COCA) [24]. Words that appear more frequently are considered less difficult. The entire corpus of target words includes 1,013 terms divided into 9 levels of difficulty ranging from Level 0 (occur very frequently in the English language) to Level 8 (occur least frequently). An average of 120 distinct words are available within each level.

For all students, the game begins at Level 0. Target words are randomly selected from the Level 0 corpus and presented to the student, and students earn points (10 points per correct answer) and make progress by correctly selecting the synonym of a target word. At predetermined score thresholds (e.g., 50 points for level 1, 150 points for level 2), students "level up" and transit to a higher level, and target words are randomly selected from that more difficult corpus. However, incorrect answers lead to the deduction of points (5 points per incorrect answer), and result in shifting down to a lower level of difficulty when students' points reach the thresholds. Thus, as in computer-adaptive testing (e.g., [18], successful gameplay results in gradually more challenging tasks and errors result in less-challenging tasks), students can fluctuate between levels of difficulty but more skilled students will encounter more difficult items.

Game performance was measured by the overall proportion of correct answers out of the number of attempted words (i.e., accuracy). We also calculated performance within each difficulty level based on the proportion of correct answers out of the number of the attempted words at a specific level. The highest level attained by any participant was Level 5, but few participants ever attained Levels 4 or 5. Therefore, these two levels were combined, resulting in five level-specific performance scores for each participant (i.e., Level 0 to Level 4).

Game Survey. Upon completion of the game, participants were asked to report their attitudes and perceptions of the game (see [14, 15]). Six items were extracted from measures used in two previous studies: "This game was fun to play," "This game was frustrating," "I enjoyed playing this game," "This game was boring," "The tasks in this game were easy,", and "I would play this game again." Participants rated their degrees of agreement with these statements on a 6-point Likert scale ranging from "1" (strongly disagree) to "6" (strongly agree).

2.3 Statistical Analyses

A principal component analysis was conducted on the game survey data to explore the dimensions of the items, given that the items were extracted from two previous studies [see 14, 15]. An oblique (nonorthogonal) rotation was applied in the analysis because we did not hypothesize the factors to be independent. After the principal components were revealed, participants' scores on each component were computed based on the regression coefficients of the items. The scores were then standardized and used in later analysis.

Hierarchical linear regressions were performed to test H1. Specifically, participants' vocabulary test scores were regressed on their game performance scores of each difficulty level and game attitude component scores. Hierarchical linear regressions were likewise conducted to test H2. Specifically, participants' reading comprehension test scores were predicted as a function of their game performance scores at each difficulty level and game attitude scores.

3 Results

3.1 Principal Component Analysis

A principal component analysis was performed to investigate the dimensions of the game survey. The analysis yielded two factors explaining a total of 70.1% of the variance for the entire set of variables. The means, standard deviations, as well as the loadings and communalities of the variables on the two factors are shown in Table 1. Factor 1 was labeled as "enjoyment" due to the high loadings by the following items: the game was fun to play; I enjoyed playing this game; I would play this game again. The first factor explained 45.4% of the variance. Factor 2 was labeled as "dissatisfaction" because of the high loadings by the following items: the game was frustrating; the game was boring. The variance explained by the second factor was 24.7%.

Table 1. Factor analysis on the game survey data

	M	SD	Loadings		Communality
			Factor 1 enjoyment	Factor 2 dissatisfaction	
This game was fun to play	4.75	1.05	.85	.09	.73
This game was frustrating	3.62	1.58	−.36	.79	.76
I enjoyed playing this game	4.83	1.17	.85	.11	.73
The tasks in this game were easy	4.56	1.14	.59	.42	.52
This game was boring	3.19	1.58	−.44	.77	.78
I would play this game again	4.73	1.24	.78	.27	.68

Note: 1 = strongly disagree; 6 = strongly agree

3.2 Descriptive Statistics of Predictor and Predicted Variables

Table 2 provides descriptive statistics of Vocab Flash game performance accuracy, game enjoyment, game dissatisfaction, and literacy skills, as indicated by GMRT vocabulary and comprehension subtests scores. Students were generally not dissatisfied with the game (Dissatisfaction Weighted M = 3.41) and tended to enjoy playing the game (Enjoyment Weighted M = 4.77). Game performance was highly correlated with vocabulary test scores ($r = .76$), and moderately correlated with reading test scores ($r = .60$). Game enjoyment was weakly correlated with vocabulary tests scores ($r = −.16$), and it was not significantly correlated with reading test scores or game performance. Game dissatisfaction, however, was moderately correlated with vocabulary test scores ($r = −.49$), reading test scores ($r = −.39$), and game performance ($r = −.51$).

3.3 Hierarchical Linear Regressions

First, a hierarchical linear regression analysis examined the extent to which the variance in vocabulary skill was explained by game performance, enjoyment, and dissatisfaction (i.e., H1; see Table 3). Model 1 included only game performance and Model 2 included both game performance and attitudes. Results indicated that game performance was the strongest predictor, with a significant but negligible added value for attitudes (i.e., very small R^2 change).

Table 2. Descriptive statistics and correlations between predictor and predicted variables

	M	SD	Min	Max	1	2	3	4
1	19.17	13.01	2.00	45.00				
2	17.35	10.42	6.00	48.00	.76***			
3	0.48	0.27	0.00	1.00	.76***	.60***		
4	4.77	1.00	1.00	6.00	−.16**	−.07	−.05	
5	3.41	1.40	1.00	6.00	−.49***	.−39***	−.51***	−.24*

1 = Gates MacGinitie Vocabulary Test Score, 2 = Gates MacGinitie
Reading Test Score, 3 = Vocab Flash Performance Accuracy (proportion
correct), 4 = Game Enjoyment (Factor 1), 5 = Game Dissatisfaction
(Factor 2).
***$p < .001$, **$p < .01$, *$p < .05$.

Table 3. Hierarchical multiple regression analysis for predicting vocabulary test scores

Variable	β	t	R^2	R^2 change
Model 1			.76***	.76***
Level 0 accuracy	.33	6.17***		
Level 1 accuracy	.08	1.65		
Level 2 accuracy	.30	4.55***		
Level 3 accuracy	.26	3.90***		
Level 4 & 5 accuracy	.05	.98		
Model 2			.78***	.02***
Level 0 accuracy	.28	5.25***		
Level 1 accuracy	.04	.91		
Level 2 accuracy	.28	4.41***		
Level 3 accuracy	.25	3.91***		
Level 4 & 5 accuracy	.06	1.25		
Enjoyment	−.10	−2.68**		
Dissatisfaction	−.15	−3.58***		

***$p < .001$, **$p < .01$

Second, a hierarchical regression analysis explored the extent to which the variance
in reading comprehension skill was explained by game performance, enjoyment, and
dissatisfaction (i.e., H2; see Table 4). Results revealed that game performance was the
strongest predictor, with no effect of attitudes (i.e., no R^2 change).

Table 4. Hierarchical multiple regression analysis for predicting reading comprehension test scores

Variable	β	t	R^2	R^2 change
Model 1			.74***	.74***
Level 0 accuracy	.03	.44		
Level 1 accuracy	−.01	.11		
Level 2 accuracy	.40	4.66***		
Level 3 accuracy	.05	.51		
Level 4 & 5 accuracy	.46	6.17***		
Model 2			.74***	.00
Level 0 accuracy	.02	.24		
Level 1 accuracy	−.01	.19		
Level 2 accuracy	.42	4.80***		
Level 3 accuracy	.05	.51		
Level 4 & 5 accuracy	.46	6.06***		
Enjoyment	.06	1.24		
Dissatisfaction	−.02	.32		

*** $p < .001$

4 Discussion

This study investigated the feasibility of implementing stealth assessment within Vocab Flash - a vocabulary game in iSTART. Specifically, we examined the extent to which participants' literacy skills (i.e., GMRT vocabulary and reading comprehension test scores) were predicted by game performance. We also explored whether the prediction of literacy skills by game performance may be moderated by students' attitudes toward the game. We hypothesized that performance in the vocabulary game would be strongly predictive of students' performance on the Gates MacGinitie vocabulary test (H1). We also expected game performance to be predictive of students' reading comprehension skills as measured by the Gates MacGinitie reding test (H2). At the same time, we attempted to rule out the possibility that students' attitude towards the game would moderate the relation between game performance and literacy skills.

Our results supported our two main hypotheses. Specifically, participants' game performance accounted for 76% and 74% of the variances in the standardized vocabulary and comprehension tests scores, respectively. The lower levels of game performance (levels 0, 2, 3) are significant predictors of vocabulary knowledge. In contrast, only higher levels of game performance (levels 2, 4 & 5) are predictive of reading comprehension skill. While vocabulary skill is directly reflected by students' knowledge of common words, higher level reading comprehension skill seems to be more strongly associated with less frequent words.

We further ruled out the possibility that students' attitude towards the game moderated the relation between game performance and literacy skills. Students tended to enjoy the game, and game attitudes (i.e., enjoyment and dissatisfaction) were not meaningfully predictive of literacy skills. Game enjoyment and dissatisfaction only accounted for 2% of the variance of vocabulary test scores beyond game performance. Additionally, attitudes did not account for significant variance in comprehension test scores.

These findings demonstrate the potential for integrating stealth assessments of literacy within games, which are more rapid, engaging, and enjoyable compared to completing standardized reading assessments. Stealth assessment is a type of assessment seamlessly embedded in game-based environments so that students can be assessed unobtrusively. Prior research suggested the possibility of integrating stealth assessment in generative games which typically embed open-ended questions. The findings from this study indicate that games such as Vocab Flash provide a stealth means of assessing literacy skills, which can complement the use of linguistic features of constructed responses (e.g., self-explanations, explanatory retrievals) [6, 7]. In the context of a tutoring system such as iSTART, stealth assessment of literacy skills offers a means to assess students while they are engaging in tutoring, and to update the student model. In the context of a classroom, these alternative means of assessment provide a way for students to be assessed without risking test fatigue.

Overall, the results of this study suggest that short, dynamic games have the potential to be a good platform for stealth literacy assessment. In addition to the vocabulary game explored in this study, there are other identification games in iSTART focusing on main ideas, summary, and questions asking. With the promising results from the current study, the next step is to investigate these and similar practice games. The ultimate goal of this research is to implement effective and efficient literacy stealth assessments in game-based learning environments to facilitate the adaptivity of ITS.

Acknowledgements. This research was supported by the Office of Naval Research through Grant N000142012623 and N000141712300. The opinions expressed are those of the authors and do not represent views of the Office of Naval Research.

References

1. Psotka, J., Massey, L.D., Mutter, S.A., Brown, J.S. (eds.). Intelligent Tutoring Systems: Lessons Learned. HoPsychology Press (1988)

2. Bayindir, R., Colak, I., Sagiroglu, S., Kahraman, H.T.: Application of adaptive artificial neural network method to model the excitation currents of synchronous motors. In: Wani, M.A., Khoshgoftaar, T., Zhu, X., Seliya, N. (eds.) Proceedings of the 11th International Conference on Machine Learning and Applications, vol. 2, pp. 498–502. IEEE (2012)
3. Shute, V.J., Ventura, M.: Measuring and Supporting Learning in Games: Stealth Assessment. The MIT Press, Cambridge (2013)
4. Kim, Y.J., Ifenthaler, D.: Game-based assessment: the past ten years and moving forward. In: Ifenthaler, D., Kim, Y.J. (eds.) Game-Based Assessment Revisited, pp. 3–11. Springer, Cham, Switzerland (2019)
5. Wang, L., Shute, V., Moore, G.R.: Lessons learned and best practices of stealth assessment. Int. J. Gaming Comput. Mediated Simul. (IJGCMS) **7**(4), 66–87 (2015)
6. McCarthy, K.S., Allen, L.K., Hinze, S.R.: Predicting Reading Comprehension from Constructed Responses: Explanatory Retrievals as Stealth Assessment. In: Bittencourt, I.I., Cukurova, M., Muldner, K., Luckin, R., Millán, E. (eds.) AIED 2020. LNCS (LNAI), vol. 12164, pp. 197–202. Springer, Cham (2020). https://doi.org/10.1007/978-3-030-52240-7_36
7. Allen, L.K., Snow, E.L., McNamara, D.S.: Are you reading my mind? Modeling students' reading comprehension skills with natural language processing techniques. In: Baron, J., Lynch, G., Maziarz, N., Blikstein, P., Merceron, A., Siemens, G. (eds.) Proceedings of the 5th International Learning Analytics and Knowledge Conference, pp. 246–254. ACM, Poughkeepsie (2015)
8. McNamara, D.S.: SERT: self-explanation reading training. Discourse Process. **38**, 1–30 (2004)
9. McNamara, D.S.: Self-explanation and reading strategy training (SERT) improves low-knowledge students' science course performance. Discourse Process. **54**(7), 479–492 (2017)
10. Johnson, A.M., Guerrero, T.A., Tighe, E.L., McNamara, D.S.: iSTART-ALL: confronting adult low literacy with intelligent tutoring for reading comprehension. In: Andre, E., Baker, R., Hu, X., Rodrigo, M.M.T., du Boulay, B. (eds.) International Conference on Artificial Intelligence in Education, pp. 125–136. Springer, Cham (2017). https://doi.org/10.1007/978-3-319-61425-0_11
11. Ruseti, S., et al.: Scoring summaries using recurrent neural networks. In: Nkambou, R., Azevedo, R., Vassileva, J. (eds.) ITS 2018. LNCS, vol. 10858, pp. 191–201. Springer, Cham (2018). https://doi.org/10.1007/978-3-319-91464-0_19
12. Ruseti, S., et al.: Predicting question quality using recurrent neural networks. In: Penstein Rosé, C., et al. (eds.) AIED 2018. LNCS (LNAI), vol. 10947, pp. 491–502. Springer, Cham (2018). https://doi.org/10.1007/978-3-319-93843-1_36
13. Magliano, J.P., Todaro, S., Millis, K., Wiemer-Hastings, K., Kim, H.J., McNamara, D.S.: Changes in reading strategies as a function of reading training: A comparison of live and computerized training. J. Educ. Comput. Res. **32**(2), 185–208 (2005)
14. Jackson, G.T., McNamara, D.S.: Motivational impacts of a game-based intelligent tutoring system. In: Murray, R.C., McCarthy, P.M. (eds.) Proceedings of the 24th International Florida Artificial Intelligence Research Society (FLAIRS) Conference, pp. 519–524. AAAI Press, Menlo Park (2011)
15. Jackson, G.T., McNamara, D.S.: Motivation and performance in a game-based intelligent tutoring system. J. Educ. Psychol. **105**(4), 1036 (2013)
16. Morgan, P.L., Fuchs, D.: Is there a bidirectional relationship between children's reading skills and reading motivation? Except. Child. **73**(2), 165–183 (2007)
17. McCarthy, K.S., Watanabe, M., Dai, J., McNamara, D.S.: Personalized learning in iSTART: past modifications and future design. J. Res. Technol. Educ. **52**(3), 301–321 (2020)
18. Meijer, R.R., Nering, M.L.: Computerized adaptive testing: overview and introduction. Appl. Psychol. Meas. **23**(3), 187–194 (1999)

19. Chall, J.S., Jacobs, V.A., Baldwin, L.E.: The Reading Crisis: Why Poor Children Fall Behind. Harvard University Press, Cambridge (1990)
20. Just, M.A., Carpenter, P.A.: The Psychology of Reading and Language Comprehension. Allyn & Bacon, Boston (1987)
21. Stahl, S.A., Fairbanks, M.M.: The effects of vocabulary instruction: a model-based meta-analysis. Rev. Educ. Res. **56**(1), 72–110 (1986)
22. Joshi, R.M., Aaron, P.G.: The component model of reading: Simple view of reading made a little more complex. Read. Psychol. **21**(2), 85–97 (2000)
23. Phillips, L.M., Norris, S.P., Osmond, W.C., Maynard, A.M.: Relative reading achievement: a longitudinal study of 187 children from first through sixth grades. J. Educ. Psychol. **94**(1), 3 (2002)
24. Davies, M.: The 385+ million word corpus of contemporary American English (1990–2008+): design, architecture, and linguistic insights. Int. J. Corpus Linguist. **14**(2), 159–190 (2009)
25. Jackson, G.T., Davis, N.L., Graesser, A.C., McNamara, D.S.: Students' enjoyment of a game-based tutoring system. In: Biswas, G., Bull, S., Kay, J., Mitrovic, A. (eds.) Proceedings of the 15th International Conference on Artificial Intelligence in Education, pp. 475–477. AIED, Auckland (2011)

Skill Mastery Measurement and Prediction to Adapt Instruction Strategies

Priya Ganapathy[1]([✉]), Lakshmi Priya Rangaraju[1], Gautam Kunapuli[2], and Jacob Yadegar[1]

[1] UtopiaCompression Corporation, Los Angeles, CA, USA
priya@utopiacompression.com
[2] Verisk Analytics, Jersey City, NJ, USA

Abstract. In this paper we present the design, development, application and validation of our skill mastery measurement software to help instructors adapt their instruction strategy to teach Visual AirCraft recognition (VACR) skill. Visual AirCraft recognition (VACR) is a critical skill required by soldiers operating surface-to-air missile defense systems to quickly recognize the aircraft and make engagement decisions. The current computer-based trainer to teach VACR has no intelligence to help instructors deliver personalized instructions or to track skill gaps. We compare our candidate automated support system that utilizes Dynamic Bayesian Network (DBN) models to measure skill progression to other conventional tutors and report our findings in terms of improved skill transfer and retention. The instruction delivery format incorporated in our automated support system is equivalent to Wings, Engine, Fuselage and Tail (WEFT) training that is provided by the instructors in a classroom setting. The goal of this study is to measure utility of our skill-tracking based automated system prior to its adoption by VACR instructors to impart WEFT training at Air Defense Artillery, Fort Sill, OK. We performed an Amazon Mechanical Turk (AMT) study to compare efficacy of our DBN-based VACR trainer with baseline and incremental tutors. The results indicate that our system increased overall transfer and retention performance of AMT participants by 19% and 16%, respectively compared to other tutors. We present the rationale behind design of these candidate tutors, implementation of DBN model for VACR and the AMT study design with final results.

Keywords: Skill-based automated support · Dynamic Bayesian network models · Visual aircraft recognition training

1 Introduction

The purpose of this study is to examine automated support systems to improve delivery of instructions to teach Visual Air Craft Recognition (VACR) (Pliler 1996a and Pliler 1996b), i.e., being able to identify an aircraft from a picture or in air. VACR is essential to air defense and is a critical component of various military operational specializations. This skill is especially important for ground-based soldiers who operate shoulder-mounted surface-to-air missiles. These personnel are required to quickly and

© Springer Nature Switzerland AG 2021
R. A. Sottilare and J. Schwarz (Eds.): HCII 2021, LNCS 12793, pp. 45–61, 2021.
https://doi.org/10.1007/978-3-030-77873-6_4

accurately recognize a visible aircraft as friend, neutral, or foe in order to rightly engage and simultaneously avoid incidents of friendly fire.

Typically, VACR training proceeds in two stages. The first stage is an instructorled classroom session where trainees are introduced to the four feature components that can be used to distinguish aircraft from each other: wings, engine, fuselage and tail, collectively known as WEFT features. In this stage, instructors use a slide presentation to introduce relevant aircraft and teach trainees to recognize the basic WEFT features. The WEFT features are not identified using technical terms but rather, layperson terms that are easily understandable and are identifiable even at a distance (Campbell 1990). The second stage consists of unsupervised, self-paced repetitive memory drills using computer-based training similar to using self-study based flash cards. Research literature on the efficacy of this training approach is sparse. One study, performed by Tubbs et al. (1981) reports that this two-stage approach (instructor-based classroom followed by self-paced flashcard method) resulted in a poor outcome, with only 30% of 900 trainees achieving the required minimum passing accuracy of 90%.

The computer-based training tool used currently to teach VACR was first deployed in 1986 and has not been updated significantly since. The system currently in use is outdated, which gives us an opportunity to leverage recent and significant advances in learning management systems, machine learning, and pedagogical strategies (Mayer 2008) to design, develop and test an intelligent support system for instructors to teach VACR via WEFT procedure. The WEFT instruction procedure is aimed at introducing structure for systematically distinguishing aircraft based on the composite of the WEFT elements as opposed to relying on memorization of each individual aircraft.

In addition, the proliferation of unmanned air systems and the rate of fratricide reported in recent conflicts (VACR 2016) have led to renewed interest in VACR. Our candidate support system examined in this study is intended to help instructors remediate in a timely fashion by providing appropriate WEFT instructions as trainee progress on their skill level.

1.1 Background and Related Work

In Juvina et al.'s study the VACR task was contrasted using real-world unfamiliar stimuli (i.e., aircraft) with a control task that used real-world familiar stimuli like trucks, boats, trains, etc. Both tasks are associative learning tasks with consistent stimulus response mapping (i.e., a visual object is associated with its name).

The main findings from that study suggested that learning in the aircraft task progresses differently than learning in the control task. The control task reached high levels of automation, which was associated with decreases in most brain regions, as reported in many laboratory studies (Chein and Schneider 2005). In contrast, the aircraft task recruited more brain resources as the participants learned to master it, particularly from brain regions involved in memory, representation, and control. Based on their findings, we hypothesized that learners might change the visual representation of the aircraft and also resolve interference from similar-looking stimuli as they practice. We expected that learners would benefit from an instructional process aimed at aiding memory encoding and retrieval, making correct associations, and resolving ambiguity and interference among representations and associations.

1.2 Current Study

The important feature of our proposed VACR training system is an assessment algorithm based on dynamic Bayesian networks (DBN) (Murphy 2002) to estimate mastery of each individual aircraft by trainees. Based on estimated mastery by the algorithm, the instruction delivery (timing and content) was adjusted to foster better learning. In this paper, we discuss the development of the DBN-based skill-mastery assessment algorithm and interface features. We also present the results from a study that was performed to evaluate the efficacy of our candidate training system against conventional VACR tutor and other incremental tutors without the skill-mastery assessment algorithm. We summarize our key conclusions from this validation study and discuss next steps for adoption of our support system by instructors in a classroom setting.

2 Design of an Automated VACR Training Support System

The design of the smart support system was formulated partly based on requirements gathered from end users at Fort Sill, OK. The end users (VACR instructors and subject matter experts) mainly wanted a better-looking interface (with high fidelity) that can be easily updated with new aircraft models. In addition, the instructors wanted a dashboard to track individual trainee's performance over different aircraft and also inform them when WEFT procedure to discriminate confusing aircraft must be introduced. To obtain a buy-in from the VACR instructors, we incorporated the WEFT procedure training in the proposed support system to demonstrate its overall effectiveness compared to other non-skill assessment based trainers.

2.1 Description of Different Candidate Tutors

As summarized in Table 1, we created four different tutors including our candidate VACR training support system. The front-end for the four trainers were developed using

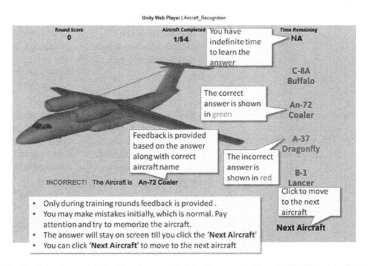

Fig. 1. Interface and feedback provided in the conventional VACR tutor (2D).

Unity 3D (Unity Technologies, San Francisco, CA). During a training round (TR) each tutor would present the same 50 aircraft in random sequence. Each aircraft presented in a given TR round is denoted as a trial. Each trial has two phases: (a) response phase followed by a (b) feedback phase. In response phase, an aircraft image/3D-model along with four name options is shown to the trainee. The trainee must then select the correct aircraft name from the four options within a period of 4 s. In the feedback phase, the trainee is informed if their choice is correct or incorrect and the correct aircraft name is displayed (Fig. 1). There is no time limit for the feedback phase; to proceed to next aircraft in the given TR round the trainee must press the "Next" button.

The tutors vary in terms of (a) front-end interface design, (b) difficulty level in terms of multiple choice options presented, (c) type of WEFT instructions presented and (d) the internal logic used to change the difficulty level in terms of multiple choice options and type of WEFT instructions presented (Table 1).

Table 1. Design details of four different tutors.

Tutor	Interface design	Difficulty of multiple-choice options	Type of feedback/WEFT instructions provided
Minimal, flashcard based (**2D**)	• Static 2D aircraft images presented • No interactive features	Random multiple-choice options; low probability of confusion between aircraft	• Correct/Incorrect and Name of Aircraft
3D with no assessment (**3DL1**)	• 3D aircraft models presented • User can inter-act with the models	Random multiple-choice options; low probability of confusion between aircraft	• Role of aircraft; • Correct/Incorrect and Name of Aircraft; • Level 1 instructions (distinctive WEFT feature);
Performance-based assessment (**3DL2**)	• 3D aircraft models presented • User can inter-act with the models	Switches from random multiple-choice options to confusing options at Day 3. The switch happens after reaching a 60% overall accuracy	• Role of aircraft; • Correct/Incorrect and Name of Aircraft; • Level 1 instructions (distinctive WEFT feature); • Level 2 instructions (comparative WEFT features)
Skill-mastery based assessment (**3DL3**)	• 3D aircraft models presented • User can interact with the models	Switches from random multiple choice options to confusing options as determined by the DBN skill mastery tracking model	• Role of aircraft; • Correct/Incorrect and Name of Aircraft; • Level 1 instructions (distinctive WEFT feature); • Level 2 instructions (comparative WEFT features);

2D VACR Tutor (Denoted 2D). A tutor featuring 2D static aircraft images similar to the computer-based system currently used for training soldiers (Fig. 1). The aircraft is presented along with four answer choices. Once the participant selects an answer, the tutor tells the trainee if their selection was correct or incorrect, and also provides the correct aircraft name. No WEFT instruction is provided.

We then used inputs from experts in learning science and education psychology to help design the interface for the remaining three tutors (Table 1, 3DL1, 3DL2 and 3DL3). Based on Juvina et al.'s study the experts conjectured that interaction with the aircraft model (as in rotate, zoom in and zoom out) could facilitate perception of the distinguishing features of the aircraft and thus accelerate learning and make the interface more engaging. As a result, all the three following tutors (Table 1, 3DL1, 3DL2 and 3DL3) would allow trainees to interact with the aircraft 3D models during the feedback phase (Fig. 2) so they can observe aircraft features from various angles if they choose.

We describe the differences between the three tutors as follows:

3D Level 1 VACR Tutor (Denoted 3DL1). During the feedback phase, the tutor gives the correct answer as with tutor 2D, but also provides an additional instruction that describes a distinctive WEFT feature and also the role or category of aircraft (Fig. 2). These instructions are called Level 1 instruction (first-level instruction).

3D Level 2 VACR Tutor (Denoted 3DL2). A game-like trainer that extends 3DL1 in two important ways; based on a trainee's observed performance (threshold at 60% accuracy), the tutor changes (1) the difficulty of the multiple-choice answer options presented to the trainee and (2) the detail of the instruction provided during the feedback phase.

When trainees are below 60% accuracy, 3DL2 functions exactly as 3DL1. Once a trainee crosses the 60% accuracy threshold across all aircraft, multiple-choice options begin to include the name of another similar/confusing aircraft, which represents an increase in difficulty as it makes selection by elimination harder and the training more engaging. In addition, in the feedback phase, trainees also begin to see Level 2 instruction if they make a mistake (Fig. 3). This second-level instruction included making pairwise comparison of distinguishing WEFT feature to discern the subtle differences between similar looking aircraft (correct and incorrect aircraft). The distinguishing WEFT component was highlighted on both aircraft accompanied with a text description. This design decision was also motivated by neuroimaging results presented in Juvina et al. 2015 showing higher activity in the anterior cingulate cortex during VACR learning, suggesting conflict resolution between similar aircraft prior to decision-making.

3D DBN-based VACR tutor (denoted 3DL3). In 3DL3, the switch in difficulty level of multiple choice options and therefore, presentation of Level 1 to Level 2 instructions is based on the assessment of trainee's skill mastery on each aircraft as predicted by a dynamic Bayesian network (DBN) algorithm. In this way, the tutor is able to provide a fully personalized learning experience, by changing the difficulty and instruction details for each trainee over each aircraft. In Sect. 2.2, we briefly describe the motivation to use DBN models and their implementation for VACR tutor. The 3DL3 interface looks identical to 3DL2 (Fig. 3).

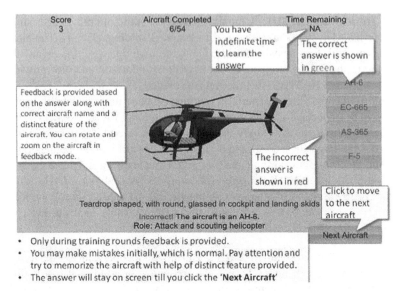

Fig. 2. Interface and feedback provided in the 3DL1 tutor.

2.2 Dynamic Bayesian Network (DBN) Algorithm to Track Aircraft Mastery

"Skill mastery" is defined as the ability to perform a given task with high accuracy and fast response time with low cognitive load (Hernandez-Meza et al. 2015). Research has shown that skill mastery gained during a training regimen directly translates to better performance in the field ("National Research Council", 1992; Proctor and Dutta 1995). Tracking skill mastery ideally and exactly would require the use of neuroimaging techniques, which are expensive and cannot be used for real-time training (Anderson et al. 2010). The goal of skill tracking is to avoid performing expensive neuroimaging studies and rely on data-driven algorithms that can be used to accurately infer innate skill mastery or decay. We have implemented such a data-driven approach for our smart VACR tutor based on dynamic Bayesian Networks (DBN).

Bayesian network-based probabilistic algorithms were first introduced in cognitive (ACT-R based) tutors (Anderson et al. 1982, Corbett and Anderson 1995) as an integral part to perform skill tracking in students. The algorithms are lightweight; thereby enabling real-time tracking of student's knowledge gaps and conceptual flaws as training ensues. These tutors have demonstrated significant improvements over traditional computer-based tutors (Koedinger and Anderson 1993) and can be at par with one-on-one training, were students receive individual instruction from teachers (VanLehn 2011).

Design of DBN Models for VACR Training. Typically, a Bayesian network model can assess trainee (in general, a "student") performance for a given instant (t). However, with a DBN model we can capture influence of trainee performance at time t on next time instants (t + 1, t + 2, and so forth).

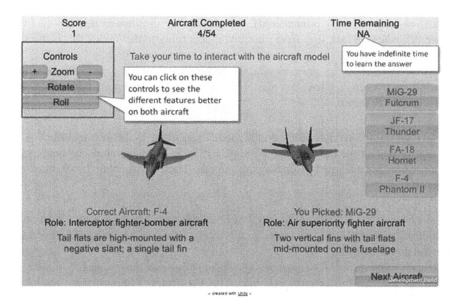

Fig. 3. Interface and feedback provided in the tutors: 3DL2/3DL3.

Learning of an aircraft is assumed to be independent of other aircraft, and thus each aircraft has a DBN model associated with it. At each learning episode, the DBN tracks two variables: Skill (S), which is a latent (hidden) variable and Answer (A), which is an observable (Fig. 4). Intuitively, Skill, or aircraft mastery is a variable that describes whether a trainee has mastered that aircraft or not; as a person's skill is not directly observable, it is treated as a hidden variable. Answer is an observable that represents how the trainee answered in the current episode: incorrectly or correctly.

We implemented a 2-slice DBN (Fig. 4) were:

1. Performance (A) observed at t is used to infer the skill level at t.
2. Skill (S) inferred at t is used to predict skill level at t + 1

We alter the pedagogy depending on our inference of skill level at t and prediction for t + 1. The variables and the links that represent how they interact with each other form a directed graph, or the structure of the DBN.

The power of DBNs lies in their ability to probabilistically capture interactions between the variables through the parameters of the DBN: the prior mastery probability, the transition probabilities and the observation probabilities. The initial probability mastery (θ_{S0}), is the probability that the trainee has already mastered the skill prior to training (in our case, this is the probability that the trainee knows the aircraft *a priori*).

The *observation probabilities* $P(A_t \mid S_t)$ can be used to predict what the trainee's answer will be in episode t. The observation probabilities contain two parameters of interest:

1. $P(A_t = incorrect \mid S_t = mastered)$, the probability the trainee misidentifies the aircraft, when, in fact, they have mastered it according to the model; this is the *slip probability P(slip)*.
2. $P(A_t = correct \mid S_t = unmastered)$, the probability the trainee correctly identifies the aircraft, when they have not mastered it according to the model; this is the *guess probability P(guess)*.

After the trainee gives the answer, the model transitions to the next episode, $t + 1$. This is governed by the *transition* probabilities, $P(S_{t+1} \mid S_t)$, which indicate how likely the trainee is to have learned to identify this aircraft. These also contain two parameters of interest:

1. $P(S_{t+1} = mastered \mid S_t = unmastered)$, the probability that the trainee has transitioned from unmastered to mastered state on this aircraft, that is, the *probability they have learned P(learn)*.
2. $P(S_{t+1} = unmastered \mid S_t = mastered)$, the probability that the trainee has unlearned, that is, *forgotten this aircraft P(forget)*. This parameter is important for modeling skill decay.

Each of the 50 aircraft has its own DBN model that estimates a trainee's mastery as they interact with the tutor. All the DBN models share the same structure but have different parameters. This captures the fact that trainees learn different aircraft at different rates and are more likely to confuse or forget certain aircraft; however, the underlying cognitive mechanism of learning remains the same. Together, these probabilities govern the dynamics of how trainees of differing skill levels learn identification of 50 aircraft during training. We estimated DBN parameters for each of the 50 aircraft using the Bayes Net Toolbox developed by Murphy (2001). Data collected from 3DL1 tutor was used to learn and test the DBN model parameters for each aircraft. The model parameters once learnt was incorporated in the 3DL3 tutor to track skill mastery (Van de Sande 2013).

DBN Model Implementation for VACR Training. The learned DBN parameters enable us to track mastery, that is, the probability that a trainee has mastered a particular aircraft, $P(S_t = mastered)$ across training rounds. The idea is that if the trainees reach a certain mastery level, we can introduce confusing aircraft names as options and switch the pedagogy from *Level 1 instructions* to *Level 2 instructions* (Table 1). To do this we had to identify the appropriate threshold on mastery for each aircraft.

To avoid individual computations of thresholds for 50 aircraft, we automatically group the average $P(S_t = mastered)$ curves generated for individual aircraft across all 3DL1 participants into three clusters (Fig. 5, left) using K-means clustering algorithm (MacQueen 1967). We see that the tracked masteries for these three clusters follow classical laws of acquisition (Newell and Rosenbloom, 1993; Delaney et al. 1998) that is, the power law of practice. The average mastery curves in Fig. 5 indicate that the difficulty in learning increases from Cluster 1 to Cluster 3.

Our goal is to identify appropriate thresholds that suggest that, improvement in mastery is slowing down (Fig. 5, right). Improvement in mastery is calculated by taking the difference in mastery levels P(St = mastered) between two consecutive training rounds.

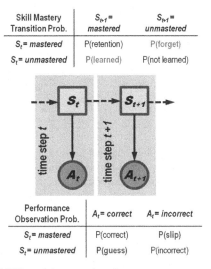

Skill Mastery Transition Prob.	S_{t+1} = mastered	S_{t+1} = unmastered
S_t = mastered	P(retention)	P(forget)
S_t = unmastered	P(learned)	P(not learned)

Performance Observation Prob.	A_t = correct	A_t = incorrect
S_t = mastered	P(correct)	P(slip)
S_t = unmastered	P(guess)	P(incorrect)

Fig. 4. DBN models to track trainee mastery on one aircraft.

Based on visual plateauing of mastery improvement we select the threshold to be at 6% (represented by the horizontal line at 0.06 in Fig. 5, right). For Clusters 1 and 2, rate of mastery improvement drops to 6% around Round 7. This corresponds to an average skill mastery threshold of $\tau 1 = 0.784$ and $\tau 2 = 0.524$ for Cluster 1 and 2, respectively (Fig. 5, left). While for Cluster 3 aircraft, the improvement in mastery is below 6% from Round 2 onwards; note that at least two rounds are needed to even compute improvement in mastery so the switch can only happen after Round 2. As a result, a lower mastery threshold $\tau 3 = 0.267$ was selected for Cluster 3. Therefore, the switch to Level 2 instruction from Level 1 instruction for Cluster 3 aircraft happened earlier compared to Cluster 2 and 1, respectively to allow the 3DL3 tutor to focus on the most difficult aircraft longer. This provides the learners more sessions with pairwise comparative (Level 2 instruction) instructions, thus providing longer time to help them distinguish between similar/conflicting aircraft.

We plot the p(Learn) and p(Guess) parameters estimated for individual aircraft belonging to the three clusters (Fig. 6). We see that the aircraft naturally cluster into three groups, i.e., the DBN model parameters successfully capture the differences in learning Cluster 1, Cluster 2 and Cluster 3 aircraft. In Fig. 7 left, we can visually confirm that Cluster 1 aircraft are indeed easy to identify and learn because they have distinct and easily identifiable characteristics and therefore, Level 2 instructions are required less for them. Cluster 3 aircraft (Fig. 7, right) are difficult to identify, as they are very similar to each other, and therefore, require more of Level 2 instructions that highlight the subtle individual differences between them. This reaffirms that the implemented DBN models can accurately track skill mastery and the resultant personalized WEFT instruction delivery must also foster learning.

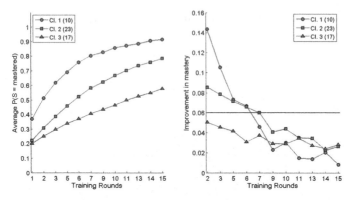

Fig. 5. (Left) Clustered skill mastery plots obtained for three groups of aircraft. (Right) Plot of improvement in mastery across rounds. When the improvement in mastery drops below 6% we change the level of difficulty and present Level 2 instructions.

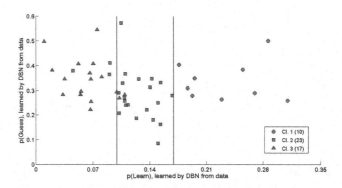

Fig. 6. Plot of DBN parameters for individual aircraft belonging to the three clusters

2.3   Study Aim and Research Questions

Through this study, we want to compare the efficacy of the four different systems to train in VACR. We also want to answer the following research questions:

1. Does DBN skill-based trainer outperform other tutors in terms of training and transfer accuracy?
2. Does DBN skill-based tutor improve retention compared to other tutors?

In Sect. 3, we describe participant recruitment strategy and study design.

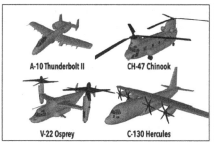

Fig. 7. Comparing easy (left) and hard (right) aircraft clusters visually.

3 Method

3.1 Participants

Amazon Mechanical Turk (AMT) platform was mainly used to recruit, send emails with study links, and make payments to workers after the study is complete. An IRB-approved disclosure/consent sheet to inform participants of study rules, payment structure, and data collection strategy was posted on AMT website for each human intelligence task (HIT). HIT refers to each task posted on AMT platform to inform and recruit workers for that individual task. To recruit participants for each tutor (2D, 3DL1, 3DL2 and 3DL3), separate HITs via the standard AMT survey feature were posted. Only participants who agreed to the posted study rules/payment structure were recruited.

Ideally, recruitment for all conditions (2D, 3DL1, 3DL2 and 3DL3) should have been done simultaneously. However, the investigators required data from 3DL1 tutor to learn DBN parameters for the 3DL3 tutor. Further, due to lack of resources (labor, budget) during study deployment, the investigators could deploy only one tutor at a time (2D-3DL1-3DL2-3DL3). As a result, the 3DL3 was the last study to be conducted. N = 100, 100, 100 and 85 AMT workers accepted the 'HIT' to participate in 2D, 3DL1, 3DL2 and 3DL3 tutoring conditions respectively.

3.2 Procedure

Data Collection. The IDs of participants who accepted the HIT were manually entered into backend MySQL database by the team. A web link of each tutor created using Unity3D was sent via email to consented participants via AMT platform. Participants were asked to enter their worker ID to log on to the website. Only those participants whose ID matched with the database where allowed to log in to the website and practice on respective tutors. The data from participants was stored in the MySQL database as text files denoted by their worker ID. The research team hosted the website and the MySQL database on the Amazon EC2 servers.

Payment Structure. Each of the tutors was evaluated by their respective group of participants over a period of five days. Each session (per day) lasted for about 30–40 min.

Participants were paid $2 for each session and were free to withdraw from the study at any point. Subjects who completed the 5 days of study were paid a total of $12 (5 sessions × $2 per session + $2 completion bonus).

Base (Training and Test) Rounds. Over the first four days, participants trained on 50 aircraft that comprised the *base set*. This set is used to collect participant behavior (accuracy, response time, feedback time, user interaction). Each day is divided into four rounds: three training (TR) rounds and one test (TE) round. Within each TR, the participant trains on a random sequence of the same 50 aircraft. They have 4 s (fix-paced) to choose the correct answer from four multiple-choice options, after which they are given the appropriate feedback (correctness, answer and useful instructions). There is no time limit on feedback (self-paced), making all the four tutors mix-paced tutors. Following three training rounds, the participants then undergo one round of testing; this is identical to the training round except participants identify aircraft without knowing their progress until they complete all 50 aircraft. Also, no feedback is provided. During test rounds, they have 10 s (fix-pace) to choose the correct answer as opposed to 5 s during training rounds.

Transfer (Training and Test) Rounds. After four days of training, on the fifth day, participants are presented with an entirely new set of 20 aircraft that they have not seen during training, i.e., 20 aircraft distinct from the base set. The purpose of Day 5 is to evaluate if participants can effectively transfer visual aircraft recognition skills, that is, this *transfer set* is used to evaluate if the participants have "learned to learn" aircraft. Day 5 also included 3 TR rounds and 1 TE round; however in TR round feedback given for all groups was limited to the correct name of the aircraft shown and the accuracy of that trial. No additional instruction unlike base TR rounds was given to the 3DL1, 3DL2 and 3DL3 participants during transfer TR rounds.

Retention Rounds. After 3 months of completing the training regimen, subjects who completed Day 1 to Day 5 in each experimental group (3DL1, 3DL2 and 3DL3) were emailed via AMT to participate in a follow-up retention study. Here, the study was limited to a day (about 15 min) with 3 test rounds to measure how well participants remembered the 50 aircraft they were trained on. The investigators could not perform retention study on 2D participants due to automated deletion of stored HIT on AMT website (beyond 120 days of posting the original HIT). As a result, the investigators could not use the AMT website to send out individual emails to 2D participants and request them to participate for the retention study. All the 3D retention studies were therefore conducted at 90 days (approx. 3 months) of posting the corresponding original HITs.

Attention Trials. To measure participants' attention level during each base and transfer rounds, attention trials were added (4 trials each round). The 4 trials were randomized but spaced out so that there is 1 attention trial after 12–15 aircraft during base rounds (total 54 trials) and 5–7 aircraft being shown during transfer rounds (total 24 trials), respectively. The interface for attention trials remained the same as for the aircraft. Subjects were notified of these attention trials in the consent form as a means to ensure that participants do not randomly click on answers while doing the training and thereby, get disqualified.

4   Results and Discussion

Research Question 1. Does DBN skill-based trainer outperform other tutors in terms of learning and transfer accuracy?

The final data analyzed in this study are of participants who completed all the 5 sessions across 2D, 3DL1, 3DL2 and 3DL3 tutors (N = 41, 35, 32 and 23, respectively). We hypothesized that participant's training on DBN-based skill tutor will show higher performance across base and transfer test rounds.

Base test accuracy. An ANOVA test was performed to compare the average participant's accuracy (performance) obtained across multiple sessions for the four tutors (groups). (Fig. 8, x-axis: Trials/Rounds; y-axis: average accuracy across rounds and Fig. 9 x-axis: base train, base test, transfer train, transfer test; y-axis: average accuracy) indicate that the participants in the four groups did not differ in performance on the end test accuracy (Round 16) on base set.

The interface for 3DL2 and 3DL3 is consistent with 3DL1 (Fig. 2 and Fig. 3, Table 1). 3DL2 tutor increases the game complexity after subject hit an overall 60% accuracy (typically Day 3 of the study). The complexity is increased by displaying aircraft names from the same category as options compared to the aircraft model shown. As a result, during training rounds (Day 3, Day 4), we see a drastic dip in base training performance due to overload of Level 2 instructions and making learning more difficult for the subjects (Fig. 8).

In case of 3DL3, the complexity of the training is increased gradually depending on the subject's predicted mastery on individual aircraft. As discussed for hard aircraft (Fig. 7), Level 2 instructions are presented much earlier on to provide sufficient practice time to learn those aircraft. Due to gradual increase in complexity of the training material, we do not see any drastic dip in base training round performance unlike in 3DL2.

Transfer Test Accuracy. 3DL3 (DBN-based trainer) fosters deeper learning of the aircraft recognition task compared to the other groups based on transfer test accuracy (Round 20) (F $(3,127)$ = 2.6, p = 0.03, η^2 = 0.057). The transfer test accuracy for 2D (mean difference: -0.11, 95% CI: $[-0.26 -0.01]$), 3DL1 (mean difference: -0.15, 95% CI: $[-0.29 -0.007]$) and 3DL2 (mean difference: -0.10, 95% CI: $[-0.24 -0.01]$) were significantly lower than 3DL3. 3DL3 participants showed 19.7% improvement in average (mean accuracy = 0.76 ± 0.18) performance compared to pooled performance of remaining groups (mean accuracy = 0.64 ± 0.21).

We hypothesize that the timing of instruction delivery as dictated by the underlying DBN model tracking mastery of participants on individual aircraft fosters "deeper declarative knowledge" and conflict resolution between aircraft. As a result, the 3DL3 tutor trains the participants to learn aircraft in terms of WEFT features better compared to all other tutors (2D, 3DL1, 3DL2). Results on the transfer round is key as in reality, soldiers performing VACR task in the field often face different aircraft then the ones they are trained in the classroom. In additional, the hotlist of aircraft keeps changing over years. Therefore, it is important that soldiers learn the skill of accurately recognizing or at least describing aircraft based on their W, E, F and T components to their remote supervisor who can then ID the aircraft for them. The design of the 3DL3 tutor is successful in assisting instructors teach VACR skill, i.e., to learn to recognize aircraft based on WEFT features compared to all other tutors.

Research Question 2. Does DBN skill-based tutor improve retention compared to other tutors?

It is our hypothesis that 3DL3 tutor will foster deeper learning compared to other tutors which will in turn will lead to better retention of studied material. An ANOVA test was performed to compare the mean performance of participants across three test rounds. The performance of subjects across 3DL1, 3DL2 and 3DL3 on retention study (3 Test rounds) are shown in Fig. 10 (x-axis: Test 1, Test 2 and Test 3; y-axis: average performance).

The results indicate that 3DL3 (mean % accuracy $= 62 \pm 3$) results in better retention compared to 3DL1 (mean % accuracy $= 51 \pm 2$) and 3DL2 (mean % accuracy $= 55\pm2$) ($F (2, 65) = 3.03$, p $= 0.04$, $\eta2 = 0.09$).

The means of 3DL1 (mean difference: -0.1105, 95% CI: $[-0.2183 -0.0027]$) and 3DL2 (mean difference: -0.06, 95% CI: $[-0.1738 -0.001]$) were significantly lower than 3DL3.

This confirms that 3DL3 helps in improving retention (16.6% higher) by providing personalized delivery of feedback in terms of WEFT instructions compared to 3DL1 and 3DL2 tutors.

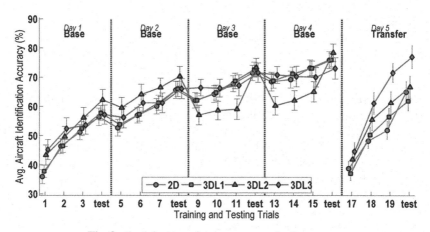

Fig. 8. Participant performance across the four tutors.

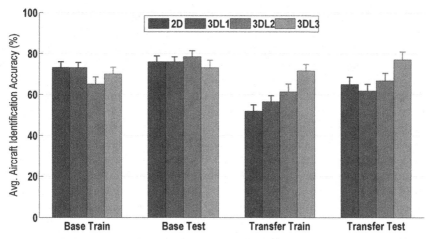

Fig. 9. Average performances of participants on Base (Train, Test) rounds and Transfer (Train and Test) across the four study groups.

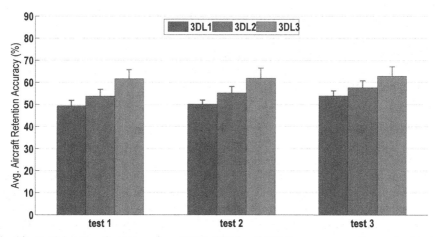

Fig. 10. Participant performances from 3DL1, 3DL2 and 3DL3 groups across three retention test rounds.

5   Conclusions

Currently, the VACR computer-based train used at Air Defense Artillery (eventual customer for this technology) is similar to a 2D tutor presented in this paper. The goal of this research is to establish the efficacy of a DBN-based tutor (over conventional 2D tutor) that tracks skill mastery and thereby, inform instructors to provide appropriate scaffolding to improve learning (Level 1 vs. Level 2 style WEFT training). We are also interested to compare intermediate tutors (3DL1 and 3DL2) which are developed with better interactive features and pedagogy delivery compared to 2D tutor but do not involve a machine learning algorithm as in the case of 3DL3 (DBN-based tutor) to track skill mastery. The goal of the automated system for VACR is to inculcate the skill of "learning to learn the WEFT features of an aircraft" as opposed to memorizing an aircraft. Our study has demonstrated that our candidate 3DL3 tutor (based on DBN model-based prediction of skill mastery) outperforms other tutors (2D, 3DL1, 3DL2) in terms of transfer and retention. The study further validates that providing personalized instruction based on skill-assessment (3DL3) is more effective than a performance-based assessment (3DL2).

The DBN models for the 3DL3 tutor was built on data from 3DL1 study as the interface was similar to 3DL3 (Fig. 2 and Fig. 3) and there was no change in instruction delivery based on performance. The model learns the parameters (probability of learn, forget, guess and slip and initial mastery) for each individual aircraft from 3DL1 data. The independence assumption to learn one DBN model for each aircraft allows us to train the model with less data. As more data is collected, better DBN models that capture similarity between training aircraft can be built. The automatic assignment of the aircraft to respective "easy", "intermediate" and "hard" cluster (Fig. 6) based on learned DBN parameters (probability of learn and guess) is similar to visually inspecting the aircraft and then clustering (Fig. 7). This to some degree confirms that the developed DBN models can also accurately predict skill mastery which is a latent parameter.

Further study is warranted to see if transfer test results on the conventional 2D tutor can be significantly boosted by adding a skill mastery assessment algorithm similar to 3DL3 along with instructional scaffolding. The result of this study will clearly prove or disprove the impact of introducing 3D interactive aircraft models and delineate the influence of skill mastery assessment algorithm and instruction delivery on performance.

Our goal is to develop a commercial VACR training support product based on these study insights for the Air Defense Artillery community.

6 Future Work

DBN-based skill assessment models are data-driven models. As a result, data from initial class cohorts (typically, at least $N = 18$–30 trainees) is required to train the DBN models for any learning task. Research is ongoing to determine if instructor-instantiated DBN model parameters will reduce the need for large number of initial trainee traces. This will facilitate easier integration and use of DBN model-based skill assessment for a range of military training courses.

References

Anderson, J.: Acquisition of cognitive skill. Psychol. Rev. **89**(4), 369–406 (1982)

Campbell, L.W.: An Intelligent Tutor System for Visual Aircraft Recognition. Master's Thesis, Naval Postgraduate School, Monterey, CA (1990)

Corbett, A., Anderson, J.: Knowledge tracing: modeling the acquisition of procedural knowledge. User Model User Adapt. Interact. **4**, 253–278 (1995)

Chein, M.J., Schneider, W.: Neuroimaging studies of practice-related change: fMRI and meta-analytic evidence of a domain-general control network for learning. Cogn. Brain Res. **25**, 607–623 (2005)

Delaney, P.F., Reder, L.M., Staszewski, J.J., Ritter, F.E.: The strategy specific nature of improvement: the power law applies by strategy within task. Psychol. Sci. **9**(1), 1–8 (1998)

Hernandez-Meza, G., Slason, L., Ayaz, H., Craven, P., Oden, K., Izzetoglu, K.: Investigation of functional near infrared spectroscopy in evaluation of pilot expertise acquisition. In: Schmorrow, D.D., Fidopiastis, C.M. (eds.) AC 2015. LNCS (LNAI), vol. 9183, pp. 232–243. Springer, Cham (2015). https://doi.org/10.1007/978-3-319-20816-9_23

Juvina, I., et al.: Neurocognitive correlates of learning in a visual object recognition task. In: Schmorrow, D.D., Fidopiastis, C.M. (eds.) AC 2015. LNCS (LNAI), vol. 9183, pp. 256–267. Springer, Cham (2015). https://doi.org/10.1007/978-3-319-20816-9_25

Koedinger, K., Anderson, J.: Effective use of intelligent software in high school math classrooms. In: Brna, P., Ohlsson, S., Pan, H., (eds.) Proceedings of the world conference on Artificial Intelligence in Education. Charlottesville, VA: AACE, pp. 241–248 (1993)

Mason, W., Suri, S.: Conducting behavioral research on Amazon's mechanical turk. Behav. Res. **44**(1), 1–23 (2011)

MacQueen, J.B.: Some methods for classification and analysis of multivariate observations. In: Proceedings of 5th Berkeley Symposium on Mathematical Statistics and Probability. University of California Press, pp. 281–297 (1967)

Mayer, R.E. Technology and training. In: Blascovich, B.J., Hartel, C.R. (Eds.), Human Behavior in Military Contexts, pp. 39–45. Washington, DC: National Academies Press (2001)

The Bayes Net Toolbox for MATLAB. Computing Science & Statistics, 33. URL: https://code.google.com/p/bnt/. Assessed 12 Apr 2020

Murphy, K.P.: Dynamic Bayesian Networks: Representation, Inference and Learning, Ph.D. Thesis, UC Berkeley, Computer Science Division (2002)

National Research Council: In the mind's eye: Enhancing Human Performance "Optimizing long-term learning and retention", Druckman, D., Bjork, R., (eds.), pp. 23–52 (1992)

Newell, A., Rosenbloom, P.S.: Mechanisms of skill acquisition and the law of practice. In: Anderson, A.R. (ed.), Cognitive skills and their acquisition, pp. 1–55. Erlbaum press, New Jersey (1993)

Pliler, J.: Aircraft Recognition Training: A Continuing Process. Air Defense Artillery, HQDA PB 44–96–2, 15–17 (1996a)

Pliler, J.: VACR Goes Multimedia. Air Defense Artillery, HQDA PB 44–96–2, 17–20 (1996b).

Proctor, R.W., Dutta, A.: Skill Acquisition and Human Performance. Sage, Thousand Oaks (1995)

Tubbs, J., Deason, P., Evertt, E., Hansen, A.: CHAPARRAL training subsystem effectiveness analysis. In: Proceedings of 23rd Annual Conference of the Military Testing Association (1981)

VanLehn, K.: The relative effectiveness of human tutoring, intelligent tutoring systems, and other tutoring systems. Educ. Psychol. **46**(4), 197–221 (2011)

Visual Aircraft Recognition (VACR) Field Manual, No. 3–01.80. http://armypubs.army.mil/doc trine/DR_pubs/dr_a/pdf/tc3_01x80.pdf . Accessed 02 Apr 2021

Van de Sande, B.: Properties of the Bayesian knowledge tracing model. J. Educ. Data Min. **5**(2), 1–10 (2013)

Measuring Flow, Immersion and Arousal/Valence for Application in Adaptive Learning Systems

Ehm Kannegieser[1]([✉]) [iD], Daniel Atorf[1] [iD], and Joachim Herold[2]

[1] Fraunhofer IOSB, Fraunhoferstr. 1, 76131 Karlsruhe, Germany
{ehm.kannegieser,daniel.atorf}@iosb.fraunhofer.de
[2] Hochschule Furtwangen University, Robert-Gerwig-Platz 1, 78120 Furtwangen, Germany
joachim.herold@hs-furtwangen.de

Abstract. Flow and Immersion are states of deep focus and thorough concentration on an activity, in which the subjective perception of performance reaches an optimum and intrinsic motivation peaks. High intrinsic motivation and deep focus does not only influence learning effects positively, deriving or enriching user models with raw and processed physiological data might also prove invaluable for successful adaptation processes that may be used to further improve learning outcome. So far, there is no reliable method to underpin states of deep focus with physiological characteristics, which would allow detecting such states objectively. Both Flow and Immersion are therefore classically measured using questionnaires. Given that the subjects are not answering the questionnaires during the activity, thus potentially breaking chances to reach states of Flow and Immersion, this method is both highly subjective and delayed - at least the latter somewhat impacting on the accuracy of the questionnaires results. To address these shortcomings, the design of a study to measure deep focus states through finding correlations between questionnaire answers and physiological sensor data (galvanic skin response, electrocardiography, eye tracking) is briefly referenced. The results of the study are discussed, motivating why the Flow model, as is, needs to be revised to allow a more fine grained measurement approach.

Keywords: Physiology of flow · User modelling · Immersion · Emotional theory · Arousal/valence

1 Introduction

The first definition of Flow as a "channel" described by Prof. Csikszentmihalyi [1], only allowed for a qualitative view, although a quantifiable way to describe Flow would be most interesting for evaluating learning systems, such as serious games, which rely on high intrinsic motivation to transfer learning content. Flow either is reached - or not - depending on the balance of the subjects' skill and challenge of the task at hand. To allow a more fine-grained mapping of deep focus states, a combined model of Flow and the three-tier model of Engagement based Immersion [2] becomes evident, as relatedness is

© Springer Nature Switzerland AG 2021
R. A. Sottilare and J. Schwarz (Eds.): HCII 2021, LNCS 12793, pp. 62–78, 2021.
https://doi.org/10.1007/978-3-030-77873-6_5

assumed, due to the similarities in definition. A way to achieve a quantitative measuring method as well as show relation between the models of Flow and Immersion would be to find correlations between those states - elicited by questionnaires, classically - and physiological measurements taken during the activity potential participants are interviewed upon. The physiological parameters with the most significance to the question, whether a participant is in an state of deep focus, should be narrowed down in an iterative approach and obtained in a non-invasive kind of way to prevent any disturbance of such states.

As the definition of Flow progressed into the eight-channel Flow model [3] later on, an emotion based, qualitative perspective becomes available, which is dividing Flow into three emotional connoted categories: positive, negative and mean/neutral level. Consequently, the approach to further extend the above mentioned combined model of Flow and Immersion by the dimensions of Arousal and Valence is taken on. This allows to incorporate video and electromyography based emotion recognition data to accompany physiological sensor data for correlation analysis with a set of questionnaires extended by the aspect of Arousal and Valence.

2 Literature Review

2.1 Presence

The term Presence was coined during the advent of VR technology. Generally, it is used to describe the psychological sense of being in a virtual environment and is based on telepresence, which was invented by Marvin Minsky: Telepresence refers to the degree a person controlling an element in a virtual environment feels as if they are really in that virtual environment. For example, when controlling a robotic arm, the term telepresence may refer to the degree the controller feels the robotic arm is their arm [4].

The generally accepted definition of Presence was given by Witmer and Singer [5] as the subjective feeling of being in a virtual environment, even when one is physically situated in another. It is synonymous with experiencing the computer-generated environment rather than the actual physical locale.

Presence is measured with questionnaires based on four factors (each divided into multiple sub factors which are omitted here): Control Factors which describe how well-controlled the virtual environment is, sensory factors which deal with perception of the environment, distraction factors which are focused on decreasing real-life distractions from the virtual environment and realism factors, which are based on the difference between the real world and the virtual environment [5]. The presence questionnaire is generally considered the most popular way to measure presence [6], although criticism was presented by Slater: while agreeing with Witmer and Singer's definition of presence, his measurement of presence is not based on the person's response to the virtual environment, but rather on attributes of the virtual environment itself. It has three aspects [7]:

- The sense of 'being there' in the environment depicted by the VE.
- The extent to which the VE becomes the dominant one - i.e., that participants will tend to respond to events in the VE rather than in the "real world".

• The extent to which participants, after the VE experience, remember it as having visited a "place" rather than just having seen images generated by a computer.

2.2 Immersion

Immersion is used to refer to two different things known as spatial Immersion and emotional Immersion [8]. The definition of spatial Immersion is synonymous with the definition of Presence defined in Sect. 2.1. As such it refers to the psychological sense of perceiving a virtual reality as real while being physically located in another.

Qin defines Immersion in a different way by analyzing Immersion in relation to narrative structure of a video game [9]: they argue that games differ from traditional narrative mediums because of their interactivity and players are not limited to the role of the audience, but additionally part of the narration, influencing the story's progression with their decisions. As such, they assess that the emotional Immersion of the player is strongly linked to the structure and content of the game story. According to that model, Immersion can also be measured by analyzing a game's narration.

This paper focusses on the definition of emotional/Engagement-based Immersion. This type of Immersion deals with the intensity of user Engagement with software. Ermi and Mäyrä [10] analyze Immersion in games as part of gameplay. When analyzing what immerses players into virtual environments, they defined three important components of the gameplay experience:

The first dimension is called sensory Immersion and refers to the audiovisual perception players have of the game. For example, a game with greater audio and better visuals will generally invoke a greater sense of Immersion in players than games with lower audiovisual quality. As such, this becomes a measurable quantity for determining how much Immersion a game may provide. Second, they identify the dimension of challenge-based Immersion which is equivalent to the definition of Csikszentmihalyi's Flow model (see Sect. 2.3), as it describes the balance of skill and challenge - which increases when a balance is struck between personal ability and the challenges presented by the game. The final dimension is called imaginative Immersion and, like the definition by Qin, considers the story and world of the game as a reason for the Immersion experienced. As such, the model includes both game-centric aspects of measuring Immersion (audiovisual quality and narrative structure) as well as player-centric aspects (Flow state).

Cairns and Jennett define this type of Immersion in their series of papers [2, 11]: Immersion, as experienced by players, is a multi-level construct. Three levels are identified: The first level is called Engagement, which is automatically achieved when the subject interacts with the software. The second level, Engrossment, is achieved when the subject becomes emotionally involved in the activity. In terms of software, it is synonymous with the feeling of the controls becoming invisible. The highest stage of Immersion is referred to as total Immersion. In this state, the subject is completely cut off from reality and experiences a loss of spatial and temporal awareness.

Based on this definition Jennett developed a questionnaire to measure Immersion [11]. They define five main factors: Cognitive involvement, real world dissociation, challenge, emotional involvement and control. Many of these factors overlap with Flow, the optimal experience of an activity - see Sect. 2.3. The main differences between Flow and Immersion are that Immersion may be a sub-optimal experience and Flow does not have levels, while Immersion, as defined by Cairns, does have levels of differing intensity.

Cheng improves upon Cairn's model of Immersion [12] by adding dimensions to each of the three layers: Engagement is broken into Attraction, Time Investment and Usability. In order to engage with software, the software must have some intrinsic or extrinsic attraction to the player. Investing time is the basic requirement for engaging with the software while easy usability increases likelihood of interaction. Engrossment, the second level of Cairn's Immersion levels is down into: emotional attachment of the user to the software and decreased perceptions of temporal and spatial surroundings. The final level of Cairn's Immersion model, total Immersion, is referred to, as the loss of spatial awareness and empathy. Cheng's improved model is shown in Fig. 1.

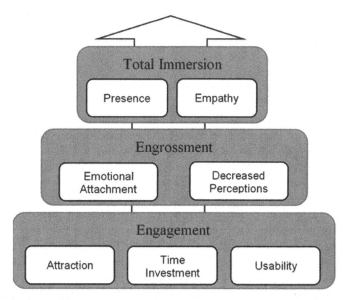

Fig. 1. Hierarchical Immersion model by Cairns and improved upon by Cheng

2.3 Flow

Flow was first described by Csikszentmihalyi as the state of the optimal experience of an activity [3]. When entering a state of Flow, even taxing activities like work no longer feel taxing, but rather feel enjoyable. Csikszentmihalyi bases Flow on the model of extrinsic and intrinsic motivation. Only intrinsically motivated actions, which are not motivated by external factors, can reach the Flow state. Flow is reachable when the challenge presented by such an intrinsically motivated action is balanced with the skill of the person performing the task.

Flow is generally measured using self-report questionnaires. Questionnaires can be employed during or after the Flow state takes place. Elicitation with questionnaires during the Flow state is difficult as the state of extreme concentration is broken by this distracting activity. These questionnaires are related to the original core aspects of Flow described by Csikszentmihalyi. They are answered using a likert scale. A likert scale is a rating scale for questionnaires that provides fixed answers in a range, providing possible answers from strongly agree to strongly disagree [13]. Different questionnaires can be used to measure Flow for different applications. They differ in length and target area they are evaluating.

For gaming targets, the most important questionnaire is the GameFlow questionnaire developed by Sweetser and Wyeth, which maps Csikszentmihalyi's original Flow aspects to gaming [14]. Additionally, Fu created the EGameFlow questionnaire based on the GameFlow questionnaire to measure Flow during serious learning games [15].

When using the questionnaire multiple times, a variation of the Flow questionnaire using fewer bullet points can be useful. For this purpose, Rheinberg developed the Flow Short Scale questionnaire [16]. It only includes 16 items and as such represents a more shallow measurement of Flow. It proves to be useful in cases where elicitation time is limited or where the questionnaire is used together with other questionnaires.

3   A Combined Model of Flow and Immersion

As explained there are a variety of definitions given for Immersion. The authors' goal is to analyze the effect of Immersion on players. As such, definitions based on analyzing game structure rather than player reaction are uninteresting for our investigation. This eliminates Qin's model, which focused on analyzing a game's narrative structure, as well as Ermi and Mäyrä's model because their audiovisual and narrative dimensions of the questionnaire focus on analyzing the game, while the challenge dimension is directly taken from Csikszentmihalyi's Flow definition – which is already part of our model.

Cairns' Immersion definition remains, as it focuses mainly on the player's reaction to the software. As mentioned in Sect. 2.2, the final level of Cairns' Immersion model, "total Immersion", has two components: loss of spatial awareness and empathy [12]. Georgiou and Kyza define empathy as synonymous with Flow [17]. This fits well with Cairns' definition of Immersion as the "psychology of sub-optimal experience" [2], while Flow is referred to by Csikszentmihalyi as the "psychology of optimal experience" [3]. In a combined model, Flow would become the highest state in Cairns' multi-level Immersion model (Fig. 2).

Looking at the components of Flow and Immersion, a large overlap can be identified. Challenge and control are a part of both Flow and Immersion. Real world dissociation is also found as part of both Immersion and Flow, both as temporal and spatial dissociation (when interacting with virtual environments). The Flow state's concentration aspect is synonymous with the most extreme version of Immersion' cognitive involvement. Flow is also strengthened by direct feedback from the interaction, which is not required in order to become immersed in an activity. This can be explained with Flow being an extreme version of Immersion (see Table 1).

At the base of the proposed model, Cairns' multi-level Immersion model is employed, augmented by Cheng's model to extend each level of Immersion with further criteria (see Fig. 1). Csikszentmihalyi's Flow model of optimal experience comes into play as part

Table 1. Comparison of similarities in Flow and Immersion definitions.

Flow	Immersion
Task	Game at hand
Concentration	Cognitive Involvement
Balance of Skill/Challenge	Challenge
Sense of Control	Control
Clear Goals	Emotional Involvement
Immediate Feedback	-
Reduced Sense of Self and Time	Real World Dissociation

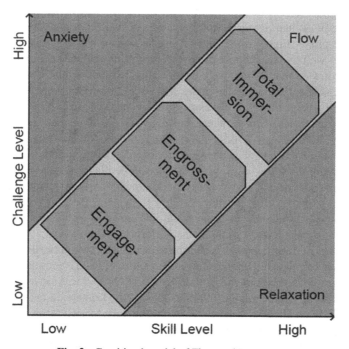

Fig. 2. Combined model of Flow and Immersion

of the highest level of Cairns' Immersion model, total Immersion: it depicts an increase in Flow among the diagonal through sub states. Given this diagonal increase, the lower levels of Immersion, Engagement and Engrossment resemble the lower to medium Flow levels in the bottom left to center area of the model, while total Immersion resembles the highest Flow level in the upper right corner (see Fig. 2). As thus, the authors' model proposal can be summed up as a unification of Flow and Immersion, which treats Flow as the most extreme state of Immersion.

4 Measuring Flow and Immersion

To validate or falsify the assumptions made in Sect. 3, a study is proposed to measure participants experiencing during a period of computer gameplay by employing the questionnaires according to the discussion in Sect. 2 and 3. During gameplay physiological measurements will be taken, to verify whether correlation between physiological data and occurrences of states of deep focus exist. The authors' hypotheses are as follows:

- H1: The state of Flow will be experienced as the state of total Immersion is experienced (and vice versa).
- H2: Physiological data will correlate with occurrences of Flow and Immersion.

4.1 Study Design

The procedure of evaluating our proposal consists of two phases: a gaming phase and an assessment phase. Figure 3 presents an overview over the different phases of the experiment, as well as an additional setup phase during which the experiment is set up. Test runs showed that 30 min were enough time to reach a relatively high state of Immersion; accordingly, the gaming phase was set to 30 min of gameplay. The game can be selected freely; this choice was made in order to make it easier for test subjects to reach high states of Immersion. Players choose from a variety of game genres: Action shooter, 4X-Strategy, Artillery, Adventure, Simulation and Puzzle. During the gaming phase, gameplay and player footage are recorded along with physiological measurements. During the following assessment phase, the player watches the previously recorded gaming session and answers Flow and Immersion questionnaires periodically.

These questionnaires elicit the player's Flow state at the specified time in the video recording. The questionnaires are shown multiple times in a three level hierarchical fashion, throughout the footage evaluation at differing time intervals:

The first level of questionnaires is measuring which level of Immersion the player is currently in. It is based on the Immersion questionnaire [12] and is presented every three minutes. The original questionnaire contains 24 questions and was too long to be asked as frequently as every three minutes. For this reason, the Immersion questionnaire was split into two individual questionnaires: One questionnaire is used at the very beginning of the assessment phase and intends to elicit "immersive tendency" in players, another iterative questionnaire contains the seven questions Cheng found most contributive to the questionnaire results of the different dimensions in their CFA.

The second level of questionnaires measures Flow, based on the Flow Short Scale questionnaire [16] and is presented every six minutes. This questionnaire was chosen because it is short and was designed to be used multiple times in succession.

The final level of questionnaires is presented at the end of the game footage playback. It is based on the Game Experience questionnaire [18] and entails a complete elicitation of Flow, Immersion and related experiences. The Game Experience Questionnaire is used to elicit more general information concerning participants.

This way, the theory that Flow is an extreme version of Immersion can be tested by comparing phases of Immersion, identified in the first and third level (Immersion/Game

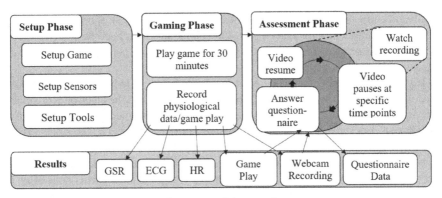

Fig. 3. Phases of the experiment

experience questionnaire) to corresponding phases of Flow, identified in the second and third level (Flow Short Scale/Game experience questionnaire).

The questionnaires were rewritten into past tense for consistency, additionally; some points were rewritten for clarity, while taking care not to change the intentions of the questions asked. As it was potentially unclear to participants, the questionnaires were also altered to reflect which span of time they refer to.

4.2 Physiological Measurements

The physiological measurements used in the study were chosen based on the idea that they should not interrupt the state of deep focus the player is in while playing the game. Additionally, measures were used in a way that they do not impede gameplay (see Fig. 4).

Fig. 4. Experiment setup showcasing the GSR+ sensor, ECG sensor, eye tracker and measurement mouse used in the study.

Galvanic skin response (GSR) uses electrodes to measure skin conductance. This has proven useful in emotion analysis, as skin conductance has been found to change in direct relation to arousal, which is the strength of the emotion perceived, either positive (such as excitement) or negative (such as fear) [19].

Measuring skin conductance in the hand region would lead to both a loss of recording precision and a constraint on player movement. To prevent this, the electrodes are placed on the inside of the participant's foot, based on the measurement method outlined by Gravenhorst. Two sensors are used to measure GSR in this study. The first sensor is the NAOS GQ mouse by Mionix, which has a built-in GSR sensor. However, test runs showed that data elicited from the mouse is not reliable. Measurement is taken at the lower palm of the hand using the mouse. During actual gameplay, participants often lift their hands or make slight adjustments to get a better grip on the mouse, which lead to wrong or missing measurements, rendering its readings unusable for evaluation. A more reliable sensor (Shimmer3 GSR+ sensor unit) was employed, which also measures electro dermal activity in the skin using electrode placements on the feet. Since it is a Bluetooth sensor, there are no cables to hinder gameplay, during test runs participants have noted that they stopped noticing the sensor while playing the game.

The second measurement type used is an ECG. This measurement type measures heart muscle activity from different angles. From heart muscle activities, useful metrics such as heart rate and changes in heart rate can be derived. As electrodes are placed on the chest, this measurement type may interrupt the player's focus on the game and prevent them from reaching the Flow state. However, test runs showed that participants were not disrupted from playing the game by the recording equipment and did not actively notice it below their clothes. Data is measured using a Shimmer3 ECG measurement unit, using five electrodes placed on the chest, while the sensor unit itself is placed near the stomach region on a belt. Clothes can be worn above the sensor electrodes without disrupting the measurement.

Eye tracking is used to track gaze position on the screen. Eye movement can be differentiated into two different categories, movement (saccades) and rest points (fixations). The amount of rest points has been found to be related to focus states [11], making it an interesting metric for analysis in the study. Eye tracking does not interfere with players, making it useful for measuring deep focus states. In this study a Gazepoint GP3 eye tracker is used, as it is cheap and can track eye movement reliably enough to derive information about rest points and the areas participants looked at. The sensor itself must be calibrated before use for each participant.

Finally, web cam footage of the player is recorded during gameplay. This gameplay footage can be used to analyze emotions displayed by a player. Like eye tracking, video recording does not disturb players playing the game. A more accurate alternative to elicit player's emotions would be measuring face muscle activities by electromyography (EMG), which was rejected for this experiment, as placing electrodes on the face of players was deemed to be a strong distraction during gameplay.

Another relevant measurement type for eliciting reactions in players is an electroencephalogram (EEG), which measures brain wave activity by means of electrodes placed on the head of the participant. EEGs come in different forms (caps, raw electrodes, headbands). Unfortunately less invasive measurements, such as headbands with a small amount of electrodes, measure brain activity less reliably than more complex measurement methods. In order to measure the data the study wants to gather, a cap with a large amount of electrodes would have to be used. As well as facial EMG, EEG measurement was rejected for the experiment, as it was deemed too distractive for players – but will be incorporated in later implementations of the study as soon as unintrusive devices become available.

4.3 Study and Results

In the first step, the recorded data was checked for correlations between Flow and Immersion. As the results from both the Flow and Immersion questionnaires did not follow a normal distribution, Spearman correlation was used [20]. The correlation analysis found a strong correlation between all three levels of Immersion and the Flow state.

The strongest correlation was found between Engagement and Flow (R = 0.69, p < .001), which is to be expected, knowing that Flow encompasses all features making up Engagement.

The second strongest correlation exists between Total Immersion and Flow (R = 0.652, p < .001) (see Fig. 5).

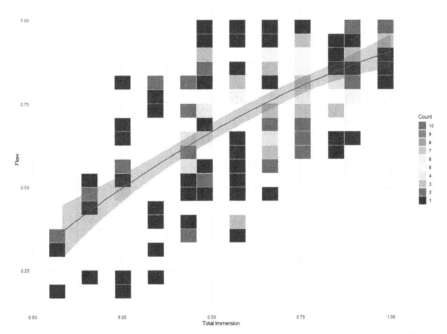

Fig. 5. Scatter plot for correlation between Flow and Total Immersion, R = 0,65; P < .001; conf = 0,95.

This is caused by the fact that players who played games without clear avatars, such as strategy games, found it difficult to emphasize with their avatar in the game, leading to reduced Total Immersion. The least correlated level of the three was Engrossment ($R = 0.56$, $p < .001$), which can be explained as Engrossment puts strong emphasis on emotional attachment of the player to the game, something Flow does not elicit. All three showed strong correlation to Flow (see Table 2), supporting H1 (see Sect. 4).

Table 2. Correlation between Flow and Immersion (Spearman-Rho-Coefficient).

	Flow	Engagement	Engrossment	Total
Flow	1	0.69	0.57	0.65
Engagement	0.69	1	0.45	0.58
Engrossment	0.57	0.45	1	0.62

Direct correlation between normalized physiological data and answers of the Flow and Immersion questionnaires showed no meaningful correlation, leaving H2 part of the hypothesis unconfirmed. The direct correlation results are shown in Table 3. Further discussion on the statistical methods employed can be found in [21].

Table 3. Correlation between Flow and physiological measurements (Spearman-Rho-Coefficient).

	GSR	HR	Fixations per minute
Flow	-0.02	-0.03	-0.07
Engagement	0.01	-0.08	-0.02
Engrossment	-0.04	-0.09	0.05
Total Immersion	-0.15	0	0.06

5 Extending the Combined Flow/Immersion Model with Arousal/Valence

When considering the combined model of Flow and Immersion [22], incorporating emotional theory allows for an additional dimension of features beside skill and challenge (see Sect. 2.3), thus making it more fine-grained and eventually more quantitative. Emotional theory includes modeling emotions in various ways: First, emotions are modelled as single discrete states. Tomkins and Karon [23] introduce nine pairs of emotion (with the second term being the stronger version of the first): interest/excitement, enjoyment/joy, surprise/startle, distress/anguish, anger/rage, fear/terror, dissmell, disgust and shame/humiliation. These emotions can be measured using brain activity, alternatively using facial expressions [24].

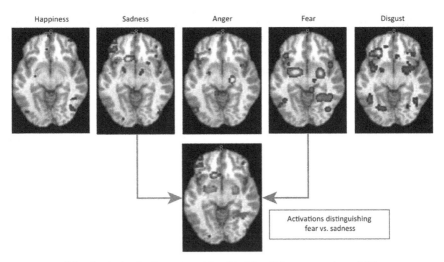

Fig. 6. Active brain regions identified for different emotions [25].

Although different emotions correspond to different active regions in the brain, identifying concrete regions accordingly isn't possible, because certain emotions share the same regions (see Fig. 6).

As emotions may not necessarily be discrete but overlapping, models were introduced that can be used to define emotions in a multidimensional kind of way. Looking at the classification of emotional dimensions, Wundt [26] proposed three emotional dimensions and their antagonists: Pleasurable (unpleasurable), arousing (subduing) and attain (relaxation). The first dimension defines the subjective feeling of how attractive the current situation is perceived as. In this context, the term valence is also important, as it also refers to the attractiveness of a situation. The second dimension refers to the strength of the emotion experienced. The final dimension refers attentiveness to the emotion experienced.

Based on these dimensions, a multitude of interpretations exist: Mäntylä [27] maps emotional states to a two-dimensional space where Valence describes how attractive an experienced situation appears to the subject while Arousal refers to the intensity of the experience. Bakker [28] defines Arousal as the emotional activation level, described as a combination of mental alertness and physical activity by using the adjectives sleep, inactivity, boredom and relaxation at the lower end and wakefulness, bodily tension, strenuous exercise and concentration at the higher end. Lane states "Valence refers to the direction of behavioral activation associated with emotion, either toward (appetitive motivation, pleasant emotion) or away from (aversive motivation, unpleasant emotion) a stimulus" and divides it into three levels: pleasant, unpleasant and neutral [29].

A fitting foundation for the model extension is Russell's Circumplex Mode of Affect [30] (see Fig. 7): a two-dimensional model with Arousal and Valence as the dimensions, representing emotional states at any level of the two dimensions. Through the central and orthogonal positioning of the axes, four quadrants are the result portraying:

- low Arousal, low Valence with emotions like sadness, depression, and boredom,
- low Arousal, high Valence with emotions like relaxation, satisfaction, and serenity,
- high Arousal, low Valence with emotions like frustration, distress, and anxiety, and
- high Arousal, high Valence with emotions like arousal, excitement, and happiness.

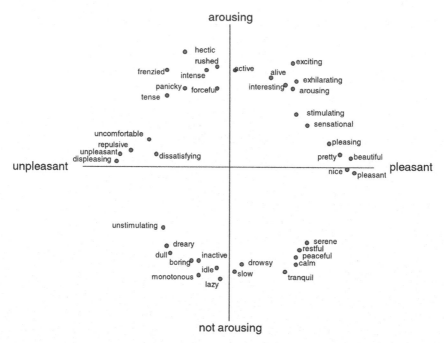

Fig. 7. Circumplex Mode of Affect [31]

When comparing Csikszentmihalyi's eight channels Flow model to Russell's Circumplex Mode of Affect (CMA), the channels' definitions can be associated to at least one of the emotions depicted in any of the CMA's quadrants. Accordingly, the Flow model may be overlaid with the two dimensions Arousal and Valence (see Fig. 8), the dimension Arousal is renamed into Intensity to avoid confusion with the Flow model's channel name.

As such the channels are each categorized as Valence positive (see Table 4) /negative (see Table 5) and Intensity (Arousal) low/high (see Table 6).

This leads to the authors' hypothesis:

– H3: There are relations between deep focus states, elicited as detailed in Sect. 4 and the additional two emotional dimensions Arousal/Intensity and Valence,

which – if found true in further studies – would greatly help quantifying deep focus states like Flow and Immersion by eliciting and examining the participants' emotional states, in regard of their Arousal/Intensity and Valence characteristics.

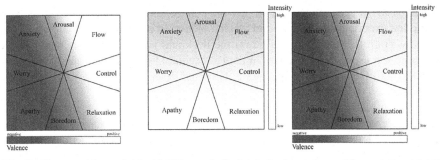

Fig. 8. Flow model, overlaid with Valence (left), Intensity (center), resulting notation (right)

Table 4. Flow channels, positive Valence connotation

Positive Valence	CMA association
Arousal	Active, alive arousing, exciting, exhilarating, interesting, intense
Flow	Stimulating, sensational
Control	Pleasing, pretty, beautiful, nice, pleasant
Relaxation	Serene, restful, peaceful, calm, tranquil

Table 5. Flow channels, negative Valence connotation

Negative Valence	CMA association
Anxiety	Hectic, frenzied, panicky, tense, forceful, rushed
Worry	Uncomfortable, repulsive, unpleasant, displeasing
Boredom	Boring, monotonous, inactive, idle, lazy, drowsy, slow
Apathy	Unstimulating, dreary, dull

Table 6. Flow channels, Intensity connotation

Intensity	High	Low
	Arousal	Control
	Flow	Relaxation
	Anxiety	Boredom
	Worry	Apathy

5.1 Measuring Intensity (Arousal)/Valence

Measuring Intensity (Arousal) and Valence is a well-researched topic. Skin conductivity can be used to measure the intensity of an emotion. It corresponds to Intensity (Arousal) in the Arousal-Valence model. The higher the conductance, the higher the intensity of the emotion experienced. Valence can also be measured using muscle contraction. An electromyogram (EMG) may be used on the neck and jaw. In this case, high muscle contraction represents high valence. In their procedural horror game Vanish, Nogueira calculates both from a mix of heart rate, GSR and EMG to alter the game world in response to how the player feels [32].

Similar in nature, Ravaja and Kivikangas present an attempt to measure galvanic skin response and an EMG on the facial muscles of participants during gaming [33]. Their underlying theory is that positive and negative emotions elicit reactions from different facial muscles. They found that positive emotions result in higher muscle activity in the cheek region, while negative emotions correlate with higher muscle activity in the brow region of the face. However, they found no correlation between GSR and valence. Two issues that have to be kept in mind, when using the EMG approach are: head movement resulting in bad readings (as with GSR) as well as the intrusiveness of the sensor/electrodes itself. Additionally, changes in muscle contractions are relatively small, making this type of measurement difficult when used without external supporting factors.

6 Future Work

Concluding, this paper concerned itself with existing definitions of deep focus states, like Flow and Immersion. Processes of measurement were brought forward and a hypothesis how Flow and Immersion might be related was discussed. A study to validate the aforementioned relation was introduced and its result presented, which induced the idea to further enhance the combined model of Flow and Immersion by emotional theory aspects like Arousal and Valence.

Future work will, first and foremost engage with the design and implementation of a study, which is to be incorporated into the existing one, to test for the validity of H3. Independently, whether the hypothesis is confirmed or falsified, the overall goal will be finding other ways to enrich the combined model of Flow and Immersion, establish a measurement method solely on physiological measurements to allow for a more accurate, in-time, objective measurement method of deep focus states, while abstaining from the use of questionnaires.

References

1. Csikszentmihalyi, M.: Beyond Boredom and Anxiety: Experiencing Flow in Work and Play. Jossey-Bass, San Francisco (1975)
2. Cairns, P., Cox, A., Berthouze, N., Jennett, C., Dhoparee, S.: Quantifying the experience of immersion in games. In: CogSci 2006 Workshop: Cognitive Science of Games and Gameplay (2006)
3. Csikszentmihalyi, M.: Flow: The Psychology of Optimal Experience. Harper Perennial, New York (1991)
4. Minsky, M.: Telepresence, pp. 45–51 (1980)

5. Witmer, B.G., Singer, M.J.: Measuring presence in virtual environments: a presence questionnaire. Presence Teleoperators Virtual Environ. **7**(3), 225–240 (1998). https://doi.org/10.1162/105474698565686

6. Nordin, A.I., Denisova, A., Cairns, P.: Too many questionnaires: measuring player experience whilst playing digital games. In: The Seventh York Doctoral Symposium on Computer Science and Electronics (2014)

7. Slater, M.: Measuring presence: a response to the Witmer and singer presence questionnaire. Presence **8**(5), 560–565 (1999)

8. Zhang, C., Perkis, A., Arndt, S.: Spatial immersion versus emotional immersion, which is more immersive? In: 2017 Ninth International Conference on Quality of Multimedia Experience (QoMEX), pp. 1–6 (2017)

9. Qin, H., Rau, P.-L., Salvendy, G.: Player immersion in the computer game narrative. In: Ma, L., Rauterberg, M., Nakatsu, R. (eds.) ICEC 2007. LNCS, vol. 4740, pp. 458–461. Springer, Heidelberg (2007). https://doi.org/10.1007/978-3-540-74873-1_60

10. Ermi, L., Mäyrä, F.: Fundamental components of the gameplay experience: analysing immersion. In: Proceedings of the DiGRA International Conference: Changing Views: Worlds in Play (2005)

11. Jennett, C., et al.: Measuring and defining the experience of immersion in games. Int. J. Hum.-Comput. Stud. **66**(9), 641–661 (2008)

12. Cheng, M.-T., She, H.-C., Annetta, L.A.: Game immersion experience: its hierarchical structure and impact on game-based science learning. J. Comp. Assist. Learn. **31**(3), 232–253 (2015)

13. Sullivan, G.M., Artino, A.R.: Analyzing and interpreting data from likert-type scales. J. Grad. Med. Educ. **5**(4), 541–542 (2013)

14. Sweetser, P., Wyeth, P.: GameFlow: a model for evaluating player enjoyment in games. Comput. Entertain. **3**(3), 3 (2005)

15. Fu, F.-L., Su, R.-C., Yu, S.-C.: EGameFlow: a scale to measure learners' enjoyment of e-learning games. Comput. Educ. **52**(1), 101–112 (2009)

16. Rheinberg, F., Vollmeyer, R., Engeser, S.: Die Erfassung des Flow-Erlebens. In: Diagnostik von Motivation und Selbstkonzept, pp. 261–279. Hogrefe, Göttingen (2003)

17. Georgiou, Y., Kyza, E.A.: The development and validation of the ARI questionnaire. Int. J. Hum.-Comput. Stud. **98**(C), 24–37 (2017)

18. IJsselsteijn, W.A., de Kort, Y.A.W., Poels, K.: The Game Experience Questionnaire. Technische Universiteit Eindhoven, Eindhoven (2013)

19. Gravenhorst, F., Muaremi, A., Tröster, G., Arnrich, B., Grünerbl, A.: Towards a mobile galvanic skin response measurement system for mentally disordered patients. In: Proceedings of the 8th International Conference on Body Area Networks 432–435. (2013)

20. Landau, S., Everitt, B.S.: A Handbook of Statistical Analyses Using SPSS. Statistics (Chapman & Hall/CRC). Taylor & Francis (2004)

21. Kannegieser, E., Atorf, D., Meier, J.: Conduction an experiment for validating the combined model of immersion and flow. In: Proceedings of the 11th International Conference on Computer Supported Education, vol. 2, pp. 252–259 (2019)

22. Kannegieser, E., Atorf, D., Meier, J.: Surveying games with a combined model of immersion and flow. In: Proceedings of the International Conferences on Interfaces and Human Computer Interaction, Game and Entertainment Technologies, pp. 353–356 (2018)

23. Tomkins, S.S., Karon, B.P.: Affect, Imagery, Consciousness, vol. I. Springer, New York (1962)

24. Ekman, I., Chanel, G., Järvelä, S., Kivikangas, J.M., Salminen, M., Ravaja, N.: Social interaction in games: measuring physiological linkage and social presence. Simul. Gaming **43**, 321–338 (2012)

25. Hamann, S.: Mapping discrete and dimensional emotions onto the brain: controversies and consensus. Trends Cogn. Sci. **16**(9), 458–466 (2012)

26. Wundt, W.: Outlines of Psychology (1897)
27. Mäntylä, M., Adams, B., Destefanis, G., Graziotin, D., Ortu, M.: Mining valence, arousal, and dominance: possibilities for detecting burnout and productivity? In: Proceedings of the 13th International Conference on Mining Software Repositories, pp. 247–258. ACM, Austin (2016)
28. Bakker, I., van der Voordt, T., Vink, P., de Boon, J.: Pleasure, arousal, dominance: Mehrabian and Russell revisited. Curr. Psychol. **33**, 405–421 (2014). https://doi.org/10.1007/s12144-014-9219-4
29. Lane, R.D., Chua, P.M., Dolan, R.J.: Common effects of emotional valence, arousal and attention on neural activation during visual processing of pictures. Neuropsychologia **37**, 989–997 (1999)
30. Russell, J.A.: A circumplex model of affect. J. Pers. Soc. Psychol. **39**, 1161 (1980)
31. Russell, J.A., Lanius, U.F.: Adaptation level and the affective appraisal of environments. J. Environ. Psychol. **4**(2), 119–135 (1984)
32. Nogueira, P.A., Torres, V., Rodrigues, R., Oliveira, E., Nacke, L.E.: Vanishing scares: biofeedback modulation of affective player experiences in a procedural horror game. J. Multimodal User Interfaces **10**(1), 31–62 (2015). https://doi.org/10.1007/s12193-015-0208-1
33. Ravaja, N., Kivikangas, J.M.: Psychophysiology of digital game playing: effects of competition versus collaboration in the laboratory and in real life (2008)

Modelling and Quantifying Learner Motivation for Adaptive Systems: Current Insight and Future Perspectives

Fidelia A. Orji and Julita Vassileva[✉]

University of Saskatchewan, Saskatoon, Canada
`Fidelia.orji@usask.ca, jiv@cs.usask.ca`

Abstract. Adaptation and personalization of learning systems are promising approaches aiming to enhance learners' experience and achievement of learning objectives. Adaptive learning systems support and enhance learning through monitoring important learner characteristics in the learning process and making appropriate adjustments in the process and the environment. For example, intelligent tutoring systems (ITSs) provide adaptive instruction to a learner based on his/her learning needs by tailoring learning materials and teaching methods to each learner based on information available in the learner's model. However, present ITSs predominantly emphasize the role of instructional content adjustment to the modelled cognitive processes of a learner, disregarding the significance of motivation in learning processes. According to research, motivation is essential in the knowledge building process and in fostering high academic performance. This paper reviews the literature on modelling of motivational states and adaptation to motivation on ITSs, mapping research progress in terms of techniques and strategies for modelling motivational states and adapting to motivation. A new approach for adapting and increasing motivation through the use of machine learning techniques and persuasive technology is proposed. The approach addresses learner knowledge and motivational states to improve learning and sustain the learner's motivation.

Keywords: Adaptive systems · Intelligent tutoring systems · Learner model · Student model · Motivation to learn · Motivational states · Machine learning · Multimodal machine learning approach · Persuasive technology

1 Introduction

There is increasing interest and investments in using adaptive educational systems to promote learning. Over the past years, research focused on developing adaptive educational systems that automatically adjust online content delivery methods and the sequencing of learning materials to the individual needs of each learner. For instance, adaptive instruction and adaptive learning environments, adaptive hypermedia, and adaptive game-based learning systems are just a few of the many user-adaptive systems available today. Intelligent tutoring systems (ITSs), for example, are adaptive instructional systems providing

© Springer Nature Switzerland AG 2021
R. A. Sottilare and J. Schwarz (Eds.): HCII 2021, LNCS 12793, pp. 79–92, 2021.
https://doi.org/10.1007/978-3-030-77873-6_6

personalized instruction to learners based on their learning needs by tailoring learning materials and teaching methods to the learner's needs based on information available in the learner model. Thus, ITSs monitor the individual learner's characteristics and context to dynamically adapt the learning processes to the inferred learning needs of the individual. Hence, appropriate modelling of the learner's characteristics and relevant knowledge representation within the systems are essential in detecting the learner's needs to adjust instructional content. Several studies conducted systematic literature reviews to identify various learner characteristics modelled in adaptive educational systems for adaptation and existing techniques that were applied [1, 2]. According to the studies, many learners' characteristics (such as age, gender, cognitive abilities, personality, emotions and affect, motivation, past learning activities, domain knowledge etc.) were employed in learner models. Adapting learning based on these characteristics helps in improving the learning experience and achievement of learning objectives for learners [3]. Popular interest in ITSs research focuses on adaptive instruction that tailors learning materials and teaching methods based on the individual learning needs of learners. Often neglected is the role of motivation in empowering learners by improving how they perceive, learn, remember concepts and master skills learnt. Due to the importance of learner motivation in learning with ITSs, there is a concern to summarize research contributions in this area to provide current insight and future perspective. The ITSs monitor learner's activities, create learner models based on different learner characteristics, determine which teaching activities should be selected for each learner, choose the type of hints and feedback to be provided, and pick the next exercise for each learner. These processes help in providing one-on-one personal tutors based on individual learner needs. The learner model quantifies current knowledge state and its variations over time based on instructional actions. The future for ITSs is thought-provoking especially when it comes to creating more efficient learner models that will enhance adaptivity and learning outcomes. Although *motivation to learn* has been mentioned among the identified learner characteristics which are modelled in adaptive educational systems, there is a need for comprehensive literature analysis to identify existing techniques applied to model and adapt learning based on motivation.

Motivation is among the learner's characteristics that influence learning processes. It is a major driver of engagement in learning, particularly in online educational systems [4–7] where the learners plan and coordinate their learning process without teachers' intervention. Lack of motivation and inability to engage learners for a reasonable period of time required to achieve the desired learning objectives are among the top and most frequently cited barriers to online education [5, 8–10] and a major reason for the high drop-out rate experienced by many online educational platforms compared to the traditional education system [11–13]. Improving and maintaining learner motivation has consequently emerged as a key challenge in both traditional and online educational systems because motivation constantly changes over time. As a result, sustaining focus to engage in learning for a continuous amount of time in online educational systems is a difficult task, even in adaptive systems.

Therefore, there is a need to include automatic detection of motivational issues into ITSs learner models. This will allow the systems to self-improve and respond with appropriate intervention without the need for direct human intervention.

Thus, in this paper, we present a review of current literature on modelling learner's motivational states and strategies for maintaining them to enhance learning processes. To achieve our research goal, we formulated research questions to help us understand and focus this study on modelling motivation to learn on ITSs. Thus, we intend to answer the following research questions:

RQ1. How can the motivational states of a learner be detected?
RQ2. What are the strategies for adapting in response to motivation?
RQ3. What features should be adapted?

Research question RQ1 helps us to understand the main techniques that are used for accessing learner's motivation in ITSs. The second and third questions intend to identify the main components of ITSs which are adapted in response to motivational states of a learner and how.

The contributions of this work to adaptive educational systems are two-fold. First, we summarize and highlight emerging trends in modelling and adapting learning processes of ITSs based on learner's motivation. Secondly, we pinpoint the challenges that remain to be solved and explore how machine learning algorithms and persuasive technology could be applied in modelling and responding to learner's motivational problems. Incorporating motivation models with algorithms for modelling and predicting the learning needs of learners will help to find the right time to adapt the system with an appropriate persuasive intervention to maintain or enhance learner motivation while at the same time adaptively addressing the current learning needs.

2   Research Background

This section provides a brief review of the existing research on the impact of motivation on learning and the current state of the art of persuasive technologies targeting learner motivation.

2.1 Motivation

Motivation has over the years been increasingly recognized as one of the factors affecting learning both in the traditional and online educational systems. As a result, many assessment scales [14–16] have been developed for determining learners' motivation during learning processes. The motivation assessment scales use a range of approaches in capturing motivation and learning variables in the context of learning environments. Several studies have adopted and used these scales for different purposes to reveal their usefulness and reliability in measuring the motivation of learners. For example, using the Students' Motivation toward Science Learning (SMTSL) questionnaire [17], a study [18] revealed that students' motivational levels affect their achievement and attitude in learning science. Other research [19] employed the Motivated Strategies for Learning Questionnaire (MSLQ) [16], which was developed for assessing academic motivation and learning strategies, in investigating motivational levels of students learning in a traditional and online educational system. The study reported that for students learning through an online educational system, motivational variables correlated stronger with their performance than the learning strategies deployed in the system. A growing number of studies have shown that motivational variables are relevant to students' success in online educational systems. For example, Barba et al. [20] revealed that the strongest predictors of students' performance in an online educational system are participation and motivation. The research indicated that participation and motivation influenced each other. Similarly, Waschull [21] investigated factors associated with success of students in an online psychology course and reported that self-discipline and motivation were the predictors of the students' success. The importance of learner motivation for online educational systems has been also shown in [22]. According to the research, motivation is a significant factor in determining learners' persistence, engagement and achievement levels.

The complexity and multifacet nature of motivation [23] have resulted in adoption of different perspectives in exploring its influence on learners using online educational systems. According to literature, motivation is viewed from three perspectives: instructional design perspective, as a form of learner's trait, and as dynamic and responsive depending on different contexts [22]. Research that explored motivation from the perspective of instructional design focuses on the design of motivational strategies that could improve students' interest in learning with online education systems [24, 25]. As a result, several instructional design frameworks such as the ARCS model [15] have been developed to be used in online educational systems to influence learners' motivation. Furthermore, some studies viewed motivation as a personal characteristic of a learner [26, 27]. Those studies based their investigation on well-established theories of motivation such as the self-efficacy [28] and self-determination theories [29]. The majority of existing studies [24, 27] are based on one of these two perspectives and are the most commonly used in assessing learner's motivation. A limited number of studies [23, 30] have tried to explore motivation to learn in terms of its dynamic and responsive nature. This approach tries to capture the mutifacet nature of motivation instead of adopting cognitive or behavioural perspective. Research using this approach emphasizes the effect of contextual factors on the relationship between a learner and their learning environment. While research has established that motivation to learn is an important factor affecting learners, the need to understand the complexity involved in its assessment in online educational systems is highlighted.

In traditional educational systems, teachers facilitate and promote learning processes through monitoring engagement and motivational states of learners [31]. Teachers recognize different behaviours of learners through interaction, questions, and facial expressions. They use various tactics and teaching strategies to motivate and encourage students to engage in more active learning. However, in online educational systems including ITSs, learners coordinate and carry out learning on their own and they rely on motivation to perform the learning activities. This creates the need for the systems to track and detect motivational issues of learners. Vicente et al. [32] expressed the need for ITSs to monitor and detect motivational states of learners in order to improve their effectiveness. Many researchers have worked on enhancing ITSs in various ways which include modelling learner motivation for adaptation of learning processes. However, detecting the motivation of learners in the systems and the factors which influence it is a complex process involving multiple dimensions such as cognitive, emotional and physiological [23].

2.2 Persuasive Technology

According to Fogg [33], technologies and techniques built into systems which help users to change their attitude, opinion, and behaviour without using coercion or deception are called Persuasive Technology (PT). The systems are usually developed to encourage users to accomplish a positive goal. Persuasive technology strategies have been shown to be effective in systems at encouraging users to achieve specific goals in various domains such as health [34], energy conservation [35] and education [36]. Persuasive technologies have the potential to be used in online educational systems to encourage and sustain learners to realize the learning objectives, as several studies show. For instance, research has shown that persuasive strategies could be incorporated into an online educational system to promote students' engagement and improve learning [37]. Similarly, persuasive technology was applied in teaching and learning through creating learning objects with embedded persuasive concepts [38].

Though research has shown that PTs can motivate users to accomplish specific goals, it has also been revealed that users differ in their susceptibility to PT strategies, and personalization can amplify the effect of PT [39]. Modelling users according to their susceptibility to persuasive strategies result in persuasion profiles that can be used to tailor or personalize the persuasive strategies to the individual user to improve its efficiency. The persuasion profile contains user features such as gender, age, cultural background or personality, as well as shown susceptibility/preference to certain persuasive strategies. The user features can be obtained through implicit or explicit measures such as questionnaires, online interactions, application logs, and sensors.

Several studies have shown that personalized PTs are more effective than the one-size-fits-all approach [40–42]. Hence, construction of user persuasion profile is important in developing personalized persuasive applications.

3 Modelling of Motivation to Learn in Intelligent Tutoring Systems

A variety of studies investigated the effect of different learner characteristics on teaching and learning on ITSs [43, 44]. However, limited studies investigated the impact of modelling motivational states of students to enhance learning experience and outcome. Modelling motivational states of learners have been recognized as an important component that could be incorporated into ITSs. The scope of motivational states modelling involves a range of measurement tools, techniques, and methodologies. An overview of studies performed in this area is provided in the following section.

3.1 Techniques for Learners' Motivational States Diagnosis in ITSs

Studies that modelled student motivation to learn in ITSs used several techniques involving explicit and/or implicit measures. For example, Vicente et al. [45] employed motivational slider technique and self-report in assessing the motivational level of university students learning with ITS called MOODS (Motivational Diagnosis Study). In detecting students' motivational states at various interaction stages with MOODS, the researchers issued short self-reports of motivation to students. McQuiggan et al. [46] modelled self-efficacy in ITS using decision tree models. The research explored how to build a dynamic self-efficacy model that will automatically update itself using an inductive approach. The dynamic model learns from pre-test data, physiological data of students captured with a biofeedback apparatus, and interaction data of students in their learning environment. The result of the research shows that the dynamic self-efficacy model predicted students' self-efficacy more accurately than a static model generated from data obtained using a validated self-efficacy instrument. The researchers suggested that the dynamic model could be used to predict student's level of self-efficacy at runtime to inform pedagogical decisions in their learning systems. Qu et al. [47] investigated the use of Bayesian model which combines focus of attention data (obtained through a combination of learner's eye gaze and interface activities) and interactions of learners in ITS in detecting learner's degree of confidence, confusion and effort. To evaluate the model the researchers performed an experimental study, which revealed that the model using human tutor's observation as baseline and the one that used learner's self-reports as baseline have recognition accuracies of above 70% for the learner's motivation. The research suggested that the model could be used in providing accurate information about learner motivation. Santos et al. [48] explored the use of convolutional networks in detecting levels of intrinsic motivation using visual cues from student's facial expressions. The research shows that the level of intrinsic motivation of students could be detected with visual input only. Johns et al. [49] investigated inferring student's motivation from a hidden Markov model (HMM) and student proficiency from an Item Response Theory (IRT) model. They generated a dynamic mixture model and used students' log data from ITS in validating the model. The researchers reveal that their model accounted for student motivation.

Monitoring and detecting motivational states of students learning with ITSs is not a common feature in many ITSs. The broader idea of motivational states modelling is concerned with trying to replicate the sort of assistance human tutors provide to students when they detect that their motivation to learn has dropped. Based on the ITSs literature surveyed only a few studies are available in this area and the techniques used for estimating the student's motivational states range from static to dynamic. An overview of studies and techniques for modelling motivational states is presented in Table 1. The studies employed different variable requirements obtained from the following: self-report data, learning interaction data, and physiological data. The techniques used for motivational states detection include self-report analysis, decision tree models, Bayesian models, and convolutional networks. Using techniques that provide more accurate evaluation of learner's states through a combination of surveys, physiological, performance, and interaction data will enhance the adaptability of ITSs.

According to [50], focus on dynamic adaptation to motivation of learners using ITSs is increasing. Existence of available techniques for automated diagnosis of learner's level of motivation is a step towards achieving the dynamic adaptation. The ability of these techniques to monitor what learners are doing, how they are feeling, and how they are managing their learning context are important in detecting when the need to adapt arise.

Table 1. An overview of research and techniques for modelling motivation

Techniques for modelling motivation	Data collection methods	Studies
Motivational slider	Self-report	[45]
Decision tree model	Mixed (self-report, biofeedback apparatus, system logs)	[46]
Motivation diagnosis rule	Mouse movement, history of interactions and performance	[51]
Natural language processing (semantic cohesion measure)	Mixed (self-report and non-intrusive Dialog) Measure	[52]
Bayesian model	Eye gaze and interface activities logs of learners	[47]
Hidden Markov model	Learning logs of learners	[49]
Convolutional network	Visual cues from facial expression	[48]

One of the notable insights about the current techniques for motivation modelling is that multiple types of data could be explored to make the models generated more robust in representing motivational states of learners. However, excluding studies that used pre-and post-surveys for motivation measures, the proportion of papers that explicitly stated how motivational states were modelled is small, and this suggests that researchers were not discussing their modelling technique or little work has been done in this area. A wider exploration of techniques for inferring motivational states of learners has the potential to advance ITSs research.

3.2 Strategies and Features for Adapting to Learner Motivation

Motivationally-intelligent tutoring systems consider the motivational states of a learner during adaptation [50]. Varying forms of adaptation such as macro-adaptation or micro-adaptation are employed. Micro-adaptation dynamically monitors and tracks changes in motivational states of a learner over time while macro-adaptation is often a one-off adaptation usually done prior to a task using existing motivational measures. Due to the complexity of motivational state and difficulty in assessing it, covering all aspects of motivation might not be feasible. Thus, researchers focus on adapting to a specific aspect of motivation. They have tried to model motivational states of learners in ITSs using validated instruments, affective states monitoring, and engagement in learning activities. For instance, Matsubara et al. [53] incorporated into ITS a motivation system that focuses on student's motivation levels in learning processes to give appropriate encouragement, praise or reproach messages. The students' motivation levels were represented as action parts and fuzzy rules were used for inferencing. The research presented that the system considered the learner model and the motivation rules in generating appropriate messages for each learner.

Research presented that main feelings associated with motivational states present a useful way to refer to the states [54]. Several studies have detected and differentiated feelings such as frustrated, excited, confident, and interested [55], states of boredom, confusion, frustration, eureka, neutral, and flow/engagement [56] that occur during learning. Equally, research has shown that emotions play important role in motivation. And that responding to affective states of learners accordingly will improve motivation and learning processes. Hence, some researchers adapt to affective states of students to improve their motivation. As such research developed a dynamic decision network for emotions based on personality theories and teachers' expertise and incorporated it to an ITS for learning mobile robotics. The research revealed that contextual adaptation based on cognitive and emotional states of learners helps to maintain motivation to learn at high level [57]. Also, D'Mello et al. [58] investigated how students can be assisted to regulate negative states such as boredom, frustration, and confusion when they arise so that positive states (flow/engagement and curiosity) can persevere. The researchers used sensors in estimating the probability value of the type of emotion a student is experiencing. They developed rules based on theories, experts' guidance, and intuition which helped them in mapping students' cognitive (dynamically assessed student ability and quality of current response) and affective states with suitable tutor actions. When the tutor detects that a student has a negative affect state, it responds with empathetic and motivational messages which will encourage the student to continue with the tutor. Thus, for the tutor to be motivationally intelligent, it needs to recognize cognitive and emotional consequences of tutorial intervention to be more efficient. Furthermore, an overview and discussion on some intelligent tutoring systems that adapted to learner's motivation dynamically or as a one-off thing were presented in research [50] to highlight progress in the area of motivationally adaptive intelligent tutoring systems.

Besides the cognitive needs of students, diagnosing their motivational states and adapting the tutor to keep them motivated will strongly impact their learning outcomes. The connection between observable learning outcomes and behavior of a learner reveals actions contributing to improving ability to engage in tutoring. According to research, regular positive emotions (affect) of students are associated with higher levels of engagement whereas negative emotions correlated with low levels of engagement. The effect of adaptivity partially mediated the correlation between positive emotions and student engagement [59].

4 Proposed Architecture for Integrating Motivation Modelling into ITSs

Over the years, surveys and interviews are the most commonly used method for assessing motivation to learn. The methods require students to report their motivation levels. Pretest and posttest surveys are often used in the methods. Using surveys in assessing motivational states of learners at different intervals in ITSs are intrusive and could negatively impact motivation to learn. In traditional learning systems, teachers can perceive the current motivational states of students and adapt the teaching strategies to increase motivation. According to research [32], the ability of ITSs to automatically detect motivational states of learners will bring numerous advantages. This leads to the need to build a tool for measuring real-time motivational states of students dynamically using their digital traces in ITSs. Current advances in technology such as cheap miniature sensors, digital cameras, and deep learning algorithms, enable unobtrusive continuous measurement of physiological and interaction data of students during learning, offering the possibility of modelling motivational states of learners over time. Recent studies are making progress in this area to create more efficient student models that will enhance adaptivity to improve students' learning.

We present a new approach that could be adopted in monitoring and improving motivation of learners in ITSs. The approach targets dynamic detection of motivational states of learners in ITSs over time. For this purpose, we rely on machine learning techniques that could use a set of behavioural indicators (objective measures) of students in ITS for measuring motivation. Our approach will involve the development of a Multimodal Machine Learning (MML) mechanism that will automatically predict motivational states of a learner at intervals during learning processes in ITS using a combination of the learner's behavioural responses on ITS. As mentioned previously, traditional methodologies for assessing learner motivation rely on data collected through questionnaires only. The MML approach will use a combination of subjective responses and unobtrusive objective measures of learner's digital traces in developing an integrated model comprising of predictive features from each measure. According to research [60], "*a deeper understanding of the learner behaviours, traits, and preferences (learner data) collected through performance, physiological and behavioural sensors and surveys will allow for more accurate evaluation of learner's states (e.g., engagement level, confusion, frustration) which will result in a better and more persistent model of the learner*" (see Fig. 1). Also, research has shown that multimodal affect detection (using a combination of data sources) yields more accurate results than the best unimodal counterparts [61]. In addition, McQuiggan et al. [46] revealed that a multimodal decision tree model predicted students' self-efficacy more accurately than the model built using students' self-reported data (unimodal). Thus, our multimodal technique will use the following data sources: data on students' motivation will be collected through self-report using the Motivated Strategies for Learning Questionnaire (MSLQ), physiological data of students are captured through eye-gaze and facial expressions, and their interaction and performance data will be provided by the ITS. Features extracted from the provided data sources through appropriate feature engineering techniques are passed to a decision tree model to predict student motivational states at intervals during learning processes with ITS, as the motivational states of learners likely change during learning interactions. Using learner's self-reports as baseline, corresponding motivational states are calibrated and mapped to any of the levels (threshold, low, and high) as a linear scale. The threshold value divides the scale into two subscales - low and high. When a low motivational state is detected the system selects an appropriate persuasive strategy that could help to increase the motivational state.

The architecture of ITS consists of four main components: domain model, learner model, tutoring model, and user-interface model. Current learner model depends more on cognitive assessments. A more efficient learner model will enhance the capability of ITSs to provide individualized help to learners when needed. Therefore, we propose to modify ITS architecture and integrate motivation detection (using MML), labelling and

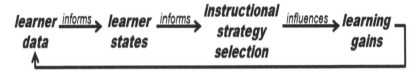

Fig. 1. Adaptive tutoring learning effect chain (Sottilare [60])

response (see Fig. 2) since motivation plays a vital part in learning. The response part takes into consideration the persuasive strategy that could motivate each learner. The learner model part of ITS architecture is modified such that modelling of motivational states during learning processes and persuasive profiles of learners are incorporated as shown in Fig. 2. The tutoring model updates the current knowledge while the module for motivational states monitoring updates learner's motivational states at intervals during learning processes. The decision model in the figure combines the cognitive (current knowledge) and motivational states of a learner in establishing appropriate pedagogical and persuasive actions that will be sent to the tutoring model and then to the interface model. Thus, the current state of a learner determines the tutoring model activities. The persuasive intervention and the pedagogical process will be delivered to a learner when the decision model diagnoses a motivational issue. The learner's persuasive profile is used in tailoring the persuasive intervention to make it more efficient. The intervention is to encourage learners to get more involved and complete the tutoring process.

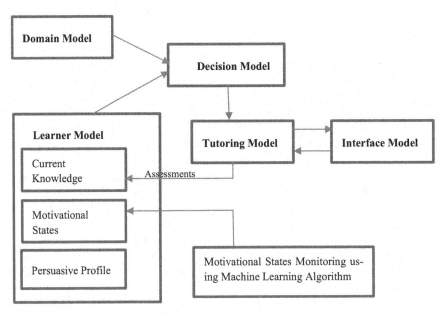

Fig. 2. Architecture of motivationally-adaptive intelligent tutoring system

Future Perspectives. Adaptive educational systems such as intelligent tutoring systems could be improved in the future through implementation of an adaptive mechanism that takes into consideration, not only the cognitive states but also the motivational states of learners. Developing a framework that will dynamically determine changes in a learner state as a guide to what will be adapted is an important area. Hence, there is need for more efficient modelling technique for determining and confirming different states to improve the effectiveness of adaptation. Existence of a more comprehensive learner model will allow adaptation to be better align to learner's needs and this will probably affect learning experience and outcome. Moreover, the type of motivational tactics that could be applied in encouraging and sustaining learners in the process of learning when negative motivational states occur is another area that needs to be explored. Research in this direction is using non-intrusive (such as physiologic sensors and interaction data) and multimodal machine learning approach for dynamic detection of learner emotional states. This category involves learner models that capture motivational/ affective states.

5 Conclusion

In view of supporting a more individualized learning experience in ITSs, this paper surveyed literature on modelling of motivational states to establish the various techniques and methods employed. Based on the current research trend in this area, we proposed an architecture for an intelligent tutoring system that will monitor and adapt learning based on the cognitive and motivational states of a learner. Thus, the architecture addresses knowledge and motivational needs and employs a dynamic technique for motivating learners using persuasive technology. Dynamic motivation is enriched with the use of persuasive strategies that a learner is susceptible to. The architecture represents an initial attempt on how motivational states of a learner could be integrated into learner model in ITS and how persuasive technology could be incorporated and adapted based on motivational states while preserving the usually ITS adaptation. The future research will involve the following: 1) implementation of ITS framework based on this approach, 2) system evaluation to determine the efficiency of the approach and its effect on students' learning. An evaluation of a system built with this architecture will be compared with similar conventional ITS that did not have motivational states modelling, persuasive technology and decision model incorporated.

References

1. Afini Normadhi, N.B., Shuib, L., Md Nasir, H.N., Bimba, A., Idris, N., Balakrishnan, V.: Identification of personal traits in adaptive learning environment: systematic literature review. Comput. Educ. **130**, 168–190 (2019)
2. Nakic, J., Granic, A., Glavinic, V.: Anatomy of student models in adaptive learning systems: a systematic literature review of individual differences from 2001 to 2013. J. Educ. Comput. Res. **51**, 459–489 (2015)
3. Granić, A., Nakić, J.: Enhancing the learning experience: preliminary framework for user individual differences. In: Leitner, G., Hitz, M., Holzinger, A. (eds.) USAB 2010. LNCS, vol. 6389, pp. 384–399. Springer, Heidelberg (2010). https://doi.org/10.1007/978-3-642-16607-5_26

4. Bauer, M., Bräuer, C., Schuldt, J., Niemann, M., Krömker, H.: Application of wearable technology for the acquisition of learning motivation in an adaptive e-learning platform. In: Ahram, T.Z. (ed.) AHFE 2018. AISC, vol. 795, pp. 29–40. Springer, Cham (2019). https://doi.org/10.1007/978-3-319-94619-1_4

5. Priego, R.G., Peralta, A.G.: Engagement factors and motivation in e-learning and blended-learning projects. In: ACM International Conference Proceeding Series, pp. 453–460. ACM Press, New York (2013)

6. Keller, J.M.: Motivational Design for Learning and Performance. Springer US, Boston (2010). https://doi.org/10.1007/978-1-4419-1250-3

7. Malone, T.W., Lepper, M.R.: Making learning fun: a taxonomy of intrinsic motivations for learning. In: Aptitude, Learning, and Instruction: Conative and Affective Process Analyses, pp. 223–253 (1987)

8. Kim, K.J., Frick, T.: Changes in student motivation during online learning. J. Educ. Comput. Res. **44**, 1–23 (2011)

9. Pappas, C.: Top 8 eLearning Barriers that Inhibit Online Learner Engagement with eLearning Content. eLearning Industry (2016)

10. Blanchard, E., Frasson, C.: An autonomy-oriented system design for enhancement of learner's motivation in e-learning. In: International Conference on Intelligent Tutoring System, vol. 3220, pp. 34–44, August 2004

11. Levy, Y.: Comparing dropouts and persistence in e-learning courses. Comput. Educ. **48**, 185–204 (2007)

12. Lykourentzou, I., Giannoukos, I., Nikolopoulos, V., Mpardis, G., Loumos, V.: Dropout prediction in e-learning courses through the combination of machine learning techniques. Comput. Educ. **53**, 950–965 (2009)

13. Rostaminezhad, M.A., Mozayani, N., Norozi, D., Iziy, M.: Factors related to e-learner dropout: case study of IUST elearning center. Procedia Soc. Behav. Sci. **83**, 522–527 (2013)

14. Guay, F., Vallerand, R.J., Blanchard, C.: On the assessment of situational intrinsic and extrinsic motivation: the Situational Motivation Scale (SIMS). Motiv. Emot. **24**, 175–213 (2000)

15. Keller, J.M.: Development and use of the ARCS model of instructional design. J. Instr. Dev. **10**, 2–10 (1987)

16. Pintrich, P.R., Smith, D.A.F., Garcia, T., Mckeachie, W.J.: Reliability and predictive validity of the motivated strategies for learning questionnaire (MSLQ). Educ. Psychol. Meas. **53**, 801–813 (1993)

17. Tuan, H.L., Chin, C.C., Shieh, S.H.: The development of a questionnaire to measure students' motivation towards science learning. Int. J. Sci. Educ. **27**, 639–654 (2005)

18. Cavas, P.: Factors affecting the motivation of Turkish primary students for science learning. Sci. Educ. Int. **22**, 31–42 (2011)

19. Stark, E.: Examining the role of motivation and learning strategies in student success in online versus face-to-face courses. Online Learn. J. **23**, 234–251 (2019)

20. de Barba, P.G., Kennedy, G.E., Ainley, M.D.: The role of students' motivation and participation in predicting performance in a MOOC. J. Comput. Assist. Learn. **32**, 218–231 (2016)

21. Waschull, S.B.: Predicting success in online psychology courses: self-discipline and motivation. Teach. Psychol. **32**, 190–192 (2005)

22. Hartnett, M.: The importance of motivation in online learning. In: Motivation in Online Education, pp. 5–32. Springer Singapore (2016). https://doi.org/10.1007/978-981-10-0700-2_2

23. Hartnett, M., George, A., Dron, J.: Examining motivation in online distance learning environments: complex, multifaceted, and situation-dependent. Int. Rev. Res. Open Distance Learn. **12**(6), 20–38 (2011)

24. ChanLin, L.J.: Applying motivational analysis in a web-based course. Innov. Educ. Teach. Int. **46**, 91–103 (2009)
25. Keller, J.M., Suzuki, K.: Use of the arcs motivation model in courseware design. In: Instruction Design for Microcomputing Courseware, pp. 401–434 (2013)
26. Wighting, M.J., Wighting, M.J., Liu, J., Rovai, A.P.: Distinguishing sense of community and motivation characteristics between online and traditional college students. Q. Rev. Distance Educ. **9**, 285–295 (2008)
27. Yukselturk, E., Bulut, S.: Predictors for student success in an online course. Educ. Technol. Soc. **10**, 71–83 (2007)
28. Bandura, A.: Self-efficacy. In: Ramachaudran, V.S. (ed.) Encyclopedia of Human Behavior (1994)
29. Deci, E.L., Ryan, R.M.: Self-determination theory: a macrotheory of human motivation, development, and health. Can. Psychol. **49**(3), 182–185 (2008)
30. Rienties, B., Giesbers, B., Tempelaar, D., Lygo-Baker, S., Segers, M., Gijselaers, W.: The role of scaffolding and motivation in CSCL. Comput. Educ. **59**, 893–906 (2012)
31. Du Boulay, B., Del Soldato, T.: Implementation of motivational tactics in tutoring systems: 20 years on. Int. J. Artif. Intell. Educ. **26**, 170–182 (2016)
32. de Vicente, A., Pain, H.: Motivation diagnosis in intelligent tutoring systems. In: Goettl, B.P., Halff, H.M., Redfield, C.L., Shute, V.J. (eds.) ITS 1998. LNCS, vol. 1452, pp. 86–95. Springer, Heidelberg (1998). https://doi.org/10.1007/3-540-68716-5_14
33. Fogg, B.J.: Persuasive Technology: Using Computers to Change What We Think and Do. Morgan Kaufmann Publishers (2002)
34. Orji, R., Moffatt, K.: Persuasive technology for health and wellness: state-of-the-art and emerging trends. Health Inf. J. **24**, 66–91 (2018)
35. Gustafsson, A., Bång, M., Svahn, M.: Power explorer - a casual game style for encouraging long term behavior change among teenagers. In: ACM International Conference Proceeding Series, pp. 182–189. ACM Press, New York (2009)
36. Goh, T.T., Seet, B.C., Chen, N.S.: The impact of persuasive SMS on students' self-regulated learning. Br. J. Educ. Technol. **43**, 624–640 (2012)
37. Orji, F.A.: Data Analytics and Persuasive Technology to Promote Students' Engagement and Learning, University of Saskatchewan (2018)
38. Behringer, R., et al.: Persuasive technology for learning and teaching – The EuroPLOT Project. In: International Workshop on EuroPlOT Persuasive Technology Learning, Education and Teaching, pp. 3–7 (2013)
39. Kaptein, M., Markopoulos, P., Ruyter, B., Aarts, E.: Can you be persuaded? Individual differences in susceptibility to persuasion. In: Gross, T., et al. (eds.) INTERACT 2009. LNCS, vol. 5726, pp. 115–118. Springer, Heidelberg (2009). https://doi.org/10.1007/978-3-642-03655-2_13
40. Orji, R., Tondello, G.F., Nacke, L.E.: Personalizing persuasive strategies in gameful systems to gamification user types. In: Proceedings of the 2018 CHI Conference on Human Factors in Computing Systems - CHI 2018, pp. 1–14. ACM Press, New York (2018)
41. Kaptein, M., Markopoulos, P., De Ruyter, B., Aarts, E.: Personalizing persuasive technologies: explicit and implicit personalization using persuasion profiles. Int. J. Hum. Comput. Stud. **77**, 38–51 (2015)
42. Orji, F.A., Greer, J., Vassileva, J.: Exploring the effectiveness of socially-oriented persuasive strategies in education. In: Oinas-Kukkonen, H., Win, K.T., Karapanos, E., Karppinen, P., Kyza, E. (eds.) PERSUASIVE 2019. LNCS, vol. 11433, pp. 297–309. Springer, Cham (2019). https://doi.org/10.1007/978-3-030-17287-9_24
43. Jiménez, S., Juárez-Ramírez, R., Castillo, V.H., Ramírez-Noriega, A.: Integrating affective learning into intelligent tutoring systems. Univ. Access Inf. Soc. **17**, 679–692 (2018)

44. Zapata-Rivera, J.-D., Greer, J.E.: Inspecting and visualizing distributed bayesian student models. In: Gauthier, G., Frasson, C., VanLehn, K. (eds.) ITS 2000. LNCS, vol. 1839, pp. 544–553. Springer, Heidelberg (2000). https://doi.org/10.1007/3-540-45108-0_58

45. Vicente, A.De., Pain, H.: Motivation self-report in ITS. In: Proceedings of 9th International Conference on Artificial Intelligence in Education, pp. 651–659 (1999)

46. McQuiggan, S.W., Mott, B.W., Lester, J.C.: Modeling self-efficacy in intelligent tutoring systems: an inductive approach. User Model. User Adap. Inter. **18**, 81–123 (2008)

47. Qu, L., Wang, N., Johnson, W.L.: Using learner focus of attention to detect learner motivation factors. In: Ardissono, L., Brna, P., Mitrovic, A. (eds.) UM 2005. LNCS (LNAI), vol. 3538, pp. 70–73. Springer, Heidelberg (2005). https://doi.org/10.1007/11527886_10

48. Santos, P.B., Bhowmik, C.V., Gurevych, I.: Avoiding bias in students' intrinsic motivation detection. In: Kumar, V., Troussas, C. (eds.) ITS 2020. LNCS, vol. 12149, pp. 89–94. Springer, Cham (2020). https://doi.org/10.1007/978-3-030-49663-0_12

49. Johns, J., Woolf, B.: A dynamic mixture model to detect student motivation and proficiency. In: Proceedings of the National Conference on Artificial Intelligence, pp. 163–168 (2006)

50. Boulay, B.D.: Intelligent tutoring systems that adapt to learner motivation. In: Tutoring and Intelligent Tutoring Systems, pp. 103–128. Nova Science Publishers Inc. (2018)

51. de Vicente, A., Pain, H.: Informing the detection of the students' motivational state: an empirical study. Int. Conf. Intell. Tutoring Sys. **2363**, 933–943 (2002)

52. Ward, A., Litman, D., Eskenazi, M.: Predicting change in student motivation by measuring cohesion between tutor and student. In: Proceedings of the Sixth Workshop on Innovative Use of NLP for Building Educational Applications, pp. 136–141. Association for Computational Linguistics (2011)

53. Matsubara, Y., Nagamachi, M.: Motivation system and human model for intelligent tutoring. In: Frasson, C., Gauthier, G., Lesgold, A. (eds.) ITS 1996. LNCS, vol. 1086, pp. 139–147. Springer, Heidelberg (1996). https://doi.org/10.1007/3-540-61327-7_110

54. Boulay, B.D: Towards a motivationally intelligent pedagogy: how should an intelligent tutor respond to the unmotivated or the demotivated? In: New Perspectives on Affect and Learning Technologies, pp. 41–52. Springer, New York (2011)

55. Arroyo, I., Cooper, D.G., Burleson, W., Woolf, B.P., Muldner, K., Christopherson, R.: Emotion sensors go to school. In: Frontiers in Artificial Intelligence and Applications, pp. 17–24. IOS Press (2009)

56. Graesser, A.C., et al.: The relationship between affective states and dialog patterns during interactions with auto tutor. J. Interact. Learn. Res. **19**, 293–312 (2008)

57. Hernández, Y., Noguez, J., Sucar, E., Arroyo-Figueroa, G.: Incorporating an affective model to an intelligent tutor for mobile robotics. In: Proceedings - Frontiers in Education Conference, FIE, pp. 22–27. Institute of Electrical and Electronics Engineers Inc. (2006)

58. D'Mello, S.R., Graesser, A.C.: AutoTutor and affective AutoTutor: learning by talking with cognitively and emotionally intelligent computers that talk back. ACM Trans. Interact. Intell. Sys. **2**(4), 1–39 (2012)

59. Reschly, A.L., Huebner, E.S., Appleton, J.J., Antaramian, S.: Engagement as flourishing: the contribution of positive emotions and coping to adolescents' engagement at school and with learning. Psychol. Sch. **45**, 419–431 (2008)

60. Sottilare, R.A., Brawner, K.W., Goldberg, B.S., Holden, H.K.: The generalized intelligent framework for tutoring (GIFT). In: Galanis, G., Sottilare, R., Best, C., Galanis, G., Kerry, J., Sottilare, R. (eds.) Fundamental Issues in Defense Training and Simulation, pp. 223–233. CRC Press (2017). https://doi.org/10.1201/9781315583655-20

61. D'Mello, S.K., Kory, J.: A review and meta-analysis of multimodal affect detection systems. ACM Comput. Surveys. **47**(3), 1–36 (2015)

Competency-Based Experiential-Expertise and Future Adaptive Learning Systems

Kevin P. Owens[✉]

Applied Research Laboratories, The University of Texas at Austin, Austin, USA
kowens@arlut.utexas.edu

Abstract. In the near future an international career and life-long learning ecosystem will be developed to not only support the growing dependence of international/global remote work teams and roles but to facilitate new technology that will enable learning to be more ubiquitous and available at the point-of-need. This paper describes the competency-based experiential-expertise (CBEE) learning and performance management support model that is designed for this future learning ecosystem. The model stems from applied research conducted with the military over the last decade, and other research going as far back as the early 1970's [1] that argued today's industrial education system does not prepare people for real occupational work, and limits access to those most in need of education. It's suggested the current academic model simply cannot keep up with the growing or changing performance ability demands from new industries or new jobs in old industries [2, 3]. There are efforts in play to change the industrial-based academic model of learning for all its obsolescence, and to adopt a more competency-based approach [4–7]. However, even if successful, the academic model still doesn't provide a means to manage the development and tracking of ability regarding existing, new or future workers in the nation's occupational labor force. Therefore, many hours and lots of money will still be required and spent for learning that either is not needed, doesn't meet expectations or does not fix problems in occupational performance. This condition can be avoided if a single, data-driven, competency standard is followed and integrated into a joint academic/vocational training approach. To help support this idea, this paper describes a model and methodology of learning that works within the coming learning ecosystem, and consists of new ALS technology that must be researched further, and invested in to make learning more cost-effective regarding our future labor force, and provide learners with a greater return-on-investment.

Keywords: Competency · Competence · Expertise · Experience · Adaptive-learning · Andragogy · Neuroscience

1 Introduction

Human learning capability has evolved in many ways over the last twenty-years. First, much has been discovered about how humans learn from neuroscience. Second, technology that expands how we learn has been developed that began at the door-step of the

© Springer Nature Switzerland AG 2021
R. A. Sottilare and J. Schwarz (Eds.): HCII 2021, LNCS 12793, pp. 93–109, 2021.
https://doi.org/10.1007/978-3-030-77873-6_7

millennium with the internet. This technology includes internet-based learning management systems (LMS) that organize and deliver learning content anywhere and anytime, as well as tracks learning. There is also the ability to access content "in the wild", such as videos, blogs, wikis, as well as massive-online "webinars". Modern learning technology has been revolutionary, and has become so ubiquitous that it produced a vision of a future life-long learning ecosystem [8]. However, the learning model being implied with this ecosystem doesn't seem much different than how academic institutional learning occurs today.

Traditional academic learning includes serial, sequenced, scripted and instructor or tutor-controlled curriculum that works from custom learning objectives. This design-pattern often includes learning passively through slide-presentations, video productions or even electronic text-books, and often in a scheduled classroom or episodic online session. While pedagogic learning is still necessary for early phases of competence development, what is more important is recursive active practical and physical contextual exercises that applies and refines academic learning, and most importantly develops real experience; including time-constrained decision-making and team-coordination while performing non-scripted real work-based tasks.

Enter experiential learning. The idea of experiential learning goes as far back as Aristotle in ancient Greece but in the modern era is a manifestation of the education philosopher John Dewey. Dewey argued against what he witnessed become the very industrial American national education system at the beginning of the 20th-century; a system that enabled and promoted the academic learning methods as noted above, and what is still used world-wide in the 21st-century. Dewey argued against a "… single course of studies; it would mean abandoning the fundamental principle of connection with life-experiences". Dewey discussed the need for learning to "live fruitfully and creatively in future experiences…" based upon what he called "… the principles of the continuity of experience or … the experience continuum" [9]. Dewey also noted the need for "real experience to guide educational innovation vs. dogmatic instruction that is separated from real life". The latter being exactly what is occurring with the future learning ecosystem vision.

An effort to transform academic institutional learning to a more progressive or experiential model has been taken on by many others in academia but have remained rooted in the academic process; perhaps out of self-interest or perhaps because of the limits of technology at the time. Meanwhile, the need for new and existing workers to adopt, and be able to learn and perform rapidly changing 21st-century technological tasks, services, knowledge and skills in the modern job market demands the old academic model of learning to evolve.

Another motivating premise to produce a new learning model is that students should no longer be required to pay large sums of money and time to attend extended course-based learning sessions for credentials (e.g., a degree) that implies a promise to provide the needed knowledge and skills for future work options but are often found to be obsolete or forgotten before they attend their first job-interview or perform their first real-job [10]. Based on demands by today's employers and Generation Z students, some universities are coming up with improvements to move away from the traditional academic learning model, and more toward developing skills for jobs directly, as well as lowering education costs [11]; however, these efforts are lacking a common competency structure (from industry) to focus their learning on.

A key goal of this paper is to suggest a more practical and experiential learning approach, and to make learning more cost-effective (greater return-on-investment) by exposing learners to many concurrent "channels" of active tasks, as well as supporting knowledge, skills, attitudes and tacit abilities (KSAA) - instead of only sequenced, serial presentations. In addition, instead of using content based on exclusive learning objectives, learning content would now be based-on, and associated with, externally/centrally governed and "crowd sourced" *competency* standards that are containerized, reusable, defined and maintained by today's (or future) work environments. This new competency-based learning model would be a central feature of a future career & life-long learning ecosystem, and its associated technology like adaptive learning systems (ALS).

2 Discussion

The needed learning model described above is referred to here-in as competency-based experiential-expertise (CBEE). This model is an extension of competency-based learning, in that it provide specificity in many ways: (1) it integrates and blurs the lines between academic and vocational training, (2) it presumes task-based vs. course-based learning; (3) it is team AND individual-centered - as opposed to only focused on individual learners; (4) it is data-informed, meaning competence standards and rubrics to assess them are defined from data continuously collected and analyzed. (5) it assesses performance via Artificial Intelligence (AI) based automated assessment, as opposed to subjective check-sheet observed or felt measures; (6) it extends the traditional pedagogical (child-focused) learning method to include andragogy [12] or adult learning methods (learning-by-doing); finally (7), it is technology enabled and facilitated through live, synthetic or semi-live micro-lessons or exercise-based experiences. These experiences incorporate many of the same technologies online gaming uses today (but are NOT game-based), and are served through a new form of ALS technology. Before discussing the methodology of CBEE, lets discuss the necessary ontology of underlying terms, concepts and principles CBEE is based upon.

2.1 Competency

CBEE begins with "competency". According to Merriam-Webster [13], the term *competency* is defined as one *"in possession of sufficient knowledge or skill"*. According to Spencer and Spencer, a competency is an ability that is causally related to a criterion-reference performance in a job [14]. From this, we can define a *competency* to be an ability (a task, KSAA) associated with a team or individual role in a team. A competency can also be measured against a set criterion, for a given organization-mission or personal purpose. Additionally, the term *competence* is defined as, "the quality or *state* of having sufficient knowledge, judgment, skill, or strength (for a particular duty)". Therefore, competencies can be thought of as a list of ability requirements for teams and/or people assigned to them, and the learning to perform in specific occupational job-based duties. *Competence states* are the measured summative quality indicators of competency or ability [15], as demonstrated through cognitive and/or physical task-based performances, and their supporting KSAA. In CBEE, these *ability state* indicators are derived from recorded data-evidence (as opposed to subjective/biased opinion) to support any asserted claims of competence.

Competency objects. As stated earlier, in a future vision that CBEE is designed to support, career/life-long learning will be part of a global learning ecosystem [8]. Without getting into the massive process of competency analysis and definitions for this ecosystem (a separate model), competency standards will reside in cyber-space using an international technology standard called a *reusable competency definition* or RCD [16]. This standard will allow competency statements to be searchable across the world-wide-web, have links to other associated competency standards, learning resources and assessment rubrics, and will be compiled into what are machine-readable *competency-objects*. An "object" is a term borrowed from computer-software development vernacular that describes an instantiated (cloned) item from an original template (a.k.a. a class).

Competency objects are instantiated with metadata or terms that describe the unique application an object was created to support (e.g., specific occupations, types of abilities, etc.). Competency objects also contain variable links to other online resources (including other competency objects) that together form all that's needed to learn a competency. As stated, many competency objects will often be clustered together to support a specific function or purpose (like a job or team-role), within what's called a *competency-framework* as shown in Fig. 1. Competency-frameworks simply allow many related competency-objects to be queried and accessed at once, and with a common set of metadata. Competency-frameworks and/or objects will allow technology like Adaptive Learning Systems (ALS) to rapidly look-up, set-up, and access necessary resources to support an experiential learning event, as well as how to evaluate one's level of competence, based on the experiential performance-based data. Competency objects can be used for career related duties like defining organizational learning requirements, hiring requirements, performance assessments and credentialing, learning or experience-content design or development - and all accessible via the modern ubiquitous medium of cyber-space.

Competency management. In CBEE, a cloud-based competency registry (CR) is used to store and serve competency-frameworks and objects (sometimes called a competency management services or CMS). CMS are also used to edit, review, approve and manage competency standards as the latest best practices, new technologies/tools/software, or analysis of performance data demands. In addition, CMS contain algorithms and math-model that is used to calculate final competence-states and assertions of occupational work readiness. Competency management can happen at central occupational centers of excellence and/or can also be crowd-sourced with its own control process and utilities to allow anyone to update and change any standard based on local changes.

A CMS stores competency structure of frameworks and definitions based on a CBEE *competency-model* (see Fig. 2). Similar to an information model, a competency-model simply is the template schema of how frameworks, objects and other elements are intended to "fit" together like toy block pieces. A competency registry is a critical component in a modern ALS but can also be part of larger organizational HR or talent-management systems.

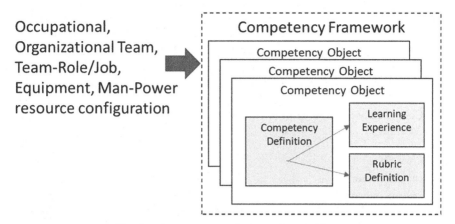

Fig. 1. The competency framework and object.

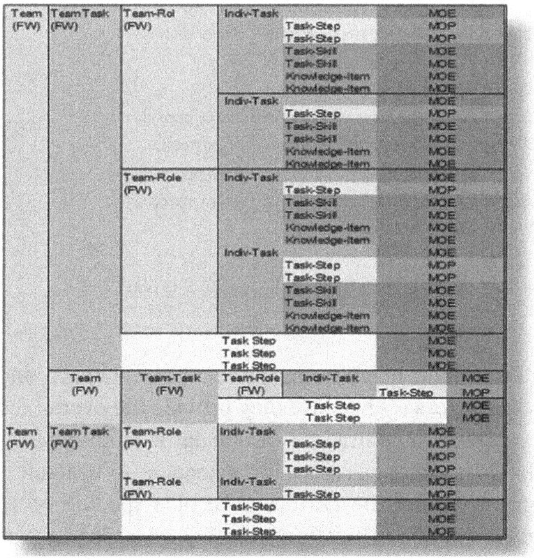

Fig. 2. The CBEE competency model.

Competency rubrics. The latest standard for competency definitions introduces an element called *competency-rubrics, which define the conditions, measures, and levels* a competency is measured. This element of a competency-object feeds new artificial intelligence-based ALS technologies so they can *adapt* to different performance conditions, and measure specific activities based on the existing level of the learner. Competency rubrics allow the ALS measurement features to be conducted objectively and unbiased, and to produce competency-specific performance data. Performance data is used by a CMS as evidence to support the production of a team or person's competency state and level using a math-model. This is a level of competency management detail never before possible from legacy LMS based learning technology or other adaptive instructional systems used in online learning.

Competency levels are used to classify actors at different levels of ability vs. today's "pass-fail" model. These levels span from when an actor first needs or wants to learns a task (novice-level) to when they are one of the few best at a task (expert-level). These discrete levels can also be aggregated to assert larger (framework-level) competence-states. Competency rubric measurement levels used in the CBEE model are described in Fig. 3 below.

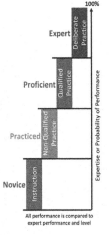

- Competence Levels:

  Competence levels specify a team or individual's summative predictive ability to perform a specific task at an expert level on demand (0-100%). Levels allow managers to predict the reliability of a team or individual to perform a given task.

  - **Expert level** – can complete all task-steps consistently at the highest criteria on-demand, AND after a significant number of experiences in the hardest conditions.
  - **Proficient level** – can complete all task-steps consistently at a qualified criteria, AND has a high number of experiences in mostly moderately difficult-conditions - a.k.a. a "journeyman".
    - Is said to be <u>QUALIFIED</u> to perform a task on their own
  - **Practiced level** – can complete all task-steps without help but not consistently at a qualified-criteria, AND/OR in mostly easier conditions. a.k.a. an "apprentice".
  - **Novice level** – an actor is learning the fundamental knowledge and skills of the task. Has minimal experience performing a task-steps and often needs help to complete tasks. Is not ready to begin solo or team practical training.

Fig. 3. CBEE competence-levels

In summary, RCDs in their machine-readable representations, and their associated standards and levels are necessary because they provide the overall learning ecosystem and "experience continuum" a central set of standards from which performance and learning is assessed. This makes it easier for managers to evaluate work completed, whom to hire, assign or predict the performance of a specific occupational team or person for a specific occupational function - e.g., when hiring or promoting someone into a team's leader role: one may need to have a higher level of competency (ability) in a given common task from the subordinates in other team-roles, from which a candidate is being selected.

Several assumptions are made from the above discussion with regard to CBEE:

(1) Competence state is based on a comparison to a vector of expertise (an experiential-expertise model). An experiential-expertise model is based on raw data collected from many performances of a given ability and condition, that are translated to one of the scaled levels based on set criteria from novice to expert. A competence state asserted for a team or individual indicates that one is "tested", and the level is "shown to be true". To ensure reliability, state is based on one's real performance data; it provides a team's or person's predictive ability to perform a task at a specific

level, and in a specific occupational role, job or specialty that a manager can plan and rely on.

(2) Because one's competency state is an indicator or decision-aid for managers to determine one's qualification for a job, team, mission, program or project, the state of competence must be presented as a stochastic probability of future performance. This is very different from that of traditional learning outcomes which are typically implied to be deterministic - i.e., a binary pass or fail (sometimes associated with subjective grades) that implies readiness to perform. This deterministic idea is even codified in traditional learning objectives (e.g., "at the end of this instruction, the learner will be able to…").

(3) Because competence-state is a predictive model of future expertise - based on empirical objective recorded data (not subjective judgement), this makes career management much less ambiguous. In the past and today, many assert their own competence (e.g., resumes) or claim competence from testimony of others (e.g., letters of recommendation or endorsements on internet platforms like LinkedIn™). These legacy practices of competence assertion not only dilute the motivation people need to learn or improve but makes it harder for managers to really predict who to place in their teams or positions with confidence about who will perform best in a critical task.

(4) A competence-state is determined or calculated not only based on one's performance outcome (how well) but a moving accumulation of experience (repetitions) performing a given activity, and a range of performance difficulties (conditions). Modern neuroscience has shown how expertise physiologically forms in the human brain and body through the nervous system based on these three data types [17].

(5) Once a competence-state is validated with evidence, and an occupational qualification credential is awarded, that state is *never* permanent. Human atrophy or forgetting occurs, and in fact is literally necessary for our brain's survival; therefore, an ability must be exercised and measured repeatedly within an appropriate periodicity in order to maintain a claim of competence or be automatically degraded to the next lower level based on a rule or degradation (math) function.

2.2 Experiential-Expertise

Learning science literature [18, 19] and neuroscience indicate two traits are tightly related: experience and expertise. Experience is quantified based on the scalars of *how often* (repetition) one performs a task within a recent window of time, and *how hard* the conditions were in those repetition-based assessments. The term *expert* is borrowed from the Latin phrase *expertus* or "tested, shown to be true" and the past participle of *experīrī* or "to put to the test, to have experience". More generally, an expert is defined as somebody who has broad, explicit and implicit competence in terms of task-work and KSAA, attained through practice and experience in a particular field of performance.

An expert has also historically been called or known as a "master" at a task; however, that term is not well received today internationally because of its negative connotation [20] so CBEE won't use it either. In CBEE, one's competence-state and expertise are synonymous. CBEE suggests expertise, more specifically experiential-expertise, is a vector indicating a probability of performing as an expert. As shown in Fig. 4 below, one's experiential-expertise state vector is based on the set of three scalars: *how well*, *how often*, and *how hard* one has performed a given competency or ability when they were measured.

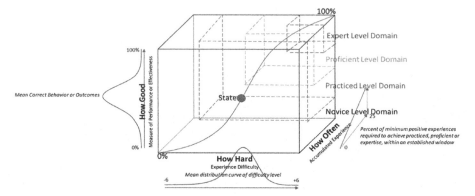

Fig. 4. CBEE algorithmic competence-state indicator

The default growth-pattern of an experiential-expertise vector is suggested to follow a sigmoid-pattern typically observed in biological material like foliage as shown in Fig. 5 below.

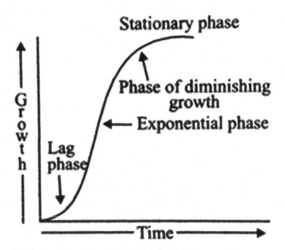

Fig. 5. The natural biologic-material growth pattern

The idea is that just as plants naturally and slowly grow taller at first so they build strong root systems to become more resilient with repeated exposure to sunlight, moisture, and environmental conditions over time, an actor's experiential-expertise grows slower at first as well, as they develop the necessary KSAA "root system" through both passive and active based learning methods, that are always focused on performing specific task-steps. As time goes on, and more experience gained, expertise grows more rapidly. This idea is supported by the principles of neuroscience (more below).

In the three-dimensional experiential-expertise model illustrated in Fig. 4, each dimension is a scalar of experiential-expertise and are specifically: (a) the mean level of performances measures, (b) the mean degree of difficulty those measures were taken from, and (c) the number of accumulated performances one has performing a task in a sliding window of time. Inside this model the spectrums are broken up into domains that represent the four levels of competence discussed earlier. Where one's competence-state or experiential-expertise is indicated - based on a mathematical function (a math model) – is where an actor's current level of competency is at a single point in time.

Initially, an actor starts a task they've never performed before in a *novice* level-domain. The actor's expertise grows at a very slow rate as they focus on learning from ALS delivered and recommended lessons delivered to the learner consisting of the core fundamentals associated with a task, and assess them to measure if they know the basic KSAA related to *how* to perform a task. If an actor has or can demonstrate they already have the core competence needed for a task (e.g., if the fundamentals were learned for other tasks), they will be calculated past the novice phase altogether and begin practicing the task immediately.

Next, an actor begins the *practiced* level-domain. As the level-label implies, actors improve competence by practicing the task, and applying their learned novice fundamentals until their mean performance is at or within the proficient level-domain based on meeting a set criterion. This means the actor needs to perform the task at a minimum mean level of quality (e.g., accuracy, latency, precision), a minimum number of times (repetition), and at a minimum mean level of difficulty (conditions). Often this level-domain uses a technique called part-task training. This technique supports focused performance on a particular task-step (which is usually a competency measure) with the end-goal being that one should be able to perform the overall task without thinking about it much or at a level of "automaticity". A person at/in this level-domain is sometimes called an Apprentice, and is sometimes said to be in an "apprenticeship" state. Another use-case for being at/in this level-domain would be when an actor loses their task *proficient* competence-state or proficiency, that they had but let it atrophy over a set periodicity.

Once the actor reaches a competence-state at/in the proficient level-domain, that usually means an actor is *qualified* to perform a task on their own in live occupational job-site or situation. They are often also authorized to begin training or coaching novices or those still practiced. A person at/in this level-domain is sometimes called a Journeyman.

Eventually, after many more task experiences, higher mean scores, and mostly in the hardest difficulty conditions, an actor may reach the coveted *expert* level-domain. Growth in one's expertise now begins to slow significantly because the actor can only increase their performance score so much more at the level of difficulty they now must always perform in to maintain this level-domain. An actor must begin doing what's called deliberate practice to raise their expertise any more. It should be noted that in CBEE, because the criteria for each competence level-domain is based on data, the criteria can also "shift-up" slightly one or all of the three dimensions, especially as more difficult exercises, and/or more actors reach this level-domain of competence. Thus, some actors who were experts may fall-out of this level-domain without continuous deliberate practice.

Neuroscience and experiential-expertise. Neuroscience indicates that when new conditions are experienced, new neural pathways are formed from a chemical and physical *change* in the brain via synaptic connections. Like the biological growth indicator in Fig. 4 above, repetition makes this new change stronger by producing more synapse connections (dendrites), and building myelin sheaths around the neural axon pathways as shown in Fig. 6 below. The myelin sheath acts like insulation around a copper wire adjacent to other wires - i.e., to keep the new path from shorting out with other near-by neural pathways resulting in stronger and faster signals. This physiological *change* is what "experiential-expertise" physically looks like, and what determines our level of competency by making our perceptions more sensitive, our movements more refined, smaller details easier to see, and memory easier and faster to retrieve and/or more "automatic". The building of muscle fibers and muscular neuro connections follow the same process.

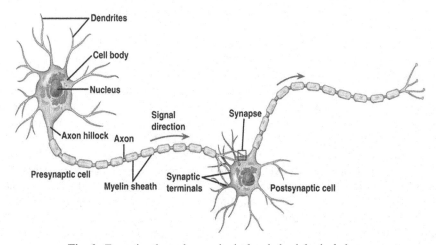

Fig. 6. Expertise through neurological and physiological change

Dr. Mike Merzenic, a leading scientist in the science of neuroplasticity provides several insights that supports the points above.

- *Learning is actually a change in neural connections and cell-to-cell cooperation.*
- *Note: this broadening network of associated brain cells that form a competency is a similar principle of how artificial intelligence is developed using weightings and node growth.*
- *The more effort made, from emotion and interest, the more one is motivated to learn, the more alert one is during execution and reflection, the more impactful the experience and the more the brain changes (i.e., learning occurs).*

- *The brain strengthens its connections between clusters of neurons representing specific knowledge and skills or experiences that consist of connected but separate discrete ideas or successive events that occur in serial time.*
- *Initial neural changes are only temporary. Your brain first records the change, then determines whether it should make the change permanent or not based on continued practice or use. Changes only become permanent if the experience is reflected on continuously or used again and again. Otherwise the brain will weaken the connection to make room for other experiences, memories (i.e., "use it or lose it").*
- *Memory guides and controls most learning. As you learn a new knowledge or skill, your brain takes note of and remembers the good attempts, while discarding the not-so-good performances, thus making incremental adjustments to the neural structures to improve the connections.*
- *Every repetition in learning provides an opportunity for the brain to stabilize and reduce the disruptive power of interfering "noise." from short-circuiting neural pathways.*
- *Each time your brain strengthens a connection that advances expertise in knowledge, skill or belief, it also weakens other connections of neurons that weren't used at that precise moment unless more neurons are produced.*
- *Brain plasticity is a two-way street; it is just as easy to generate negative changes from non-use as it is positive ones from repetitive use.*

3 Method

Now that some underlying principles of CBEE have been discussed, next is a description of the method or use-case model CBEE uses in practical applications. This description is based on applied research that is on-going as part of a US Army science and technology project, that includes adopting an existing open source Intelligent Tutoring System called the generalized intelligent framework for tutoring or GIFT [21] into a future learning ecosystem compliant ALS.

Integrated Education and Training

First, I should remind the reader that one of the goals of CBEE is to demonstrate the idea of a new future learning ecosystem, by adopting today's traditional educational institutions and work-centric vocational institutions or programs into an integrated single continuum of learning that work with and from the CBEE competence levels and learning indicator in Fig. 5 above. The former being mainly concerned with providing learning for the novice level-domain, and the latter providing learning for the remaining competency level-domains. In this way, both are "focused" on the same competency-based web-based standards, instead of creating their own unique and local learning objectives using the traditional Analysis, Design, Development, Implementation and Evaluation (ADDIE) curriculum process. CBEE assumes that occupational centers of excellence will collect data from their respective fields and produce inspectable tasks and underlying KSAA structures that are turned into the international competency models, and that they will re-use competency elements if they already exist in other occupational fields, only tailored for their specific occupation. Academia, will then focus on the lower level KSAAs that support these contextual occupations, so students understand why and how what they're learning applies in a possible future occupation, or as prerequisite before moving on to practical training as part of a chosen career field, based on the latest data driven competency standards in a given industry.

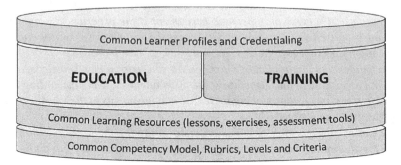

Fig. 7. Integrated learning continuum

The CBEE and ALS Methodology

CBEE is an active learning process by engaging in real-world problems, challenges, and tasking in a 10-stage cyclic process shown in Fig. 8 below. We will now discuss each of these stages of the CBEE and ALS methodology below in order.

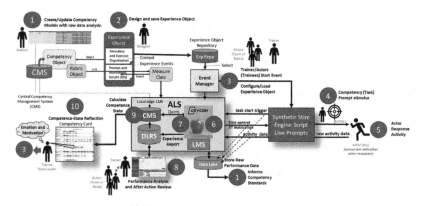

Fig. 8. CBEE and ALS methodology

1. Create competency models. This stage in the cycle is actually a continuous process. As you can see in Fig. 8, this process involves perpetual job and task analysis of the raw performance data collected from each "repetition" every actor goes through, and every task and/or KSAA based activity they perform. This stage produces the competency models discussed earlier that serve as the focus of all task-based learning.

2. Design Experience objects. CBEE is mainly focused on building one's competence-state in task performance for real work, and it envisions an ecosystem where

most learning will occur through task-based learning that are directly related to competency-objects that support their application and assessment. At this stage specially, trained *experience designers* extract real data recorded from the job site and convert it into an *experience object*. These experience objects will contain metadata for searching, and multiple experience events which is when tasks are prompted and assessed. Experience objects also point to (thus read in when used) small competency-specific based content (called *lesson objects*) that can be learned as stand-alone microlearning [22] before a training exercise or during a pause in a training exercise.

An experience-object is usually designed to support a specific high-order competency, can be instantiated from other experience objects or designed custom. Experience objects can be as simple as a recorded task-based video or as sophisticated as a device or computer-based simulations - using virtual reality or mixed reality, that immerses the learner into the occupation environment. This stage of CBEE is suggested to be a future career, and the core "curriculum" for future education and training. Using competency-standards and levels, teams and people can gradually build experiential-expertise through several "sets" and "reps" of scenario-performance, feedback, and reflective experiences, and all in the occupation environment.

3. Start an experience event. In CBEE, an "event" is a period in time when experiential-expertise is developed. What today is called a class-period or course is now a live or virtual exercise in an occupational context. Starting an experience is handled by an Event Manager function which is where the desired experience object - associated with the competencies needed to be developed - is read in from a central repository in the web-based cloud or local edge cloud learning ecosystem. This is also when/where the designated trainer (if used) and trainees (called actors) are registered into the ALS and assigned to occupational teams and roles they will perform as. Learning records are also accessed, and any necessary microlearning will happen if needed. Devices are also given and registered with each person so the ALS knows whom the raw data belongs to.

Within an experience object are multiple "assessment-events" that are conditions that trigger one or more specific competencies (task, ability, skill(s), knowledge, etc.) to be performed. These are the parts of the experience-object when competency is measured against standards, associated to a competence-level, and recorded, along with raw performance data.

At the same time, the selected experience object is sent to the ALS and Stimulation Engine (or provide a live script) so it knows how to set-up the exercise, and read-in the required competency-frameworks and/or objects so the ALS can configure the standardized criteria, and what AI informed measurements classes to use as actors activate different assessment-events throughout the occupational exercise environment. When all is ready, the trainer selects "start".

4. Prompt task performance. The execution of the experience object's script is a central function of the ALS. The ALS controls the set-up of the occupational "world" in the virtual and/or experience reality (XR) cloud-based Stimulation Engine (stem-engine) with live or synthetic entities running around or poised to prompt performance. The session actor(s) will now do what occupational duty the experience-object assigns them to do, and as they do this, the actors will "trigger" specific assessment-events in the stem-engine environment. These triggers will then not only prompt the actors to perform the competencies they need to perform but start the assessment process in the ALS using expected data it receives back from the stem-engine. It should be noted that as triggers, prompts, and response data are being sent and received between the stem-engine and the ALS, all this data is being stored in a cloud-based data-lake that is used to inform the competency analysis process discussed above for stage 1.
5. Respond to an assessment-event prompt. Similar to the idea of behaviorism, the assessment-event prompts will stimulate a response of some kind (cognitive or behavioral) from one or more actors. This will happen by synthetic (virtual or augmented) entities created in the stem-engine, or simply part of playback of recorded live data. The actor(s) resulting activity data will be recorded from respective devices they are either holding or wearing.
6. Classify and report performance data. The actor(s) response data sent from the stem-engine will be used by the ALS to assess the expected activity against a predefined criterion that comes from the competency-object's rubric method. The ALS uses the measurement class to determine which level best matches the performance.
7. Store experience and performance data. The ALS measurement class then produces output data that will be recorded in what's called experience storage (a.k.a a learning resource store or LRS). This data is reported as text-based "statements" with links to associated raw data. These statements report multiple levels of performance such as a task-step, a response to a verbal or written knowledge question, an access to micro-learning, as well as an AI based "roll-up" assertion that reports an overall task or KSAA learning outcome. The statement will also indicate the difficulty of the assessment-event that stimulated the response data. This classification (or grading) process is compared to an actor support service within the ALS that compares an actor's baseline competence-level (received when the session was started) to that of the exercise-based classified response data, and simply outputs if the actor was better, the same or worse than the baseline in a quantitative format.
8. Performance analysis and feedback. A key stage in the CBEE process is the analysis of the classified response data from each actor, for each competency being assessed, and the occupational team or role they were performing in the exercise. It is at this point that the trainer (if applicable) can identify problems in the performance in real-time and intervene or after the exercise is completed, when the trainer can properly analyze all the data of possibly many actors performing concurrently - which they would not be able to assess cognitively in real-time.

During this stage of CBEE, the trainer can not only identify points to discuss with actors as feedback but also correct AI based classifications (especially the AI class is new). This "correction" is actually a labeling process that the machine-learning algorithms use to create the AI class in the first place. Another key attribute of this stage is that actors get feedback not based on the trainer's opinion but based on real data and objective/unbiased classification, against a pre-created competency standard so they will view the feedback with maximum value, that will initiate the neural learning process described above, beginning with reflection and emotion.

Some questions the ALS may be programmed to prompt (along with the raw data to analyze) via the actor's device (per the competency-object or experience-object design) are:

a. what task activity worked (for their own or another performer)?
b. what task activity did not work and why?
c. what task experience stimulus was missed and why?
d. [For team performance] what team-task teamwork behaviors were done well or not done?
e. what competency needs to be improved (learned/practiced) before the next experience?

This stage is probably the greatest opportunity when deep experiential-expertise and task-based competence to be developed.

9. Competency model output. As classified activity statements are produced and stored in the experience storage (LRS), the CMS is being alerted so that it can consume the stored statements and associate them with all the other statements for a competency that an actor has accumulated over many exercises (or experiences). Once the exercise is over, the CMS will use these accumulated actor statements, their respective difficulty values, and a math-model (like what's conceptualized in Fig. 5 above) to produce a final competence-state and level that will be sent for review by the actor-team or individual's manager for awareness and/or approval to be placed in the actor's global learning record as an asserted state or that qualifies them for specific occupational role or job (for promotion or pay purposes). The manager will also be able to query and "playback" any team or individual exercise data as desired so they can view any of their team's or individual's actual performance themselves.

10. Competence-state reflection. Just as actors were given a chance to reflect on their performance within a specific experience-exercise, in CBEE they are always enabled to access and reflect on their current final competence-state for a given task or rolled-up team or role state. This is done through what's called a competency card that summarizes all the competency states associated with their career job, assigned roles, future career aspirations, or for a team manager or leader, how well their team's competence-state is, and what competency they need to focus on to improve or sustain those states. As noted in Fig. 7, this reflection is what leads actors and leaders to begin new experience sessions, and repeat the cycle described above, only perhaps with new competencies and associated experience-objects and events to learn through.

4 Conclusion and Recommendation

In summary the future ALS will be designed to serve this new CBEE model of occupational competency sustainment and learning. Competency objects will define all performance standards and competence-states. Experience-objects that prompt task-based assessment-events in natural occupational conditions, will be the new "curriculum" for career or life-long learning, and provide data-based feedback on each and every task performed. Most importantly, this process now allows both the academic and vocational training domains to work within the same competency-based, experiential-expertise scaled continuum. Instead of using less effective Carnegie-units of time and "butts in seats" approach to learning funding and accounting, the new ALS will produce raw data that can then be monitored for how much actual learning is happening both at individual exercise levels, and if a needed occupational competency-state is being improved or sustained (and NOT being allowed to atrophy as what happens today) so that maximum return on learning investment is gained.

Another important attribute of CBEE is that learning is much more cost-effective. Teams and people spend less time and/or money on learning what they don't need and focusing on what they do need or aspire to be in their current or future career so they can contribute to society in a positive way. Furthermore, CBEE ensures people actually *learn* more deeply and broadly based on neuroscience and modern learning science and techniques (e.g., microlearning, part-task training, etc.) and all the current and new technology the future learning ecosystem will provide.

The CBEE model will need more applied research (as the US Army is doing) to not only validate its assumptions and claims but to improve the ALS technology and methodology described above that CBEE relies upon. At the same time as new standards, practices, principles of competency-definitions, and neuroscience are discovered, those new findings need to be folded into this model as well. As the future career and life-long learning ecosystem begins to take shape, a new learning model like CBEE will be needed to optimize its learning effectiveness and return-on-investment.

References

1. McClelland, D.C.: Testing for competence rather than for intelligence. Am. Psychol. **28**, 1–14 (1973)
2. Linked In: 12 Jobs You'll Be Recruiting for in 2030 (2021). https://business.linkedin.com/talent-solutions/blog/future-of-recruiting/2018/12-jobs-you-will-be-recruiting-for-in-2030. Accessed 05 Jan 2021
3. Pew Research Center: The Future of Jobs and Jobs Training (2017). https://www.pewresearch.org/internet/2017/05/03/the-future-of-jobs-and-jobs-training/. Accessed 05 Jan 2021
4. Jaschik, S.: A Plan to Kill High School Transcripts … and Transform College Admissions (2017). https://www.insidehighered.com/news/2017/05/10/top-private-high-schools-start-campaign-kill-traditional-transcripts-and-change. Accessed 04 Feb 2021
5. Itin, C.M.: Reasserting the philosophy of experiential education as a vehicle for change in the 21st century. J. Phys. Educ. **22**(2), 91–98 (1999)
6. Breunig, M.C.: Teaching Dewey's *experience and education* experientially. In: Stremba, B., Bisson, C.A. (eds.) Teaching Adventure Education Theory: Best Practices, p. 122 (2009). ISBN 9780736071260

7. Nodine, T.R.: How did we get here? A brief history of competency-based higher education in the United States (2016). https://doi.org/10.1002/cbe2.1004. Accessed 09 Feb 2021

8. Walcutt, J.J., Schatz, S. (eds.): Modernizing Learning: Building the Future Learning Ecosystem. Government Publishing Office, Washington, DC (2019)

9. Dewey, J.: Experience & Education. Touchstone (1938)

10. James, G.: Colleges Aren't Preparing Students for the Workforce: What This Means for Recruiters (2015). https://business.linkedin.com/talent-solutions/blog/2015/07/colleges-arent-preparing-students-for-the-workforce-what-this-means-for-recruiters

11. Marcus, J.: How Technology Is Changing the Future of Higher Education (2020). New York Times: https://www.nytimes.com/2020/02/20/education/learning/education-technology.html. Accessed 09 Feb 2021

12. Knowles, M.S., et al.: The Adult Learner, 8th edn. Routledge, London and New York (2015)

13. Merriam-Webster.com Dictionary, Merriam-Webster (2021). https://www.merriam-webster.com/dictionary/proficiency. Accessed 19 Jan 2021

14. Spencer, L.M., Spencer, S.M.: Competence at Work: Models for Superior Performance. Wiley, Hoboken (1993)

15. Biech, E. (ed.): ASTD Handbook for Workplace Learning Professionals, 1st edn. Danvers (2008)

16. IEEE P1484.20.1 Working Group. P1484.20.1–2021™/D1 Draft Standard for Learning Technology-Data Model for Reusable Competency Definitions (2021). https://standards.ieee.org/content/ieee-standards/en/standard/1484_20_1-2007.html. Accessed 11 Feb 2021

17. Merzenic, M.: Soft-Wired: How the New Science of Brain Plasticity Can Change Your Life. Parnassus Publishing, San Francisco (2013)

18. National Research Council: How People Learn I: Brain, Mind, Experience, and School: Expanded Edition. National Academies Press, Washington DC (2001)

19. Board of Behavioral and Social Sciences and Education: How People Learn II: Learners, Contexts and Cultures. National Academies Press, Washington DC (2018)

20. ZDNet. GitHub to replace "master" with alternative term to avoid slavery references (2021). https://www.zdnet.com/article/github-to-replace-master-with-alternative-term-to-avoid-slavery-references/. Accessed 30 Jan 2021

21. GIFT. Generalized Intelligent Framework for Tutoring (GIFT) Documentation (2020). https://gifttutoring.org/projects/gift/wiki/Overview#Background. Accessed 16 Jan 2021

22. Brusino, J. (ed.): ATD's 2020 Trends in Learning Technology. ATD Press, Alexandria (2020)

23. Felicia, P.: Handbook of Research on Improving Learning and Motivation, p. 1003 (2011). ISBN 978-1609604967

24. Tavangar, H.: The Out of Eden Walk: An Experiential Learning Journey from the Virtual to the Real. Edutopia, 3 January 2014. Accessed 16 Jan 2021

25. Beard, C.: The Experiential Learning Toolkit: Blending Practice with Concepts, p. 20 (2010). ISBN 9780749459345

Early Prediction of At-Risk Students in a Virtual Learning Environment Using Deep Learning Techniques

Nisha S. Raj$^{(\boxtimes)}$ ⓘ, Sreelakshmi Prasad, Parvathy Harish, Maria Boban, and Nidhuna Cheriyedath

SCMS School of Engineering and Technology, Karukutty, Angamaly, Kerala, India
nishasraj@scmsgroup.org

Abstract. With the advancement of the internet and communication technologies, online learning has gained acceleration. The largely-scaled open online courses run on specific virtual platforms, where learners can engage themselves in their own space and pace. The Virtual Learning Environments (VLE) have shown rapid development in recent years, allowing learners to access high-quality digital materials. This paper aims at exploring students' affinity towards early withdrawal from online courses. The work expands by finding learner-centric factors contributing to students' early prediction at-risk of withdrawal and developing a prediction model. The current work uses the free Open University Learning Analytics Dataset (OULAD). Here, the early identification of students at risk of withdrawal is predicted based on a Deep Learning Approach using CNN Algorithm. Time-series analysis is done using data from consecutive years. The work's significant contribution is a set of influential parameters predicting at-risk students at an early learning stage. The prediction accuracy falls in the range of 83% to 93%.

Keywords: Learning analytics · At-risk student prediction · Student dropout · Deep learning

1 Introduction

A Virtual Learning Environment (VLE) is a virtual teaching-learning platform that comprises course materials, tests, assessments, and other tools. It may also have social media tools for learners and instructors to interact. VLE is often part of an advanced education institution's inclusive learning management system (LMS). Recently, online educational systems have emerged as a rising phenomenon. As we have seen, the recent COVID 19, which finally resulted in India's lockdown, gradually increased the use of virtual learning platforms. Not only in India but also throughout the world, students depend on such online classes. Predicting student dropouts in a virtual learning environment is an important issue. Statistics show that less than 13% of students are only on track [7]. It is necessary to detect students at risk as early as possible, to provide some care to prevent these students from quitting their studies.

© Springer Nature Switzerland AG 2021
R. A. Sottilare and J. Schwarz (Eds.): HCII 2021, LNCS 12793, pp. 110–120, 2021.
https://doi.org/10.1007/978-3-030-77873-6_8

Interestingly, these online educational systems generate repositories as a by-product. They contribute to the generation of educational data repositories surrounding learners' interactions, activities, and engagement patterns, which can be used to explore appropriate student behavior and predict students at risk of failure or withdrawal [12]. Traditional educational approaches are usually unable to identify large-scale numbers of at-risk students. There are various data analytics techniques, of which Deep Artificial Neural Networks (ANNs) are most commonly applied in prediction [1, 10, 13, 16]. Deep Learning consists of multiple forms of neural networks and several computational layers. It facilitates the model to learn from existing instances by filtering inputs through layers to predict and classify information. This study intends to investigate the effectiveness of deep learning practices to indicate the students at risk of withdrawal in a virtual learning environment from the easily accessible Open University Learning Analytics (OULA) dataset [11]. Convolutional Neural Networks (CNN) model is used to predict at-risk students in VLE [10]. The models have the potential to detect the students who are in danger of withdrawal at the early stage of academics. Identifying at-risk students can be used to improve the completion rate.

The rest of the paper is organized as follows: Sect. 2 discusses the recent studies related to recent developments in predictive analytics in education. Section 3 details the research questions and objectives. Section 4 briefs the dataset's characteristics, and Sect. 5 explains the methodology, which involves data preprocessing and modeling. Section 6 briefly discusses the results of the experimentation and the discussion concerning the research objective. Section 7 concludes the paper with a discussion on future work.

2   Literature Study

Several research works have explored different ways to improve student academic performance prediction using different types of variables and algorithms and identify the best way to increase the predictive model's accuracy and efficiency [4, 6]. Since the introduction of VLEs, studies investigating them have focused on the institutions' perceptions of VLEs and their implementation, especially in the context of blended learning. The author's Tamada et al. [14] propose reducing the dropout rate in Virtual Learning Environments (VLE). This generates large amounts of data about courses and students, whose analysis requires computational analytical tools. Haiyang et al. [9] focus on developing a dropout predictive model based on collecting students' behavior MOOC interactions data using a time series classification method. A study of the impact of technology-enhanced learning on student academic performance investigates the relationship between the frequency of the student VLE learning activities and the student's academic performance [5]. The study was done by Figueroa- Canas, J., and Sancho-Vinuesa, T, which helps teachers intervene to reduce dropout rates. Early prediction of course achievement helps teachers suggest new learning materials to prevent at-risk students from failing or not completing the course [8]. Several aspects might influence the performance achieved by existing learning systems. One of these aspects is a class imbalance, in which examples in training data belonging to one class heavily outnumber the models in the other class. In this situation, which is found in real-world data describing an infrequent but important event, the learning system may have difficulties learning the concept related to the minority class. A Study of the Behavior of Several Methods for Balancing Machine Learning Training Data [3] performs a comprehensive experimental evaluation involving ten methods, three them deal with the class imbalance problem in thirteen UCI data.

3 Research Questions and Objectives

The study's objective is to develop an accurate predictive model to identify students showing affinity towards early withdrawal from MOOC or VLE courses. Two research questions are designed to achieve the objective.

- RQ1: Whether the deep learning techniques are useful in predicting early withdrawal from courses?
- RQ2. What are the learner-centric factors which help to predict early withdrawal from courses?

4 Methodology

The open university learning analytics dataset is enormous [11]. For achieving better prediction from the applied model, the dataset should be preprocessed effectively. Since a vast dataset is challenging to process, we have taken the dataset's subset by feature extraction. The subgroup is further split into two sets, one for training and one for testing.

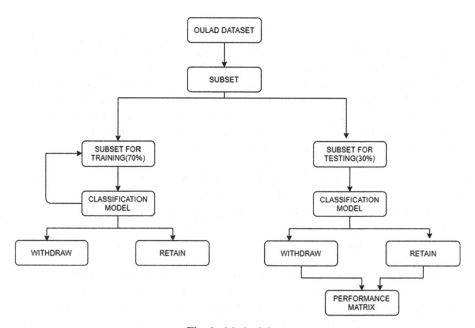

Fig. 1. Methodology

The training set will train the model, and the testing set will test the trained model. Here 70% of the preprocessed dataset is taken for training, and the remaining 30% is taken for testing. 1D Convolutional Neural Network (CNN) is used as the classification model. Figure 1 represents the methodology of the current work. The training dataset is given to the model, and it classifies whether withdrawn or retain. The fitted model then runs with the test dataset, and the test dataset will provide a balanced evaluation of the final model. Here we have taken three different subsets of the OULA dataset. So, we can conclude which all factors in the dataset are affecting the withdrawal of the student.

A confusion matrix is used to evaluate the accuracy of this prediction procedure. In the two-class label problem, the confusion matrix is a matrix with four entries, as shown in the table below (Table 1).

Table 1. Confusion matrix

True Positive (TP)	True Negative (TN)
False Positive (FP)	False Negative (FN)

TP denotes the number of actual dropout students who are predicted by the classifier. FP denotes the number of retained learners as per prediction, but actually, they are dropouts. FN denotes the count of dropout learners who has been signaled a non-dropout. TN indicates the number of engaged students who are accurately foreseen. Based on the confusion matrix, precision denotes the proportion of real dropout learners.

Accuracy is the measure of closeness of predicted value to the actual value. Here, accuracy is considered the evaluation measure as the objective is to do an accurate predictive analysis over an educational dataset.

5 Experimentation

5.1 OULA Dataset

The Open University is a public distance learning university in the UK. It provides free open data related to their online courses to the research community, which are anonymized. The OULA dataset consists of the demographical information, log-in patterns, and assessment behavior of 32,593 students over a course period of 9 months, from 2014–2015. It consists of 7 courses, referred to as modules, where each module is taught at least twice a year at different intervals [11]. The students' performances are classified into four classes: distinction, pass, fail, and withdrawal. The acquired raw data constitutes of files, with information about students' demographics, students' interaction with the online environment signified as clickstream numbers, assessments quiz performances and modules information. The students' interaction data consists of 20 different activities namely; dataplus, dualpane, externalquiz, folder, forumng, glossary, homepage, htmlactivity, oucollaborate, oucontent, ouelluminate, ouwiki, page, questionnaire, quiz, repeat activity, resource, sharedsubpage, subpage and url. Each activity signifies a particular behavior in the learning environment such as quiz for clicks on the course quiz, questionnaire for clicks on the questionnaire related to the course and so on. In general oulad distinguish three different data types: Demographics (represents the basic information about the students including their age, gender, region, previous education), performance (reflects students' results and achievements during their studies at the OU) [11].

The data is structured in seven CSV files. Figure 2 depicts the detailed structure of the dataset [11]. Table student Info can be linked to student Assessment, studentVle and student Registration tables using column id_student. Table courses links to the assessments, student Registration, vle and student Info using identifier columns code_module and code_presentation. Table assessments links to student Assessment using id_assessment and vle to studentVle using id_site.

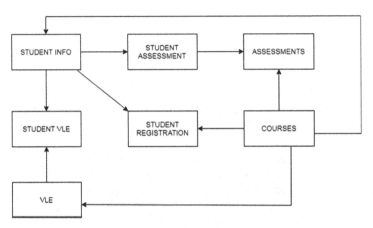

Fig. 2. Structure of OULAD

5.2 Preprocessing of Dataset

Since the dataset is large enough to train the model, we consider a subset of this OULAD. The student Info table contains the students' demographic information, and each course's results grouped as pass, fail, distinction, or withdraw. The learning environment interaction data consists of the number of clicks that the students made while studying the original dataset's VLEExtracting features. To train the model, we have created a feature vector table. Generally, there are two courses considered, a STEM course as well as a Social Science course. Code_modules AAA, BBB, and GGG are the Social science courses and the others are the STEM courses. To train our model, we have taken one social science course with code_module AAA.To get a wide range of data, we consider two different code_presentation for the code_module AAA, ie. 2013J and 2014J. These courses start in October in the years 2013 and 2014. We have considered the tables, student Vle,Vle, student Assessment, and student Info to create the feature vector table. The student info table contains the students' demographic information and the results of each course. The course table contains information about the courses in which students are enrolled. The registration table contains student record timestamps and course enrollment dates. The assessment information is recorded in the assessment table. The VLE interaction data consist of the number of clicks students made while studying the course material in the VLE. Since the dataset is large, we are taking only one course: STEM (i.e., code_module = AAA). We have extracted data based on code_module = AAA.

Studies show that demographic characteristics and students' clickstream activity, have a significant impact on student performance [2, 15]. Sample features considered are code_module, code_presentation, id_student, sum_click, activity_type, highest_education and score [10]. Tables considered are studentinfo, vle, studentVle and student_assessment. In the original dataset, there are 4 classes pass, fail, withdrawn and distinction out of those two classes are considered they are passed and withdrawn.The pass class has been obtained by merging Fail, pass and distinction. The studentVle table contains attributes code_module, code_presentation, id_student, id_site, date, sum_click. The vle contains id_site, code_module, code_presentation, activity_type, week_from, week_to. The studentinfo table contains code_module, code_presentation, id_student, gender, region, highest_education, imd_band, age_band, num_of_prev_attempts, studied_credits, disability, final_result. The studentAssessment table contains id_assessment, id_student, date_submitted, is_banked, and score.

The common attributes are code_module, code_presentation, id_student, id_site and id_assessment. A subset of the dataset is obtained, which is used for training. Since it is more convenient to input one table to the model, we have merged the tables with extracted features.studentInfo table is merged with the studentVle table. The attributes of final_result and highest_education will be included in the studentVle table. Similarly vle table is merged with studentVle table, so that the attribute Activity_type will be included in the studentVle table.There are seven attributes: code_presentation, id_student, id_site, sum_click, activity_type, highest_education, and final_result in the first input table. In the second input, the table score is taken. The two tables are fed to the algorithm as input. Both input datasets are divided according to the code presentation 2013J and 2014J and trained separately. So there are six datasets.The separate assessment thus helps us know the learner-centric factors that affect students' withdrawal from vle. The programming language used is Python. Python is an interpreted, high-level, general-purpose programming language.The non-profit Python Software Foundation manages python and CPython.

5.3 Convolutional Neural Networks

CNN is used as the classification model in this work. Convolutional neural networks help to reduce the number of parameters and adapt the network architecture [16]. Convolutional neural networks are composed of layers that their functionalities can group. The activation layer is used to raise the system's non-linearity without affecting convolution layers' receptive fields. ReLU, Softmax, and Sigmoid are the activation functions used. ReLu is used for faster training. But the major issue is that all the negative values become zero immediately, which decreases the model's ability to fit or train from the data correctly. That means any negative input given to the ReLU turns the value to zero.

6 Results and Discussions

The datasets are fed to the CNN model separately. To increase the performance of the model, we have implemented hyperparameter tuning. It is found difficult to manually change the hyperparameters and fit them on the training data always. Because it is laborious, and it is challenging to keep track of hyperparameters that have already been tried. There are mainly two types of hyper-parameter tuning techniques, Grid search and Random search. We have used GridSearchCV as the hyperparameter tuning technique. It is simple to calculate, uncomplicated to interpret, and a single quantity to recap the model's capability, making it the most common metric used to evaluate classifier models. Achieving high classification accuracy may be trivial on an imbalanced classification problem with an imbalanced dataset. Imbalanced data typically refers to a situation where the classes are not represented equally [3]. Two methods used to even-up the types are random over-sampling and random under-sampling. Here we have done random under-sampling. After obtaining a balanced dataset, the input is fed into the model, and the results are obtained. Table 2 shows the results received before balancing for the first dataset. The table also contains information about the optimizer, epochs, and batch size used.

Table 2. Dataset 1 before balancing

	Features	Optimizer	Epochs	Batch size	Sample size (Training)	Sample size (Testing)	Accuracy
Dataset 1	code_presentation, id_student, id_site, sum_click, activity_type, high-est_education, final_result	ADAM	15	6000	115828	28957	0.92
Datset1 (2013J)	code_presentation, id_student, id_site, sum_click, activity_type, high-est_education, final_result	ADAM	10	4000	115828	28957	0.92
Dataset1 (2014J)	code_presentation, id_student, id_site, sum_click, activity_type, high-est_education, final_result	RMSprop	20	8000	108361	27097	0.91

For Dataset 1, the accuracy obtained is 0.92. After splitting the Dataset 1 based on code_presentation 2013J and 2014J, the obtained subset is fed into the model. In Table 3, results obtained after balancing for the first dataset is shown. Here Dataset 1 offers an accuracy of 0.8358. The Dataset 1 is split based on code_presentation 2013J and 2014J. The obtained subset is fed into the model, and accuracy is recorded in the Table 3.

Table 3. Dataset 1 after balancing

	Features	Optimizer	Epochs	Batch size	Sample size (Training)	Sample size (Testing)	Accuracy
Dataset 1	code_presentation, id_student, id_site, sum_click, activity_type, high-est_education, final_result	RMSprop	15	5000	32612	8154	0.8358
Datset1 (2013J)	code_presentation, id_student, id_site, sum_click, activity_type, high-est_education, final_result	RMSprop	25	2000	16460	4115	0.92593
Datset1 (2014J)	code_presentation, id_student, id_site, sum_click, activity_type, high-est_education, final_result	RMSprop	10	4000	16152	4038	0.9140

For Dataset 2, the accuracy obtained before balancing is 0.86. After splitting the Dataset 2 based on code_presentation 2013J and 2014J, the obtained subset is fed into the model, and the accuracy is recorded. Table 4 shows the results obtained before balancing for the first dataset.

Table 5 shows the results received after balancing for the second dataset. The corresponding accuracy obtained is 0.8385. After splitting the Dataset 2, its accuracy is also recorded in Table 5.

This work aims to develop a predictive model to identify students showing affinity towards early withdrawal from MOOC or VLE courses, exploring the effectiveness of deep learning. Deep learning techniques are effective in early prediction of at-risk students by analyzing the results. The accuracy ranges from 83% to 93%. The balanced

Table 4. Dataset2 before balancing

	Features	Optimizer	Epochs	Batch size	Sample size (Training)	Sample size (Testing)	Accuracy
Dataset 2	code_presentation, id_student, sum_score, count, score, final_result	ADAM	10	300	450	113	0.86
Datset2 (2013J)	code_presentation, id_student, sum_score, count, score, final_result	ADAM	10	500	233	59	0.87
Dataset2 (2014J)	code_presentation, id_student, sum_score, count, score, final_result	ADAM	10	500	233	59	0.87

Table 5. Dataset2 after balancing

	Features	Optimizer	Epochs	Batch size	Sample size (Training)	Sample size (Testing)	Accuracy
Dataset 2	code_presentation, id_student, sum_score, count, score, final_result	ADAM	5	300	104	26	0.885
Datset2 (2013J)	code_presentation, id_student, sum_score, count, score, final_result	RMSprop	5	400	51	13	0.898
Dataset2 (2014J)	code_presentation, id_student, sum_score, count, score, final_result	ADAM	10	20530	53	14	0.908

datasets show a rise in accuracy. The random under-sampling method is used for balancing the dataset. As the under-sampling method deletes the rows randomly, the accuracy diminished in the first trials. Later the process is revised to delete rows showing a low correlation between the variables under study. And the projected results were obtained. The results indicate that the model is useful in predicting when a strongly correlated balanced dataset is provided. The results are in-line with the earlier works done using the OULA Dataset [2, 10, 16].

From the results, it is understood that the early prediction of at-risk students depends on students' interaction with the environment. i.e., the vle activities. Also, the intermediate scores are a strong parameter in predictive analytics. Thus, the parameters such as sum_click, activity_type highest_education, count, and the score could effectively be used to predict student dropout.

7 Conclusion

Our study presents deep learning effectiveness in forecasting early removals from the OULA dataset by considering features like students' clickstream behavior, highest education, and assessments in a VLE. In this study, we steered a thorough analysis of the learning performance patterns of higher education students. Our problem domain predicts whether the students are getting dropped out or not based on some features considered. Also, how far the deep learning method is useful for predicting the early withdrawal of students. For this, we are using the OULA dataset, which is a real-time dataset. We consider a subset of OULAD, including five tables student info, student vle, vle, student assessment, and assessment. We have merged these tables and obtained two input tables. Three features were considered in the first input table: sum_click, activity_type, and highest_education. Whereas in the second input table, features considered are count and score. Since the dataset is imbalanced, balancing is done. The deep learning model CNN is used to train the dataset. When the dataset was fed for training into the model, the output obtained was not a better result. For getting better results, we have tuned the model. From the confusion matrix and the accuracy calculated, we could conclude that parameters such as sum_click, activity_type highest_education, count, and the score could effectively be used to predict student dropout. A future viewpoint can be defining the collaboration patterns of learners at-risk of failure, noticing the marginal pass students, examining students' performance with distinction. We also plan to construct more reasonable network structures to predict the dropout and further explore the correlations between parallel higher education courses selected by the learner.

References

1. Akour, M., Al, S.H., Al Qasem, O.: The effectiveness of using deep learning algorithms in predicting students' achievements. Indonesian J. Elect. Eng. Comput. Sci. **19**(1), 387–393 (2020)
2. Aljohani, N.R., Fayoumi, A., Hassan, S.U.: Predicting at-risk students using clickstream data in the virtual learning environment. Sustainability **11**(24), 7238 (2019)
3. Batista, G.E., Prati, R.C., Monard, M.C.: A study of the behavior of several methods for balancing machine learning training data. ACM SIGKDD Explor. Newsl. **6**(1), 20–29 (2004)
4. Bekele, R., McPherson, M.: A Bayesian performance prediction model for mathematics education: a prototypical approach for effective group composition. Br. J. Edu. Technol. **4**(3), 395–416 (2011)
5. Chowdhry, S., Sieler, K., Alwis, L.: A study of the impact of technology-enhanced learning on student academic performance. J. Perspect. Appl. Acad. Pract. 2(3) (2014)
6. Coelho, O.B., Ismar, S.: Deep learning applied to learning analytics and educational data mining: A systematic literature review. In: Brazilian Symposium on Computers in Education (Simpósio Brasileiro de Informática na Educação-SBIE), vol. 28. no. 1 (2017)

7. Chen, Y., Zhang, M.: Mooc student dropout: pattern and prevention. In: Proceedings of the ACM Turing 50th Celebration Conference-China, pp. 1–6. (2017)
8. Figueroa-Canas, J., Sancho-Vinuesa, T.: Early prediction of dropout and final exam performance in an online statistics course. IEEE Revista Iberoamericana de Tecnologias del Aprendizaje **15**(2), 86–94 (2020)
9. Haiyang, L., Wang, Z., Benachour, P., Tubman, P.: A time series classification method for behavior-based dropout prediction. In: 2018 IEEE 18th International Conference on Advanced Learning Technologies (ICALT), pp. 191–195. IEEE (2018)
10. Hassan, S.U., Waheed, H., Aljohani, N.R., Ali, M., Ventura, S., Herrera, F.: Virtual learning environment to predict withdrawal by leveraging deep learning. Int. J. Intell. Syst. **34**(8), 1935–1952 (2019)
11. Kuzilek, J., Hlosta, M., Zdrahal, Z.: Open university learning analytics dataset. Sci Data. **4,** 17017 (2017)
12. Mubarak, A.A., Cao, H., Zhang, W.: Prediction of students' early dropout based on their interaction logs in online learning environment. Interact. Learn. Environ. 1–20 (2020)
13. Patil, A.P., Karthik, G., Anita, K.: Effective deep learning model to predict student grade point averages. In: IEEE International Conference on Computational Intelligence and Computing Research (ICCIC), pp. 1–6 (2017)
14. Tamada, M.M., de Magalhães Netto, J.F., de Lima, D.P.R.: Predicting and reducing dropout in virtual learning using machine learning techniques: a systematic review. In 2019 IEEE Frontiers in Education Conference (FIE), pp. 1–9. IEEE (2019)
15. Waheed, H., Hassan, S.U., Aljohani, N.R., Hardman, J., Alelyani, S., Nawaz, R.: Predicting academic performance of students from VLE big data using deep learning models. Comput. Hum. Behav. **104**, 106189 (2020)
16. Xing, W., Du, D.: Dropout prediction in MOOCs: using deep learning for personalized intervention. J. Educ. Comput. Res. **57**(3), 547–570 (2019)

An Experiential Competency Application Framework

Elliot Robson[1]([✉]), Robby Robson[1], Tom Buskirk[1], Fritz Ray[1], and Kevin P. Owens[2]

[1] Eduworks Corporation, Corvallis, OR, USA
elliot.robson@eduworks.com
[2] Applied Research Laboratories, University of Texas At Austin, Austin, TX, USA

Abstract. Implementing competency-based training, education, and talent management requires models that compute and apply competencies to answer three questions: *Does a person or team possess a given competency, how likely are they to successfully apply or demonstrate it, and what is the best way to acquire it?* This paper argues that the underlying mathematical models should be treated as separate, although interrelated, and presents a framework for creating and computing such models that includes notions such as the level of a competency and conditions under which it is performed and that takes experience, practice, knowledge and skill decay, and the spacing effect into account. The source data for the computations outlined in this paper, which are described in the most detail for the model that ascribes possession of a competency, consists of *assertions* that in practice are derived from results reported by training systems. These computations reflect current practice in competency modeling and include "rollup rules" that respect relations among competencies. This paper includes an analysis of how these models appear and are used in intelligent tutoring systems.

Keywords: Competencies · Adaptive instructional systems · Mathematical models · Experiential training · Assertions · State model · Predictive model

1 Overview

Disruptions caused by COVID-19 have accelerated transitions to remote work, learning, and training. These transitions have further catalyzed the demand for measurable, traceable, and verifiable skills attainment. For example, the American healthcare system, which was already investigating competency-based training (Andrews et al. 2018), was forced to move rapidly to adopt competency-based methods in response to COVID-19. In April 2020, the American Board of Medical Specialties (ABMS) and the Accreditation Council for Graduate Medical Education (ACGME) stated that they "endorse and rely upon the authority and judgement of Clinical Competency Committees (CCCs) and training program directors (PDs) to determine readiness for unsupervised practice and to inform specialty-board decisions regarding eligibility for initial board certification." (ABMS and ACGME 2020; Goldhamer et al. 2020). This transition was mirrored in other countries, with the UK's National School of Healthcare Science (NSHS) issuing

© Springer Nature Switzerland AG 2021
R. A. Sottilare and J. Schwarz (Eds.): HCII 2021, LNCS 12793, pp. 121–134, 2021.
https://doi.org/10.1007/978-3-030-77873-6_9

"Practical tips for supporting competency-based medical education during the COVID-19 pandemic" (Hall et al. 2020). Beyond the medical profession, competency-forward nations accelerated rollouts and updates of existing competency-based policies. Between December of 2020 and March of 2021, the Australian ministry of training released new data requirements for national education, removed or updated over 975 competencies supporting 46 underused qualifications, and updated regulatory requirements for competency-based decision publication. While the demand for competency-based education has grown, the ability to reliably use competency information to make certification, training, and advancement decisions has not kept up. The three foundational questions that inform these decisions are:

1. *At what level does an individual or team possess a given competency?*
2. *What is the probability that they will succeed if they try to apply, perform, or demonstrate a given competency at a given level?*
3. *What training or experience is best if the goal is to change the level at which a competency is held?*

Almost all organizations and systems that use competencies focus on one or more of these three primary questions, but they often fail to separate them and frequently conflate them. Clearly distinguishing these questions is a meaningful and necessary step that adds clarity, e.g., because possession of a competency does not guarantee that it will be successfully performed every time, and that increases modularity and robustness of the models used to answer each question by enabling different data and different computational methods to be used.

For an example that highlights the importance of this distinction, consider Steph Curry, a future member of the Basketball Hall of Fame. Steph is an excellent free-throw shooter who most people would agree has the highest level of competency available in this area (Question 1), but that does not mean that he will make every free throw he attempts (Question 2). Moreover, in determining Steph Curry's competence, it may suffice to look at his general history of free-throw shooting in games, whereas predicting how he will do in a particular game in a particular situation may benefit from more refined data, such as information about his practice routines and his health or injury status, the game script, his minutes on the floor, and other conditions. Furthermore, the training method that is effective for helping Steph Curry improve his free throws may be directed at competencies other than "free throw shooting", such as concentration and conditioning. Thus, the model to answer Question 3 may involve different competencies and factors than those used to answer Questions 1 and 2.

This paper introduces a set of separate but interrelated models and computational methods for answering the above three questions. These models and methods enable competencies to be applied in concrete, actionable, and computable ways. A key ingredient of these models is that they track *experience* and rely on longitudinal data. As a result, we have named the approach described in this paper the *Experiential Competency Application Framework* (ECAF). This paper focuses on computations for one of these models – the state model defined in Sect. 3 – and on how these models are used in adaptive instructional systems (AIS).

1.1   Ecaf

ECAF uses a different model to address each of the three questions posed above.

- For Question 1 (*at what level is a competency held?*) ECAF uses a **state model** that determines the state of a competency based on assertions about the competency, and on a limited set of rules (Sect. 3).
- ECAF relies on a **predictive model** for Question 2 (*how likely is it that a competency will be successfully performed?*) (Sect. 4).
- Question 3 (*what is the best training intervention?*) is answered by a **training model** that examines a set of possible interventions and applies the state and predictive models to each (Sect. 5).

All models in this paper are based on the same data, and the output of one model may be used as input to another. For example, level of competence (an output of the state model) can be a component of the predictive model. In general, however, distinguishing among models allows different data to be used in each. For example, the state model described in this paper includes experiential data, skills and knowledge decay, and institution-specific computation rules, but an alternative model based on different data could be used without impacting the predictive model. From this perspective, ECAF is both a specific method of computation and an extensible framework for understanding competency computation.

2   Terms and Definitions

In this paper, we use the term *entity* to refer to an individual or team and we use the term *competency* (*C*) as a generic term for knowledge, skills, abilities, attitudes, behaviors, beliefs, capabilities, and other characteristics of an individual or team. In simpler terms, competencies define what an entity knows and can do. Competencies are often grouped or organized into *competency frameworks* (or *competency models*).

A large variety of competency frameworks are in use worldwide, ranging from national frameworks that broadly outline job requirements (e.g. O*Net, Australian Qualifications Framework) and multi-national frameworks (e.g. Skills Framework for the Information Age) to small single-job frameworks and frameworks of learning objectives for courses. While the size and depth of these frameworks vary, they all represent a discrete unit of activity. In addition, they often contain relations among competencies that define which competencies are required for a given competency, which learning objectives enable other learning objectives, which competencies are contained in another competency, and so on. In the ECAF model, we assume that all such relations are abstracted to a single parent/child relation that turns the competency framework into a directed acyclic graph (DAG).

Although ECAF is agnostic about the competency schema used, it does take into account the real-world complexity that frameworks represent. For this reason, ECAF competencies can have *levels* (e.g. beginner, intermediate, and advanced). Levels are often used to express both what an entity knows and can do and how well they know and can do it, and different levels can represent differences in both of these aspects. *ECAF treats the levels of a competency as though they are separate competencies.* As a result, each level can have its own set of child competencies and its own set of relations to other competencies. End-user applications can display levels as if they were properties of a single competency, but ECAF computes with them separately.

In addition to levels, ECAF recognizes that competencies are often performed under different *conditions*. Conditions are often lumped together into a *condition set*. For example, the condition set "lighting" might contain the conditions *broad daylight, cloudy day, dusk, night time.* In this paper we use a capital C for a competency, a small c for a condition, and the notation $C|c$ to denote the competency C under the condition c.

3 The State Model

The state model of an entity E is defined with respect to a *domain*, which is a set of competencies. For each competency C in this domain, the state of E has two components, each of which has a timestamp indicating when the value was computed:

- A *Boolean state* for each competency whose possible values are *True, False,* and *Unknown* [T, F, U] that indicates whether E possesses C, does not possess C, or it is not known whether E possesses C.
- A *practice score* that is a function of the frequency and times at which E attempted to perform C or engaged in training C. This is the experiential component.

In applications, the state model may include additional metadata (e.g. the model name and author) and the Boolean state may be simplified to a binary True and False. A common way to reduce to this binary state is to map both U and F to F, in which case F means that E is not known to possess C, but other rules are justifiable.

Data used for the computation of competence in ECAF comes from *assertions*. Assertions are discrete claims about the competencies an entity possesses or has trained on. Assertions can say whether an entity has or does not have a competency, has practiced the competency (without concluding whether they have it or not), and must indicate the competency involved, the entity involved, a source (s) for the assertion, and a timestamp (t). Assertions may include additional elements such as the conditions, additional evidence, an expiration date, a confidence, and more. For ECAF calculations, each assertion's source may have a trust parameter. This is called the source's *authority* and is used to weight assertions made by that source. A given assertion may have both a confidence, reported by a source, and an authority, that represents the confidence in that source. Assertions are typically fed into ECAF from other systems within a training environment, but can also be captured from direct observations or expert input. An example assertion is: *The authors of this paper (agent) assert on 17-March-2021 (time stamp) that Steph Curry (entity) has the "free throw shooting" competency (competency) at the expert level (level) during the last 10 min of the game (condition) based on an examination of free throw shooting records for the last five years (evidence) with confidence .75 (because the authors are not experts on basketball).* Note that this is *not* an assertion that Steph Curry will make a free throw under the given condition 75% or any other percent of the time (in fact, he makes them more frequently than that).

3.1 Assertion Scores

When examining assertions about an entity E with respect to competency C, ECAF considers all assertions made by a given source s about possession of C and generates a single assertion score $A(s,C)$ for that source. This is normalized, so $-1 \leq A(s,C) \leq 1$. Assertion scores from each possible source are combined with weights to create a single number $A(C)$ that is also normalized and that can be compared to a threshold. If C can be performed under condition c, the same method is used to compute $A(s,C|c)$ for each source of assertions about E with respect to C under condition c and to compute a number $A(C|c)$.

As a reminder, ECAF treats different levels as different competencies, so the above a fortiori applies to levels of competencies as well.

The weights represent the contribution of each source to the opinion ECAF forms about E with respect to C (under condition c) and can be viewed as combining multiple factors such as the validity, trust, and relevance of each source. Weights are normalized so that their sum is 1. Weights can be initialized based on opinion and eventually learned from data. The conditioned assertion score of each source is calculated using the formula

$$A(s_i, C|c) = \frac{\sum_{j=1}^{m} f(t - t_j) \cdot \gamma_j \cdot \lambda_i}{\sum_{j=1}^{m} f(t - t_j)} \tag{1}$$

Here f is a function that represents skill decay (Sect. 2.5), $(t\text{-}t_j)$ represents the time elapsed, γ_j the confidence in assertion j, and λ_j, the polarity of the assertion, is $+1$ if it is asserted that E has $C|c$ and -1 if its asserted that E does not have $C|c$. Unconditioned assertion scores are calculated in a similar way, but for $A(s_j, C)$.

In addition to the assertions from each external source, ECAF also considers the children of C when computing the Boolean state of E with respect to C. This can be done in two ways in ECAF depending on the needs of the application:

1. The state of each child can generate an *implied assertion* about C. This method is used to reflect relations such as D *enables* C and the undefined or vaguely defined hierarchical relations frequently found in real-world competency models and frameworks.
2. The children of C can be used in "rollup rules" that express explicit requirements (e.g. if C *requires* D and the Boolean state of D is F, then the Boolean state of C is F).

Once the assertion score for each source s has been calculated and additional implied assertions from the child competencies have been added, the overall assertion score for E with respect to C given condition c is calculated by

$$A(C|c) = \frac{1}{n} \sum_{s=1}^{n} w_i(c) \cdot A(s_i, C|c) \tag{2}$$

Here the weights (w_i) for each source reflect our belief in the source's authority and accuracy. This equation defines the overall assertion score for $C|c$ as the weighted sum of all component assertions (from each source s plus implied assertions).

Boolean state is computed by evaluating a series of *expressions*, which could be "rollup rules," that express the state of a competency in terms of the state of its child competencies, or additional rules that compare A(C), A(C|c), or the practice score to a threshold. This allows ECAF to represent dynamic and probabilistic relationships, like those found in many AIS, as well as rules-based systems. For example, a pilot license that requires specific hours of flight time, well demonstration of certain skills in a simulator, and demonstrating certain knowledge in ground school, can be represented as a combination of thresholds for assertions from flight simulator, rollup rules that require assertions generated by a ground school assessment, and a practice requirement for in-flight training.

3.2 Practice

Obtaining a competency often requires repeated practice, and, as noted in Eq. 1, assertions from a long time ago may no longer be useful and should decay over time. These observations are captured in the ECAF state model through the practice score r and a decay function f.

As above, the competency C is practiced by entity E under condition c, and a set of sources $S = \{s_1,...,s_n\}$ report assertions about E with respect to C|c, we compute the practice score of C|c as follows:

1. We assume an *a priori* practice score r_0 valid at time t_0.
2. Consider all assertions $\{a1,..., am\}$ about C|c and E with a timestamp later than t0 and with sources in S. Let sk be the source of ak and tk the timestamp of ak and assume that the assertions are ordered by time, so that $t_0 < t_1 <... < t_m$.
3. We assume C has a decay function f: $(0,\infty) \rightarrow [0,1]$ that represents the rate at which the value of an assertion about C decays as a function of time since C was asserted. This may be considered to be the "forgetting curve" for C, but it is applied to negative as well as positive assertions. As discussed in (Averell and Heathcote 2011), a reasonably general form of such a function is $f(t) = a + (1 - a) \cdot b \cdot P(t)$ where $P(t) = (1 + \gamma t) - \beta, 0 \leq a \leq 1, 0 \leq b \leq 1, \gamma > 0, \beta > 0$, and t represents time
4. We assume C has a spacing function g that weights an assertion by the time since the last assertion was made. This function models the "spacing effect" (Ebbinghouse 1913; Bjork and Allen 1970; Dempster, 1988; Cepeda et al. 2008; Carpenter et al. 2012), which implies that more value is gained by practice sessions that are properly spaced than by repeated practice within a short period of time. We make the simplifying assumption that g depends only on how long it has been since C was last practiced (under condition c).

We assume that each source s_j has a practice value v_j that represents the weighting of the source as providing experience and practice. For example, practicing free throws in a game may have less value than doing so in an arcade, which may have less value than practicing them on a real basketball court. Using these assumptions, the practice score of C under condition c is

$$r(c) = r_0 \cdot f(t_{now} - t_0) + \sum_{j=1}^{m} f(t_{now} - t_j) \cdot g(t_j - t_{j-1}) \cdot v_j \tag{3}$$

This generates a value that represents the number of times an entity E has practiced a given competency under condition c, where each attempt at practice is weighted by the time elapsed (the decay function) and the time since the last attempt (the spacing function). If there are no relevant assertions, then $r(C|c) = 0$.

3.3 Skill Decay

There are many possible "forgetting functions" that can be used to model skill or knowledge decay, and in general a different function may be appropriate for each competency or type of competency (e.g. for a competency that represents knowledge as opposed to one that represents the ability to perform a task). In the formula given in 2.4 item 3 taken from (Averell and Heathcote 2011), the constant β in (4) is the "forgetting rate," whose effect can be scaled by γ. The constant a is a floor that represents the value of events that happened long ago. For example, if the competency is "riding a bicycle," it is reasonable to assume that having ridden one as a child will still contribute to learning how to ride one as an adult. The constant b sets a ceiling $a + (1 - a) \cdot b$ that represents the maximal contribution an experience can make. If $b = 1$, then $a < f(t) \leq 1$ for all $t \geq 0$.

3.4 Spaced Repetition

The spacing function g explains the effect of spacing on repeated training attempts. Several authors have created learning and performance models that use theories of memory activation and memory decay to predict optimal spacing, e.g. the ACT-R work of Pavlik and Anderson (Pavlik and Anderson 2008) for intelligent tutoring systems and the predictive performance optimizer developed by Jastrzembski, Gluck, and Gunzelmann (Jastrzembski and Gluck 2009; Walsh et al. 2018). Another approach is to define a spacing function of the form

$$g(t) = d \cdot [(1 + ln\,(1 + (\tau - t)^{\alpha}))^{-\beta} - c], \text{ for } t < \tau \tag{4}$$

$$g(t) = [(1 + ln\,(1 + (\tau - t)^{k}))^{-\beta} - c], \text{ for } t \geq \tau \tag{5}$$

where

$$c = (1 + ln\,((1 + \tau)^{\alpha}))^{-\beta} \text{ and } d = 1/(1 - c) \tag{6}$$

In this function,

- τ is the ideal spacing interval,
- β is the same power as in the forgetting function f, and
- α and ? are parameters that flatten out the spacing function when t is near τ and should generally be chosen to be at least 2.

Note that c is chosen so that $g(0) = 0$, $g(\tau) = 1$, $g(\tau) = 1$. Also note that $dg/dt(\tau) = 0$ for both the left and right-hand derivative (the parameters are chosen so that g is a smooth curve that is related to the forgetting rate).

3.5 ECAF State Function Calculation

In ECAF, the state of an entity contains the Boolean state of every competency C in a given domain and a practice score that indicates the extent to which E has practiced each C. The calculation of the Boolean state combines.

- Assertions about C (and the parameters within the assertions)
- The Boolean state of E at every child competency of C
- The practice value $r(C|c)$ for conditions c under which C can be performed and the unconditioned practice value $r(C)$.

This calculation follows a set of ordered steps. We assume that rollup rules and assertion rules have been defined for each competency and that the ECAF profile domain is a DAG with a parent/child relation. With these assumptions, the Boolean state of E with respect to C is computed as follows:

STEP 1: Compute the assertion score(s) and practice score(s) for all leaf nodes of the DAG represented by the ECAF profile. Then compute the Boolean state of all leaf nodes. (Ignore any rollup rules for leaf nodes, since these are not relevant.)

STEP 2: Move up one level within the DAG, which after STEP 1 takes you to the parents of leaf nodes. For each competency C at this DAG level, compute the assertion and practice score(s) for C. Then

    1.   Compute the rollup rule for C if it exists.

       - If the rollup rule evaluates to F, then the Boolean state of C is F.

       - If the rollup rule evaluates to T or U, then continue

    2.   Evaluate the assertion rule for C and set the Boolean state accordingly.

    3.   Apply the level rule.

Repeat 2 until the Boolean state of all nodes, including root nodes, is determined.

If competencies have levels, ECAF adds a step that ensures that competencies held at one level are held at all lower levels.

4 Predictive Models

The state model is used to answer questions about what competencies an entity holds, but should not be confused with a model for predicting how an entity will perform a competency. In the state model, the only uncertainty comes with respect to the source of the assertion and the confidence that source has in an assertion. In this respect, ECAF is a naïve actor that believes the data coming from various sources based on the authority level and assumed accuracy of that source. ECAF's state model does not attempt to model the distributions of belief within different assertions from a single source beyond the confidence reported by the source itself. On the other hand, the predictive model tackles probabilistic uncertainty head-on. Although the state model may tell us that Steph Curry is an excellent free-throw shooter, there is still a distribution to the success of his free throws.

There are many predictive approaches for estimating the likelihood that an entity will succeed or fail in performing a competency. The most direct is to calculate the probabilities for a given entity from repeated observation. One problem with this approach is that the amount of data needed suffers a combinatorial explosion once multiple levels and conditions are introduced, and data must be re-collected if new confounding factors are recognized. Another problem is that this approach assumes the subject is constant over time, but people learn and change. A third problem that can arise when applying ECAF to AIS is that the data collected are from training sessions and cannot be assumed to be fully predictive of performance in live sessions.

For these reasons, it is expedient to use the structure of the domain and the state model to create a predictive model. Because competency frameworks represent an expert view of a job, task, subject, etc., it is plausible that the major factors for success are represented in the framework. In other words, we can assume that if a competency framework has been properly defined, then all significant dependencies have been expressed in the children, levels, and conditions associated with a competency, and we can therefore make a conditional independence assumption. This allows us to treat competency frameworks as naïve Bayes networks, which reduces the amount of data needed.

Although using naïve Bayes is a traditional approach, a more modern approach is to go back to the question we wish to answer and to use the state model as a predictor. In this approach, Question 2 can be formulated as:

Given the practice scores and Boolean states of all competencies in a domain, what is the probability that an entity E possessing those scores and states will perform competency C?

This formulation assumes that the probability of successfully performing C depends only on data in the state model and not on any other factors (other than perhaps the condition under which C is attempted), including time. This assumption is compatible with the notion of a learner model used in intelligent tutoring systems and other AIS, i.e. that the current state of competency and history of practice predicts performance.

This is the type of problem that neural networks and similar Machine Learning (ML) tools are meant to solve. The input is a profile, which consists of a Boolean state and a practice score for each competency in the domain of the profile. The output is a probability for each such competency. Not every combination of states will appear in a training set, but this does not matter since we are making no assumptions about relations among competencies. Whatever relations exist and influence the probabilities will be learned from the data. Conditions can be added as child competencies on which other competencies are conditioned (recommended).

It is important to note that, in keeping with ECAF's separation of questions, the predictive model is not used to answer the question "is the competency framework supported by the data?" This is an important question that can often be answered using similar data inputs with techniques like structural equation modeling (SEM) or other joint probability and factor analysis approaches (Robson et al. 2017).

5 Training Model

Training Models answer the question: *What is the best way to provide training that transitions an entity E from holding a competency C at level L_i to holding it at some other level (or holding at all if they do not hold it beforehand)?* To answer this question, we must determine the likely effect of a training event Z on state transition. This formulation of the question makes it clear that a training model can be seen as a transition problem, and lends itself to a Markov model. However, the variables required for the training model include those associated with the training events in addition to information about the entity involved.

These additional variables can be exceedingly complex. In real implementations, for example, we must consider both the inner and outer loops of training events (Van-Lehn 2006) and the probabilities that a competency state transitions at each loop node. Although leveraging the structure of frameworks makes building a predictive model easier, it does not provide the same support for the training model because most competency models are designed to reflect the conceptual relationship between competencies rather than the optimal order of attainment (which may vary among entities). This is further complicated by the fact that the details of training events such as the algorithms used to adapt or adaptively select interactions in an AIS may not be available to ECAF at the time of calculation. Because of this, it may be necessary to make broad assumptions about a specific training event based on a limited set of information such as the source of the training and metadata that describes the training.

Due to the complexity of the question and interdependence with other systems, a current ECAF approach is to slightly change the core question. Rather than ask *"What is the best way to provide…"* it is much easier to answer the question: *What is an effective way to provide training that transitions an entity E from holding a competency C at level L_i to holding it at some other level?* By changing the constraint from comparing all possible training options for an entity and selecting the best one, to a more general formulation of selecting a successful route, it is possible to apply techniques that combine hidden Markov models and other sequence analysis techniques such as growth mixture models (Helske et al. 2018).

6 ECAF Implementations

The ECAF approach has been implemented with synthetic data using the Competency and Skills System (CaSS 2021), which is part of the US Advanced Distributed Learning (ADL) Initiative's Total Learning Architecture (ADL 2021) and includes methods for translating activity data reported from training systems via the experience API (xAPI) into assertions. At the time of this publication, we have verified the computational feasibility of the state model and predictive model using functions in this paper. We have not fully developed a training model.

7 Analysis of Intelligent Tutoring Systems

A key theme of this paper is that using separate models for estimating competence and for predicting performance improves conceptual clarity and implementation. It is instructive to examine how these models are used in intelligent tutoring systems (ITSs), which are among the most common (and sophisticated) AIS deployed today. There seems to be a dichotomy between ITS that focus entirely on the state model and use assessments to determine "knowledge" (which we would consider to be "competency") and those that focus on the predictive model and treat knowledge as a hidden variable that controls likelihood of getting a problem correct.

In this dichotomy, dialogue based ITS such as AutoTutor (Graesser et al. 1999) and constraint-based ITS (Mitrovic et al. 2007) belong to the first class. They evaluate answers to determine the tutor's reaction, but do not include a discernable predictive model. ITSs that use Bayesian Knowledge Tracing, or BKT (Corbett and Anderson 1994), are also interested in the state model, i.e. whether a student has achieved mastery on a knowledge component (KC). BKT is a hidden Markov model in which a binary state model informs observed success or failure on a series of exercises that test the KCs. At each step, BKT has an a priori probability of mastery, parameters that indicate the likelihood that an answer will be correct given mastery or lack of mastery, and transition probabilities that determine the chance of changing mastery state from False to True. It is assumed that mastery is retained once it is achieved and depends only on the previous state, so the probability of mastery after each exercise is the a priori probability plus the transition probability given lack of mastery. In the original versions of BKT, all of the models were skill-specific but not individualized. Many researchers subsequently created individualized versions (Yudelson et al. 2013). Since tutoring stops when the estimated mastery probability exceeds a given threshold, these implicitly compute a binary state model, similarly to ECAF, but unlike ECAF the predictive and state models are intertwined and cannot be computed separately.

Several related models, such as the Additive Factors Model (AFM), Performance Factors Model (PFM) and Instructional Factors Analysis Model (IFM) are described and analyzed in (Chi et al. 2011). In addition to observed successes and failures, these include parameters such as learning rates, difficulty, the nature of each "learning opportunity", and a "Q-matrix" that associates problem solving steps with skills and knowledge components (KCs), both of which are competencies in our terminology. Like BKT, these are predictive models with hidden state models, with the twist that Q-matrices express relations between competencies, so models that use them are implicitly using a two-level DAG. In addition, Q-matrices allow for a single concept to influence multiple KCs (Barnes 2005), which is not the case with BKT models that treat each skill independently.

More recently, Piech, Yang, and others have applied recurrent and convolutional networks with long-term short-term Memory (LSTM) to create methods they call deep knowledge tracing, or DKT (Piech et al. 2015), and convolutional knowledge tracing, or CKT (Yang et al. 2020). These are presented as predictive models that learn from a series of observations and, for CKT, consider more recent results as more predictive than older results, which is also a feature of ECAF. More importantly, as is typical in neural-network-based machine learning, these models make no assumptions about, and therefore impose no restrictions on, temporal sequencing or relations or influence among competencies. As in previous models, these also have a component that predicts learner mastery, although the main problem addressed is predicting student success on an exercise.

8 Closing Remarks and Further Research

Predictive models and state models can include a large variety of input parameters. Combining these models in interdependent ways, as is done in most AIS, is effective for adapting instruction, but there are many real-world cases where the three questions posed in Sect. 1 are asked for different purposes. As an example, it may be important to know whether a person is certified for performing a task for regulatory reasons, whereas for safety reasons it may be more important to know how likely they are to perform it correctly under stressful conditions, and if it turns out that their ability to do so is in doubt, finding an effective and efficient way to train them with the tools available may be critical. In ECAF, the three questions and their associated models are treated as separate, but potentially allowed to interact.

An important feature of ECAF is dependence on experience. Existing Markov in this space may include feed-forward elements and history, but do not explicitly model experience. Although models based on ACT-R include the cumulative effect of practice and a forgetting function, they also do not model experience explicitly. The ECAF practice score aims to introduce experiential factors into state models and predictive models in a transparent and relatively simple way. Further research, data gathering, and analysis are required to determine how well this accomplishes its goal.

In our analysis of ITS we did not address Question 3. ITS are designed to select the best next instructional move. In that sense they solve their own training problems, but only for the loops within the ITS. Selecting among multiple training interventions seems much harder and almost certainly involves interactions between the state and predictive models, which both explains why they are interdependent in ITS and why it is advantageous to separate them in general. Understanding how to create training models that at least find effective interventions, if not the most effective intervention, is an important area of research, particularly when applied to training in non-cognitive domains where practice and repetition play important roles.

Finally, we observe that whereas competency models exist for teamwork (Kozlowski and Ilgen 2006), and AIS such as the Generalized Intelligent Framework for Tutoring (GIFT) have been used for non-cognitive tasks (Kim et al. 2018), relatively little work has been done on constructing state or predictive models for team tasks that rely on combinations of cognitive skills, psychomotor skills, and team skills. This is an area of great interest to industry, the military, and public services and is an area of active research for ECAF.

References

Andrews, J.S., et al.: Education in pediatrics across the continuum (EPAC): first steps toward realizing the dream of competency-based education. Acad. Med. **93**(3), 414–420 (2018)

ABMS and ACGME. ABMS and ACGME Joint Principles: Physician Training During the COVID-2019 Pandemic, April 10, 2020 (2020). https://www.abms.org/newsevents/abms-and-acgme-joint-principles-physician-training-during-the-covid-2019-pandemic/. Accessed 29 Mar 2021

Goldhamer, M.E.J., Pusic, M.V., Co, J.P.T., Weinstein, D.F.: Can covid catalyze an educational transformation? competency-based advancement in a crisis. N. Engl. J. Med. **383**(11), 1003–1005 (2020)

Hall, A.K., et al.: Training disrupted: practical tips for supporting competency-based medical education during the COVID-19 pandemic. Med. Teach. **42**(7), 756–761 (2020)

O*Net Online homepage. https://www.onetonline.org/. Accessed 29 Mar 2021

Australian Qualifications Framework homepage. https://www.aqf.edu.au/. Accessed 29 Mar 2021

SFIA The global skills and competency framework for a digital world home page. https://www.aqf.edu.au/. 29 Mar 2021

Ebbinghaus, H.: Memory (H. A. Ruger & C. E. Bussenius, Trans.). New York, NY: Teachers College, Columbia University. (Original work published 1885) (1913)

Bjork, R.A., Allen, T.W.: The spacing effect: consolidation or differential encoding? J. Verbal Learn. Verbal Behav. **9**(5), 567–572 (1970)

Dempster, F.N.: The spacing effect: a case study in the failure to apply the results of psychological research. Am. Psychol. **43**(8), 627 (1988)

Cepeda, N.J., Vul, E., Rohrer, D., Wixted, J.T., Pashler, H.: Spacing effects in learning: a temporal ridgeline of optimal retention. Psychol. Sci. **19**(11), 1095–1102 (2008)

Carpenter, S.K., Cepeda, N.J., Rohrer, D., Kang, S.H., Pashler, H.: Using spacing to enhance diverse forms of learning: Review of recent research and implications for instruction. Educ. Psychol. Rev. **24**(3), 369–378 (2012)

Pavlik Jr, P.I., Anderson, J.R.: Practice and forgetting effects on vocabulary memory: an activation-based model of the spacing effect. Cogn. Sci. **29**(4), 559–586 (2005)

Jastrzembski, T.S., Gluck, K.A.: A formal comparison of model variants for performance prediction. In: Howes, A., Peebles, D., Cooper, R. (eds.) Proceedings of the 9th International Conference of Cognitive Modeling, Manchester, United Kingdom (2009)

Walsh, M.M., Gluck, K.A., Gunzelmann, G., Jastrzembski, T., Krusmark, M.: Evaluating the theoretic adequacy and applied potential of computational models of the spacing effect. Cogn. Sci. **42**, 644–691 (2018)

Robson, E., Ray, F., Sinatra, A.M., Sinatra, A.M.: Integrating the outer loop: Validated tutors for portable courses and competencies. In: Sottilare, R. (ed), Proceedings of the 5th Annual Generalized Intelligent Framework for Tutoring (GIFT) Users Symposium (GIFTSym5), pp. 161–168 (July 2017)

VanLehn, K.: The behavior of tutoring systems. Int. J. Artif. Intell. Educ. **16**(3), 227–265 (2006)

Helske, S., Jouni, H., Mervi, E.: Combining sequence analysis and hidden Markov models in the analysis of complex life sequence data. In: Ritschard, G., Studer, M. (eds.) Sequence Analysis and Related Approaches. Springer, Cham, pp. 185–200 (2018) https://doi.org/10.1007/978-3-319-95420-2_11

CaSS project homepage. https://www.cassproject.org/. Accessed 29 Mar 2021

ADL Total Learning Architecture Homepage. https://adlnet.gov/projects/tla/. Accessed 29 Mar 2021

Graesser, A.C., Wiemer-Hastings, K., Wiemer-Hastings, P., Kreuz, R.: Tutoring research group: AutoTutor: a simulation of a human tutor. Cogn. Syst. Res. **1**(1), 35–51 (1999)

Mitrovic, A., Martin, B., Suraweera, P.: Intelligent tutors for all: Constraint-based modeling methodology, systems and authoring. IEEE Intell. Syst. **22**, 38–45 (2007)

Corbett, A.T., Anderson, J.R.: Knowledge tracing: modeling the acquisition of procedural knowledge. User Model. User-Adap. Inter. **4**(4), 253–278 (1994)

Yudelson, M.V., Koedinger, K.R., Gordon, G.J.: Individualized bayesian knowledge tracing models. In: Lane, H.C., Yacef, K., Mostow, J., Pavlik, P. (eds.) International conference on artificial intelligence in education, pp. 171–180. Springer, Berlin (2013) https://doi.org/10.1007/978-3-642-39112-5_18

Chi, M., Koedinger, K.R., Gordon, G.J., Jordon, P., Van Lahn, K.: Instructional factors analysis: A cognitive model for multiple instructional interventions. In: Mykola P.M., Calders, T., Conati, C., Ventura, S., Romero, C., Stamper, J. (eds.) Proceedings of the 4th International Conference on Educational Data Mining, Eindhoven, 6–8 July 2011, pp. 61–70 (2011)

Barnes, T.: The Q-matrix method: Mining student response data for knowledge. In: American Association for Artificial Intelligence 2005 Educational Data Mining Workshop, pp. 1–8. Pittsburgh, AAAI Press (July 2005)

Piech, C., et al.: Deep knowledge tracing (2015). *arXiv preprint* arXiv:1506.05908

Yang, S., Zhu, M., Hou, J., Lu, X.: Deep Knowledge Tracing with Convolutions (2020). *arXiv preprint* arXiv:2008.01169

Kozlowski, S.W., Ilgen, D.R.: Enhancing the effectiveness of work groups and teams. Psychol. Sci. Public interest **7**(3), 77–124 (2006)

Kim, J.W., Dancy, C.L., Sottilare, R.A.: Towards using a physio-cognitive model in tutoring for psychomotor tasks. In: Proceedings of the AIED Workshop on Authoring and Tutoring for Psychomotor, Mobile, and Medical Domains, London, UK (2018)

Individual Differences in the Relationship Between Emotion and Performance in Command-and-Control Environments

Alina Schmitz-Hübsch$^{(\boxtimes)}$, Sophie-Marie Stasch , and Sven Fuchs

Fraunhofer Institute for Communication, Information Processing and Ergonomics FKIE,
53343 Wachtberg, Germany
{alina.schmitz-huebsch,sophie-marie.stasch,
sven.fuchs}@fkie.fraunhofer.de

Abstract. The present investigation examines the relationship between emotional user states – composed of emotional valence and arousal – and performance in command-and-control environments. The aim is to gain insights into how the integration of the emotional user state into an adaptive instructional human-machine system can take place. Based on literature, a state of neutral valence is expected to be associated with high performance (H1) and high levels of arousal with low performance (H2). However, according to previous investigations, we also assume interindividual differences in the relationship of emotional user state and performance (H3). In two laboratory experiments, subjects performed a command-and-control task in the domain of anti-air warfare. A software for recognition of emotional face expressions (Emotient FACET) assessed emotional valence. Three physiological measures (heart rate, heart rate variability, pupil width) indicated arousal. Performance was operationalized by performance decrements that occurred whenever a subtask was not accomplished in time. For the analyses, data from two experiments ($N = 24$, 19–48 years, $M = 32.0$, $SD = 7.2$; $N = 16$, 22–49 years, $M = 32.3$, $SD = 8.7$) were used. Statistical analyses confirmed H1 and H2 for many subjects, but there were interindividual differences in the relationship of emotional user state and performance that supported H3. These results indicate that individual models are necessary for the analysis of emotional user state in Adaptive Instructional Systems. Future investigations could consider personality traits in the development of individual models. Furthermore, we suggest a multifactorial approach in the detection of emotional arousal.

Keywords: Affect-adaptive instructional systems · Affective user state · Affective computing · Command-and-control · Emotional state

1 Introduction

Findings from neuroscience, psychology, and cognitive science indicate that emotions play a critical role in human behavior [1–3]. In this regard, emotion and cognition may be inseparable in a way that the emotional state is correlated with performance in cognitive tasks [4–7]. For training environments, studies have shown that stress - a state often

© Springer Nature Switzerland AG 2021
R. A. Sottilare and J. Schwarz (Eds.): HCII 2021, LNCS 12793, pp. 135–148, 2021.
https://doi.org/10.1007/978-3-030-77873-6_10

accompanied by high mental workload and negative emotions [8, 9] - can interfere with learning due to physiological, cognitive, and behavioral responses (e.g. increased heart rate, increased perspiration, attention lapses, decreased information processing, tunnel vision, and increased anxiety [10]. Moreover, a positive association of neutral valence with performance has been demonstrated by Cai and Lin [11] in a driving task.

Recent developments, such as reduced-manning initiatives despite an ever-increasing complexity of military operations, have led to higher cognitive workload in command-and-control (C2) environments and emphasize the need for adaptive automation to counteract mental overload [12]. High workload situations can be experienced as stressful and highly arousing states decreasing the operators' performance [9]. That fact is not surprising, considering Yerkes and Dodson [13] illustrated the negative influence of high arousal states on performance more than a century ago. From a physiological standpoint, states of high arousal are associated with increased heart rate, low heart rate variability, and large pupil width [14–16]. However, the relationship between stress and learning is not that simple. On one hand, low levels of stress lead to an increase in memory performance by facilitating memory formation. On the other hand, sustained levels of stress impair learning and memory performance by impeding memory updating [17].

Thus, not only cognitive states and psychomotor behaviors, but also affective states are important for task learning and performance and may have an impact on training transfer. Therefore, it is important to better understand how trainee affective states impact performance in the training environment.

In this paper, we examine the relationship of affective user states and performance in a simulated command-and-control task. Both, the valence component and the arousal component of the emotional state were analyzed.

1.1 Background

Adaptive Instructional Systems (AIS) are defined as "any form of educational intervention aimed at accommodating individual learner differences" [18]. One way of doing so are Affective Tutoring Systems (ATSs), a type of intelligent tutoring systems that can assess a learner's emotion und use this information to promote learning. Video cameras, eye tracking, physiological sensors, microphones, and self-assessments provide the information necessary to determine the learner's current affective state [19]. Woolf et al. [20] developed an emotional adaptive system measuring learner emotion by two dimensions: valence and arousal. According to the Circumplex Model of Affect [21], all affective states can be mapped to a certain point in a two-axis coordinate system, where the horizontal valence axis ranges from displeasure to pleasure and the vertical arousal axis ranges from high to low arousal. Woolf et al. [20] used these dimensions to create affect-adaptive responses of an animated agent that was able to keep up learner motivation and task engagement. Hudlicka and McNeese [22] provide an example of how an affect-adaptive Instructional System can be applied to a C2 environment: The Affect and Belief Adaptive Interface System (ABAIS) inferred the current affective state with a rule-based approach employing task context, external events, personality, individual history, training, and physiological data. ABAIS was evaluated with an Air Force Combat Task and used a four-step adaptive methodology to modify the cockpit instrument displays to counteract the pilot's anxiety.

Still, inconsistencies in recent findings indicate that the relationship between emotion and learning performance is not yet fully understood: On one hand, Shun et al. [23] emphasize the positive influence of positive emotion on learning effectiveness. Similar to Woolf et al. [20], the authors used pleasure, arousal, and dominance (PAD) as emotional input information within a virtual learning environment. By adjusting the type of task and learning information according to the learner's current emotion, the system promoted a successful learning experience. On the other hand, Picard [1] stresses the rewarding "Aha-effect" after experiencing frustration or anxiety due to increased task difficulty. With the ability to proceed beyond these negative emotions, frustration can be helpful by becoming a source of motivation.

Also, a number of challenges remain unaddressed in the field of affective computing. The design of a comprehensive multimodal affective recognition system that integrates various types of input data postulate a challenge [24]. Previous work by the authors has indicated that the relationship between affective state and performance in C2 environments is not consistent across participants [6]. Individuals may respond differently to stressors based on experience or knowledge, as psychological stressors depend on interpretation for effect, and do not themselves relate directly to affective responses.

Appraisal Theory [25] provides a possible explanation, stating that multiple processes contribute to the emotional experience, ranging from bodily sensations to situational factors. The biopsychosocial model of challenge and threat [26, 27], which is based on Appraisal Theory, states that stressful situations lead to increased physiological arousal that is often appraised negatively and may thus impair performance. When situational demands are appraised as exceeding available coping resources, the situation is experienced as a threat. With arousal reappraisal, a stressful situation can be experienced as a challenge and facilitate performance. Individual differences in appraisal emerge from general appraisal tendencies, which refer to systematic distortions in how individuals appraise their environment independent of a specific event [28, 29]. For example, with anger-prone appraisal style, events are constantly appraised in a way that leads to an anger experience [30], causing a different emotional experience. In addition, some individuals may externalize their emotional response more than others, or in different ways.

In order to be able to evaluate trainee affective state with respect to their performance level, it is therefore necessary to gain an in-depth understanding of individual differences in the relationship between emotion and performance.

1.2 Hypotheses

Based on these insights, we used data from two laboratory experiments with a simulated C2 task in the domain of anti-air warfare to test the following hypotheses:

H1: The emotional state of neutral valence is associated with high performance.

- H1a: During instances of high performance, positive valence is significantly lower than during instances of low performance.
- H1b: During instances of high performance, negative valence is significantly lower than during instances of low performance.

- H1c: During instances of high performance, neutral valence is significantly higher than during instances of low performance.

H2: High levels of arousal are associated with low performance.

- H2a: During instances of low performance, heart rate is significantly higher than during instances of high performance.
- H2b: During instances of low performance, heart rate variability is significantly lower than during instances of high performance.
- H2c: During instances of low performance, pupil width is significantly higher than during instances of high performance.

H3: There are interindividual differences in the association of emotional user state and performance.

2 Methodology

2.1 Sample Description

- **Experiment 1.** Twenty-four ($N = 24$) subjects aged between 19 and 48 years ($M = 32.0$, $SD = 7.2$) participated in the first experiment. The participants were all employees of the Fraunhofer Institute for Communication, Information Processing and Ergonomics (FKIE). Twenty-five percent of the participants were female.
- **Experiment 2.** Sixteen ($N = 16$) subjects aged between 22 and 49 years ($M = 32.3$, $SD = 8.7$) participated in the second experiment. Again, all participants were Fraunhofer FKIE employees. Thirteen percent of the participants were female.

2.2 Experimental Task

The experimental task was an air defense task on a simulated radar display. The task consisted of four subtasks:

1. Identify: The participant assigns an identification (hostile, neutral, or friendly) to all unknown tracks according to predefined parameters and rules.
2. Warn: If a hostile track enters the Identification Safety Range, it must be warned.
3. Engage: If a hostile track ignores the previous warning and enters the Weapon Range, it must be engaged.
4. NRTTs ("on real-time tracks"): The participant manually adds a track to the radar display based on written information received through a messaging interface.

The first and the second experiment were part of a larger study in which different user states and adaptation strategies were investigated. For this analysis, we used the control conditions of both experiments that did not employ any adaptation mechanisms. The first experiment's control condition had a total duration of 8 min and the second experiment's 24 min.

2.3 Variables

Performance. As a performance metric, we analyzed performance decrements that occurred whenever a task was not completed within the assigned time limit. If one or more performance decrements were present, performance was classified as low (1). In order to obtain a performance value for every second of the investigation, a performance value of 0 was assigned to indicate adequate performance when time limits were not exceeded for any task present.

Emotional User State. The construct of the emotional user state was operationalized based on valence and arousal – the two dimensions described by the Circumplex Model of Affect [21].

Emotional valence was derived from facial expressions using the emotion detection tool Emotient FACET. FACET analyzes facial expressions in real time using a regular camera (in our case a Logitech C920 webcam). A classification value > 0.5 was considered a moderate emotion [31]. FACET offers a variety of classifiers, however, only three of them – neutral, positive, and negative valence – were analyzed. The camera recorded 30 frames per second and FACET generated classification results for every frame. Classification values were aggregated to calculate a second-by-second median.

Arousal was detected using heart rate, heart rate variability, and pupil width as indicators. Heart rate and heart rate variability for every second of the investigation were recorded using a Zephyr Bioharness 3 multisensor chest strap. The Tobii X3–120 eye tracker tracked pupil width at 120 Hz. Again, raw data were aggregated to calculate a second-by-second median.

2.4 Statistical Analysis

Three participants of the first experiment and two participants of the second experiment were excluded due to missing data. From the first experiment, we used 8 min (480 s) of scenario time for the analyses, compared to 24 min (1440 s) from the second experiment. For every subject, we analyzed instances of low and high performance regarding differences in emotional valence and arousal. In order to avoid confounding within-subject and between-subject factors, one-way ANOVAs were calculated for every subject individually. One-second time windows of low performance were compared to one-second time windows of high performance regarding (a) the three FACET classifiers (positive, negative, and neutral valence), and (b) the three arousal indicators (heart rate, heart rate variability, and pupil width). The conservative Bonferroni correction was used to control for the multiple testing problem. Hence, p-values were tested against an alpha-level of .008. If a participant's performance was continuously high or low, the sample size was too small for a comparison between both states. Thus, if one sample showed less than 30 s of any performance state (either high or low performance), the participant was excluded from the analyses (resulting in the exclusion of two additional subjects in Experiment 1).

3 Results

3.1 Expected Results

Expected results according to the hypotheses are illustrated in Fig. 1. In line with Cai and Lin [11], a high percentage of subjects is expected to show high performance when positive and negative valence are low and neutral valence is high (H1). With respect to arousal, performance is expected to be low when heart rate and pupil width are high and heart rate variability is low (H2).

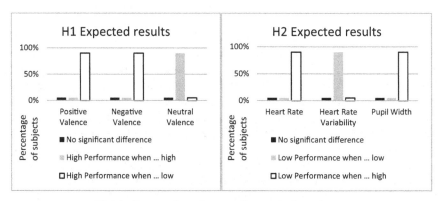

Fig. 1. Expected results according to the hypotheses.

3.2 Observed Results

Hypothesis 1. There was mixed evidence for the hypothesis regarding valence (H1: neutral valence is associated with high performance, see Fig. 2).

For data from the first experiment, H1 was partially confirmed. We found individual differences though. There was a statistical trend for positive valence being low in instances of high performance for almost half of the subjects, supporting H1a. However, there was no significant difference in 37% of subjects and evidence contrary to the hypothesis in 21% of subjects.

H1b was confirmed for 58% of subjects who performed better when negative valence was low. One third of the subjects showed no significant difference in negative valence between high and low performance. Only for 11% of subjects negative valence was associated high performance.

Neutral valence was high during instances of high performance for almost half of the subjects, supporting H1c. However, we found interindividual differences for this classifier also: There was no significant difference in 37% of subjects and evidence contrary to the hypothesis in 16% of subjects.

In data from the second experiment, H1 was partially confirmed as well. There was evidence for H1a for 57% of the subjects. We found no statistical difference in positive valence in instances of high performance vs. low performance in one third of the subjects and evidence contrary the hypothesis in only 7%.

For half of the subjects H1b was confirmed and for the other half there was no statistical difference in negative valence between high and low performance.

We found evidence for H1c (neutral valence is associated with high performance) in more than a third of subjects. Half of the subjects showed no significant difference and 14% performed better when neutral valence was low.

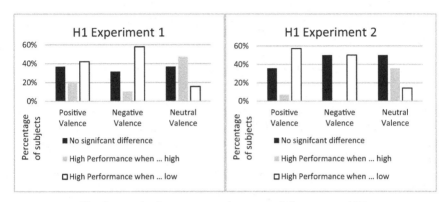

Fig. 2. Results from two experiments partially supported H1.

Hypothesis 2. The hypothesis related to arousal (H2: high levels of arousal are associated with low performance) was partially confirmed (see Fig. 3).

In the first experiment, there was supporting evidence for H2a in a third of the subjects who performed better during instances of low heart rate. More than half of the subjects showed no significant difference, and in 5% of participants we found evidence contrary to the hypothesis.

H2b was confirmed for almost half of the subjects. There was no significant difference in heart rate variability in 21% of subjects. Almost a third performed – contrary to the hypothesis - better when heart rate variability was high, showing remarkable interindividual differences.

High pupil width was associated with low performance in more than half of the subjects, supporting H2c. In the other subjects, there was no significant difference.

Findings in the second experiment were similar. H2a was confirmed for 43% the subjects, while there was no significant difference for heart rate in half of the subjects. 7% showed evidence contrary to the hypothesis.

Low heart rate variability was associated with low performance in 43% of subjects, supporting H2b. For another 43% there was no significant difference and for 14% low performance was associated with high heart rate variability.

H2c was confirmed for 43%. There were no significant differences in pupil width for the other subjects.

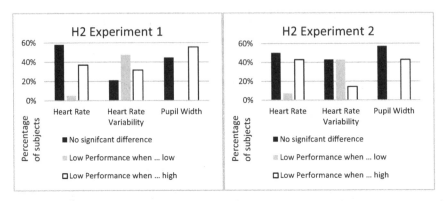

Fig. 3. Results from two experiments partially supported H2.

Hypothesis 3. Observed results show interindividual differences, especially for emotional valence but also for the arousal measures. While there was an overall tendency for neutral valence being associated with high performance and high levels of arousal with low performance, many subjects did not show any significant relationship between emotional user state and performance. Some subjects' performance benefitted from states of high positive valence or low neutral valence, supporting H3.

Only a few benefitted from high levels of arousal, however, results varied within the three different arousal measures. None of the subjects experienced low performance when pupil width was low. Few participants showed an association of low heart rate and low performance. High heart rate variability, however, was associated with low performance in many subjects in experiment 1, strongly supporting the hypothesis of individual differences in this particular arousal measure.

4 Discussion

The present investigation aimed at gaining first insights into the benefit of considering the emotional user state in an adaptive C2 system. To that end, we examined emotional valence, arousal, and performance in data from two previous experiments. Based on theoretical background, neutral valence was expected to be associated with high performance (H1) and high arousal with low performance (H2). According to previous investigations, we assumed individual differences in the relationship of emotional user state and performance (H3).

4.1 Individual Differences in the Relationship of Emotional Valence and Performance

Overall, there was supporting evidence that the state of neutral valence was beneficial for the performance of many subjects in both experiments, partially confirming H1. In experiment 1, high neutral and low positive and negative valence were associated with high performance in about half of the subjects, supporting H1. In about a third of subjects, no significant differences in valence between instances of high and low performance were found. Up to one fifth of participants experienced low neutral or high positive/negative valence during high performance. These findings support the interindividual differences in the relationship between the emotional user state and performance stated in H3. Results from experiment 2 were similar to those from experiment 1. H1a and H1b were supported in half of the subjects, H1c in about one third. We found no significant association between emotional valence and performance in 35–50% of subjects, supporting H3. Contrary to expectations, some participants benefitted from states of low neutral or high positive/negative valence.

These results pose a challenge for affect-adaptive mechanisms, as there may be a category of learners that performs best in a state of neutral valence, while another group of learners thrives in a positive or negative emotional state. About 50% of the subjects tested in this investigation would not have benefitted from an affect-adaptive mechanism, as there seemed to be no association of emotional user state and performance in these individuals. Participants who benefitted from a state of positive valence might even be hindered by an adaptive mechanism that generally promotes neutral valence, even though this was the state of emotional valence that correlated with high performance for most subjects. These findings stress the importance of the consideration of individual differences in the emotional user state. Possibly, distinct categories of learners exist that benefit from different emotional user states. An effective affect-adaptive instructional system should be able to distinguish these categories, assign learners to them, and adapt interaction or instructional content accordingly.

One approach to determining these categories could be based on Appraisal Theory. We suspect that the observed individual differences emerge at the stage of appraisal. Personality traits may have a key role in appraisal [32, 33] and thereby shape the subsequent emotional experience. Individuals differ in personality traits and in how they appraise their environment. For instance, neuroticism, one dimension of the Big Five Personality Factors, is associated with low perceived coping ability, the experience of negative emotions such as anxiety and fear, as well as emotion-focused coping strategies. In contrast, conscientiousness has been linked to problem-focused coping, and individuals with high levels of conscientiousness perceive themselves as able to meet situational demands [34]. These individual differences in the personality-appraisal relationship might help explain the individual differences we found in the relationship between valence and performance. By taking into account the users' personality traits and different appraisal styles, affect-adaptive systems may be able to better interpret the current emotional user state and provide more adequate adaptive responses.

Dennis et al. [35] investigated the role of learner personality on adaptive emotional feedback and performance. They developed a system that considers learners' levels of two personality traits – conscientiousness and emotional stability – when providing feedback through a conversational agent. For instance, individuals with low emotional stability and low performance received feedback in form of emotional reflection, reassurance, and advice, whereas individuals with high emotional stability and low performance did not receive emotional reflection support. For users that showed high performance along with high conscientiousness, emotional support was provided in form of praise.

Future research in the field of Adaptive Instructional Systems could use a similar approach and investigate whether and how the Big Five Personality Factors can account for the individual differences in the emotion-performance relationship of learners.

4.2   The Importance of Multifactorial Detection of Emotional Arousal

The second hypothesis, stating that high levels of arousal are associated with low performance, was partially confirmed also. In the first experiment, between one third and one half of the subjects benefitted from low levels of arousal. About half of the subjects showed no association of arousal measures and performance, except for HRV (only 21%). When arousal was indicated by HRV, one third of subjects benefitted from high arousal, supporting H3. However, high levels of arousal were not beneficial when indicated by pupil width or heart rate. Similar results were found in the second experiment. H2 was confirmed for 43% of subjects in all three measures. Half of the participants did not show any correlation of arousal and performance, supporting H3. Only few benefitted from high arousal.

At first, it seems puzzling that HRV results deviated from those of the other two arousal measures. A possible explanation can be found in the nature of this measure: HRV was calculated based on the past 30 s of a subject's heart rate. One might argue that this measure is not suitable for emotion detection as it detects changes very slowly. However, Nardelli et al. [36] successfully used HRV in emotion detection: They were able to achieve a recognition accuracy of 84.7% on the valence dimension, and 84.2% on the arousal dimension. Therefore, the exclusion of HRV from the emotional analysis seems unwarranted at this time.

Mauss and Robinson [37] suggest that, in order to accurately assess emotional responses, several arousal measures of the autonomic nervous system (ANS) should be combined. According to Lacey's [38] principle of *directional fractionation*, not all ANS measures map onto one single dimension. Different measures of ANS activity, like heart rate and pupil width, can operate independently or even in opposition to each other [39]. These findings offer an explanation why HRV varied from the other two arousal measures in its relationship with performance. Schwarz et al. [40] recommend combining multiple physiological sensors for effective user state detection, given that individual measures can be impacted by a variety of factors, including physical activity, task characteristics or lighting. In order to obtain a more complete and holistic assessment, we suggest a multifactorial approach in the detection of emotional arousal that considers its multiple dimensions. Multimodal machine learning approaches offer a good starting point for integrating multiple sensor data into a generalized emotion recognition algorithm [41].

4.3   Methodological Reasons

About 50% of the subjects did not show any relationship between emotional user state and performance. Methodological reasons may have contributed to these findings. Sample size in the second experiment was small after the exclusion of several subjects. More reliable results can be obtained from larger samples. In addition, some participants may have been more capable of accurately assessing their own current performance than others and we suspect that subjective performance may also have an impact on the emotional user state. For example, the impression of poor task processing could lead to frustration, whereas a complete inability to self-assess performance could explain the missing relationship between the emotional user state and performance in many subjects. Other C2 environments, like the Warship Commander Task [42], provide a performance score that allows self-monitoring of one's own performance and could serve as a model for future experiments. However, the didactic impact of a visible performance score should be considered carefully. Finally, the one-second time windows chosen for the analysis may not be suited for analyses of the emotional user state. It was chosen for practical reasons in the present investigation. The size of the time window could consider the type of experimental task used. In a C2 training environment, rapid changes can occur in the task load that can influence emotions and require instant adaptation mechanisms. Other adaptive instructional systems, like math learning platforms, might have to react slower in order to promote learning success.

5 Conclusions

The present study investigated the relationship between the emotional user state and performance in a C2 task. Results indicate that this relationship is not yet fully understood. While 47% of participants in Experiment 1 and 36% in Experiment 2 showed best performance during a neutral emotional state, 21% of participants in Experiment 1 and 7% in Experiment 2 showed best performance during a positive emotional state. About half of the participants showed no relationship between emotional state and performance at all. Low arousal was mostly accompanied with high performance; however, we observed differences between the three arousal measures investigated.

Follow-on research is underway to investigate if personality traits can offer a possible explanation for the observed differences between emotion and performance. Perhaps, distinct categories of learners, which differ in their relationship between emotion and performance, can be discovered. Future studies could aim to identify distinct category clusters in the emotional responses. Subjective traits like personality, age, or gender might assist in assigning learners to them. With an in-depth understanding of individual differences in the emotion-performance relationship, affect-adaptive instructional systems can be further improved.

The consideration of new technological advancements will facilitate the integration of the affective user state into adaptive instructional systems. With respect to diagnosing critical cognitive user states for adapting human-machine interaction, Schwarz and Fuchs [43] pointed out the importance of the multidimensional nature of user state, as well as the importance of considering impact factors from the user and the environment. Similarly, a multimodal affect recognition system may capture the multidimensional nature of the affective user state [44]. Especially the arousal component of the emotional user state seems to require multimodal detection due to directional fractionation [38].

Therefore, we will add respiration rate to the measures already used. Stemmler [45] was able to differentiate anger and fear by a combination of cardiovascular and respiratory measures, even though these two emotions are similar in terms of valence and arousal in Russell's Circumplex Modell [21], however, they deviate in a third dimension that can be added to the model: dominance [46]. Especially in an affect-adaptive instructional system, the distinction between anger and fear seems highly important due to the different cognitive biases and behaviors accompanied by these emotions. While anger induces an urge to act, fear can favor withdrawal [47]. A future adaptive training system could consider these bias differences in the adaptation of interaction or instructional content to maximize learning success, requiring an accurate assessment of the emotional user state.

References

1. Picard, R.: Affective computing. The MIT Press, Cambridge (1997)
2. Picard, R.W., et al.: Affective learning—a manifesto. BT Technol. J. **22**(4), 253–269 (2004)
3. Dolan, R.J.: Emotion, cognition, and behavior. Science **298**(5596), 1191–1194 (2002)
4. Gray, J.: Emotional modulation of cognitive control: approach–withdrawal states double-dissociate spatial from verbal two-back task performance. J. Exp. Psychol. General **130**(3), 436–452 (2001)
5. Tenenbaum, G., et al.: A conceptual framework for studying emotions–cognitions–performance linkage under conditions that vary in perceived pressure. In: Progress in Brain Research: Mind and Motion: The Bidirectional Link between Thought and Action. Elsevier, pp. 159–178 (2009)
6. Schmitz-Hübsch, A., Fuchs, S.: Challenges and Prospects of Emotional State Diagnosis in Command and Control Environments. In: Schmorrow, D.D., Fidopiastis, C.M. (eds.) HCII 2020. LNCS (LNAI), vol. 12196, pp. 64–75. Springer, Cham (2020). https://doi.org/10.1007/978-3-030-50353-6_5
7. Schmitz-Hübsch, A.: Der Einfluss situationaler affektiver Zustände auf den Zusammenhang zwischen Aufmerksamkeit und Performanz: Evidenz aus einer Command and Control Aufgabe. Master Thesis, Rheinische Friedrich-Wilhelms-Universität Bonn, Bonn, Germany (2019)
8. Spector, P., Goh, A.: The role of emotions in the occupation-al stress process. In: Research in Occupational Stress and Well Being, Exploring Theoretical Mechanisms and Perspectives, pp. 195–232. Emerald Group Publishing Limited (2001)
9. Staal, M. A.: Stress, cognition, and human performance: A literature review and conceptual framework. Citeseer (2004)
10. Orasanu, J. M., Backer, P.: Stress and military performance. In: Series in Applied Psychology, Stress and Human Performance, pp. 89–125. Lawrence Erlbaum Associates, Inc., Hillsdale (1996)
11. Cai, H., Lin, Y.: Modeling of operators' emotion and task performance in a virtual driving environment. Int. J. Hum Comput Stud. **69**(9), 571–586 (2011)
12. de Tjerk, E.G., Henryk, F.R.A., Neerincx, M.A.: Adaptive automation based on an object-oriented task model: implementation and evaluation in a realistic C2 environment. J. Cogn. Eng. Decis. Mak. **4**(2), 152–182 (2010)
13. Yerkes, R.M., Dodson, J.D.: The Relation of Strength of Stimulus to Rapidity of Habit Formation. J. Comp. Neurol. Psychol. **18**, 459–482 (1908)
14. Mulder, B., Rusthoven, H., Kuperus, M., de Rivecourt, M., de Waard, D.: Short-term heart rate measures as indices of momentary changes in invested mental effort. Human Factors Issues (2007)
15. Bradley, M.M., Miccoli, L., Escrig, M.A., Lang, P.J.: The pupil as a measure of emotional arousal and autonomic activation. Psychophysiology **45**(4), 602–607 (2008)
16. Pedrotti, M., et al.: Automatic stress classification with pupil diameter analysis. Int. J. Hum.-Comput. Interact. **30**(3), 220–236 (2014)

17. Vogel, S., Schwabe, L.: Learning and memory under stress: implications for the classroom. npj Sci Learn. **1**(1), 16011 (2016)
18. Park, O., Lee, J.: Adaptive instructional systems. In: Handbook of Research on Educational Communications and technology, 2nd ed, pp. 651–684. Lawrence Erlbaum Associates Publishers, Mahwah (2004)
19. Petrovica, S., Anohina-Naumeca, A., Ekenel, H.K.: Emotion recognition in affective tutoring systems: collection of ground-truth data. Procedia Comput. Sci. **104**, 437–444 (2017)
20. Woolf, B., Burleson, W., Arroyo, I., Dragon, T., Cooper, D., Picard, R.: Affect-aware tutors: recognizing and responding to student affect. IJLT **4**, 129–164 (2009)
21. Russell, J.A.: A circumplex model of affect. J. Pers. Soc. Psychol. **39**(6), 1161–1178 (1980)
22. Hudlicka, E., McNeese, M.D.: Assessment of user affective and belief states for interface adaptation: application to an air force pilot task. User Model. User-Adap. Inter. **12**(1), 1–47 (2002)
23. Shun, M.C.Y., Yan, M.C., Bo, A., Cyril, L.: Modeling learner's emotions with PAD. In: 2015 IEEE 15th International Conference on Advanced Learning Technologies, Hualien, Taiwan, vol. 72015, pp. 49–51 (2014)
24. Hasan, M.A., Noor, N.F.M., Rahman, S.S.B.A., Rahman, M.M.: The transition from intelligent to affective tutoring system: a review and open issues. IEEE Access **8**, 204612–204638 (2020)
25. Lazarus, R.S.: Emotion and Adaptation. Oxford University Press, Oxford (1991)
26. Blascovich, J., Tomaka, J.: The biopsychosocial model of arousal regulation. Adv. Exp. Soc. Psychol. **28**, 1–51 (1996)
27. Blascovich, J.: Challenge and threat. Psychology Press, New York (2008)
28. van Reekum, C.M., Scherer, K.R.: Levels of processing in emotion-antecedent appraisal. In: Advances in Psychology: Cognitive Science Perspectives on Personality and Emotion, pp. 259–300 (1997)
29. Matthews, G., Derryberry, D., Siegle, G.J.: Personality and emotion: cognitive science perspectives. In: Advances in Personality Psychology, vol. 1, pp. 199–237. Psychology Press, New York (2000)
30. Roseman, I.J.: A model of appraisal in the emotion system. In: Appraisal Processes in Emotion: Theory, Methods, Research, pp. 68–91 (2001)
31. iMotions: iMotions facial expressions analysis pocket guide (2016)
32. Tong, E.M., et al.: The role of the Big Five in appraisals. Pers. Individ. Differ. **41**(3), 513–523 (2006)
33. Kuppens, P., Tong, E.M.W.: An appraisal account of individual differences in emotional experience. Soc. Pers. Psychol. Compass **4**(12), 1138–1150 (2010)
34. Penley, J.A., Tomaka, J.: Associations among the Big Five, emotional responses, and coping with acute stress. Pers. Individ. Differ. **32**(7), 1215–1228 (2002)
35. Dennis, M., Masthoff, J., Mellish, C.: Adapting progress feedback and emotional support to learner personality. Int. J. Artif. Intell. Educ. **26**(3), 877–931 (2015). https://doi.org/10.1007/s40593-015-0059-7
36. Nardelli, M., Valenza, G., Greco, A., Lanata, A., Scilingo, E.P.: Recognizing emotions induced by affective sounds through heart rate variability. IEEE Trans. Affect. Comput. **6**(4), 385–394 (2015)
37. Mauss, I.B., Robinson, M.D.: Measures of emotion: a review. Cogn. Emot. **23**(2), 209–237 (2009)
38. Lacey, J. I.: Somatic response patterning and stress: some revisions of activation theory. In: Psychological Stress: Issues in Research, pp. 14–37. Appleton-Century-Crofts, New York (1967)
39. Libby, W.L., Jr., Lacey, B.C., Lacey, J.I.: Pupillary and cardiac activity during visual attention. Psychophysiology **10**(3), 270–294 (1973)

40. Schwarz, J., Fuchs, S., Flemisch, F.: Towards a more holistic view on user state assessment in adaptive human-computer interaction. In: 2014 IEEE International Conference on Systems, Man, and Cybernetics (SMC), San Diego, CA, USA, vol. 102014, pp. 1228–1234 (2009)

41. Bota, P.J., Wang, C., Fred, A.L.N., Da Placido Silva, H.: A review, current challenges, and future possibilities on emotion recognition using machine learning and physiological signals. IEEE Access **7**, 140990–141020 (2019)

42. Pacific Science & Engineering Group: Warship Commander 4.4. San Diego, CA (2003)

43. Schwarz, J., Fuchs, S.: Validating a "real-time assessment of multi-dimensional user state" (RASMUS) for Adaptive Human-Computer Interaction. IEEE (2018)

44. Wu, C.-H., Huang, Y.-M., Hwang, J.-P.: Review of affective computing in education/learning: trends and challenges. Br. J. Educ. Technol. **47**(6), 1304–1323 (2016)

45. Stemmler, G.: Physiological processes during emotion. In: The Regulation of Emotion, pp. 33–70. Lawrence Erlbaum Associates Publishers, Mahwah (2004)

46. Mehrabian, A., Russell, J.A.: An Approach to Environmental Psychology. The MIT Press, Cambridge (1974)

47. Hudlicka, E.: Computational modeling of cognition–emotion interactions: theoretical and practical relevance for behavioral healthcare. In: Emotions and Affect in Human Factors and Human-Computer Interaction, pp. 383–436 (2017)

Using Principled Assessment Design and Item Difficulty Modeling to Connect Hybrid Adaptive Instructional and Assessment Systems: Proof of Concept

M. Christina Schneider[(✉)], Jing Chen, and Paul D. Nichols

NWEA, 121 NW Everett Street, Portland, OR 97209, USA
{christina.schneider,jing.chen,paul.nichols}@nwea.org

Abstract. Coherence between adaptive instructional and summative assessment systems should provide teachers stronger support in challenging each student. Coherent systems should lead to accelerated student learning, and students being ready for the next grade. Range achievement level descriptors (RALDs) describe a state's theory of what increasing knowledge, skills, and abilities look like in their standards as students become more sophisticated thinkers on their journey to proficiency and beyond. Systems can be connected to better align interpretations of student performance using task features that align to evidence statements in RALDs. Our proposition is that through coding tasks in both systems using common schema, including RALD-to-task match, assessment and instructional system inferences about student progress can be bridged. We combined two approaches for linking inferences across systems measuring mathematics that do not rely on common students or common tasks as a proof of concept. Using RALDs and other task features, we predicted 45% of the variance in task difficulties for a secondary data source. Holding all else constant, RALDs were the strongest feature for modeling increases to task difficulty. This suggests that RALDs could be leveraged in instructional systems to support interpretations of student growth, increasing their value for teachers.

Keywords: Adaptive assessment · Adaptive instruction · Proficiency

1 Introduction

The formative assessment theory of action is situated in the context that one of the jobs to be done by a teacher is analyzing and grading student work to determine next instructional actions to increase student achievement. Sadler's [1] formative assessment theory of action is based on the notion that a teacher identifies the learning target, where a student is with respect to the learning target, and what instructional action or feedback a student needs next to close the gap between where he or she is and the intended learning outcome. However, increasing research evidence suggests that teachers need support in accurately engaging in formative assessment. Llosa [2] found

© Springer Nature Switzerland AG 2021
R. A. Sottilare and J. Schwarz (Eds.): HCII 2021, LNCS 12793, pp. 149–166, 2021.
https://doi.org/10.1007/978-3-030-77873-6_11

that teachers inconsistently interpreted standards with multiple parts. They ignored the parts of standards they did not understand, developed their own interpretation, or ignored the standard completely. Heritage et al. [3] and Schneider and Gowan [4] found that teachers struggle with determining next instructional actions. Teachers must analyze and interpret student work or analyze and interpret item characteristics and the student's responses to those item characteristics to determine where the student is with respect to the learning target. If teachers are not comfortable determining the right learning targets or determining next instructional actions, it becomes difficult for them to set up personalized learning activities or tasks that elicit the right evidence for students to reveal what they understand. This, in turn, makes it difficult for teachers to determine what they need to do next to improve the student's understanding of the content, which makes instructional planning and adaptations less effective for individual students.

A second complication is that teachers may not recognize that within a standard can be ranges of content- and thinking-skill difficulty that describe different levels of achievement [5, 6]. In addition, not all standards are equal. Some standards are precursors to others, whereas others represent more advanced levels of thinking with the content [7]. Individual standards that are measured in isolation without a content connection to other within-grade standards do not allow an individual teacher to determine what proficiency in grade-level content or "on track" performance represents. Being "on track" for success in the next grade is typically a content-centered process in which a representative group of teachers from a state defines how much content and at what level of difficulty and cognitive complexity a student should be able to successfully respond with during problem solving and/or analysis [8, 9]. In some cases, statistical modeling of future outcomes such as college and career readiness is also incorporated into the process [10]. The determination of proficiency in a state assessment is often far more complex than the common teacher belief that standards are objectives they can check off. Being "on track" for proficiency means not all content has to be answered correctly by a student, but that particular content at a particular level of difficulty, integrated with related standards, must be.

A third challenge is that teachers have little time for the complex analysis required to track the rigor of the tasks given to students and the student responses to those tasks. Teachers want support and tools that allow them to challenge more students in ways that are manageable [11]. From this perspective, adaptive tutoring systems solve a teacher problem. They offer students individual practice and repetition, feedback on where the student is on their journey to "proficiency," and automate grading and progress monitoring. Xie et al. [12] noted that such systems use students' preferences, learning achievements, and profiles for adaptive learning. However, it is our observation that such systems also have different interpretations of mastery than many state assessments, which, in turn, places the educational ecosystem out of alignment in supporting student progress interpretations over time. In other words, the tasks that students receive across instructional systems and assessment systems may not be built to the same definitions of mastery, and teachers therefore do not have a single compass to support them in interpretating student achievement across systems.

1.1 Achievement Level Descriptors

Teachers, parents, and students need a common unifying framework to identify where students are currently in their journey to proficiency and beyond in state standards and to help monitor the depth of student learning of instructional topics over time. Emerging from the accountability movement in the 1990s [13], states often use Policy achievement level descriptors (ALDs) to support educators and the public in understanding at a high level what students should know and be able to do at each achievement level with respect to the content standards in domains such as English language arts, mathematics, and science [5]. This high-level, policy-based description is common across grades and content areas except, possibly, for high school. However, Policy ALDs have limited usefulness for communicating what students are expected to know and be able to do from a context of building curriculum and instruction. For example, they do not incorporate theories of learning regarding how knowledge and skills become more sophisticated both within and across grades [14]. As Daro et al. [15] explained, Policy ALDs are of little help to teachers in designing instructional interventions to help students stay on track and continue to progress. This is one reason attempts at "data driven improvement" often come up short. Data in the form of scale scores, without specific interpretations of what those scores represent, do little to support curriculum and instruction adjustments.

Range ALDs (RALDs) have been proposed as a framework to better support educators in recognizing differences in student thinking [5, 6] and the attributes of tasks needed to elicit evidence of student thinking. RALDs provide detailed descriptions of the interactions of task features used to elicit evidence about what students understand and student response characteristics to those task features. Task features include (a) using observable, measurable verbs to denote the level of cognitive load for a task, (b) contextual features the task should possess to elevate or lower cognitive load so teachers can determine when a student can show what they know, and (c) specific content characteristics the tasks should possess given that some content attributes (e.g., identifying a simile) are easier for students than others (e.g., identifying a metaphor). RALDs describe what increasing knowledge and skill attributes are expected as students become more sophisticated thinkers in the content area on their journey to proficiency and beyond [5]. As such, it is expected that RALDs have a positive relationship with the difficulty of the task (also called item difficulty) along a test scale [16]. Under such a model, novice to mastery states are explicitly defined along with allusions to related precursor standards. This approach to constructing RALDs has been used in state assessments [17].

RALDs are the underpinning of principled assessment approaches to test design [18]. Principal assessment design shares common characteristics with Understanding by Design [19], which is often used to support curriculum design. Both approaches to design use templates to assist developers in identifying and documenting desired results and determining acceptable evidence that students have mastered the learning targets, although the granularity of the assessment evidence to be collected may differ across sources. Curriculum development moves into a third stage beyond assessment by developing the specific blueprint for learning that is determined based on desired understanding and results. However, because RALDs also identify desired outcomes of those learning experiences—coupled with ranges of content- and thinking-skill difficulty that are theories of how students grow in their development within and across standards—RALDs may be used as a tool to underpin both curriculum development learning tasks and assessment tasks, thereby encouraging horizontal and vertical educational system coherence between instructional and assessment systems and supporting interpretations of growth across time.

Our proposition is that RALDs can be the bridge that connects instructional activities and assessment activities. We argue that if teachers, curriculum developers, and test developers use the same types of evidence and standards interpretation to understand student learning, increased educational systemic validity would occur. When states develop RALDs to articulate (1) the observable evidence that teachers, curriculum developers, and assessment developers should elicit to draw conclusions about a student's current level of performance, (2) what that evidence looks like when students are in different stages of development based in learning science findings where feasible, and (3) how students are expected to grow in reasoning and content skill acquisition across achievement levels within and across grades, they better communicate how standards are interpreted for instructional purposes, how tasks can align to a standard but not be of sufficient difficulty and depth to represent proficiency, and what growth represents. That is, we believe there are synergies between RALDs and learning progressions that we describe next.

1.2 Learning Progressions

RALDs offer a deeper lens into contextualizing learning progressions that are increasingly described in the learning science and formative assessment literature as theoretical underpinnings for curriculum development, instruction, and assessment of learning. The purpose of a learning progression is to inform researchers and educators about general developmental pathways of learning so they can set reasonable, achievable learning goals and provide appropriate guidance for instruction and assessment in each content area. Assessments that are designed to measure student growth as well as inform instruction should be derived from the combination of the learning goals and within-grade developmental progressions of those goals. Clements and Sarama [20, p. 83] wrote, "Developmental progressions… [are] descriptions of children's thinking and learning… and a related, conjectured route through a set of … tasks." The outcome of instructional tasks delivered in the classroom or assessment tasks delivered on a large-scale assessment should be the same: observable evidence of what students know and can do in relation to the stages of learning of on-grade content from a state's standards. As shown in Fig. 1, RALDs show a progression of how students are expected to grow in reading development of a standard based on an RALD for an assessment.

Learning progressions describe how students learn, but they are also an interpretive aid in analyzing that information and a support for using the information for action [21]. This is a complementary view to the intended use of RALDs. For example, Schneider and Egan [6, p. 4] state that, "In terms of learning progressions, the Common Core Standards may be thought of as the learning goals for students at each grade level, and the RALDs may be considered developmental trajectories—evidentiary statements regarding children's observable thinking and skills as they pass along the path to the learning goals." Assessment developers who commingle the interpretations of RALDs with the notions

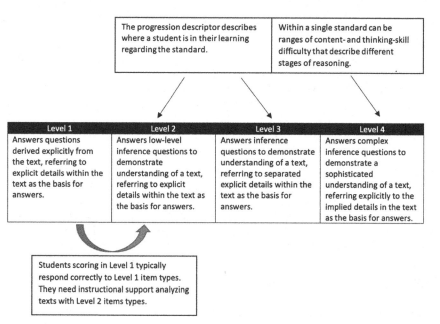

Fig. 1. Example of an RALD and interpretive guidance for what to provide students based on the type of items students answer correctly.

of learning progressions have the potential to provide a tool for teachers and adaptive instructional system providers to link the interpretation of tasks and student responses across systems to provide users a systemically valid instructional and assessment system that supports change in the development of the cognitive skills [22]. Items aligned to a particular standard and achievement level can be used to automate interpretations regarding where students are in their learning and what they need next to grow, as the blue arrow shows in Fig. 1.

1.3 Adaptive Systems

The use of RALDs can help create an instructional system that is efficient and personalized to the needs of the learner in a similar manner as an adaptive assessment personalizes items based on item difficulty and a student's ability level. As already noted, RALDs are expected to have a positive relationship with task difficulty [16]. Validity evidence using RALDs ties task features to task difficulty along a test scale. Coding task features in an instructional system in the manner we describe can likewise be an approach to support personalized instructional opportunities to learn within a curriculum. Coding task features of items in an instructional system to task features associated with RALDs could support adaption of tasks to the learner in a manner similar to the way a computer adaptive assessment personalizes a test to a student through branching algorithms or the use of predictions of task difficulty. An adaptive assessment can estimate the ability of a student with fewer items and more precision than a non-adaptive assessment. Similarly, an adaptive instructional system can personalize instructional tasks for modules to a student so that the student takes fewer tasks and practices tasks that provide just the right amount of cognitive dissonance the student needs to grow.

An adaptive instructional system is useful to buyers and users by being efficient and personalized to the needs of the learner. It is also a principal of learning science. Targeting the types of tasks a student receives to RALD classification or predicated task difficulty based on student ability aligns to the Office of Educational Technology's definition of learning technology effectiveness, where "Students who are self-regulating take on tasks at appropriate levels of challenges, practice to proficiency, develop deep understandings, and use their study time wisely" [23, p. 7].

Such an approach requires a validity framework that outlines the evidence needed to support the claims that the use of RALDs is likely to provide accurate information about where the student is in their learning. Frameworks used to validate learning progressions may be borrowed to design, collect, and evaluate validity evidence for RALDs. Validity frameworks for learning progressions proposed by Confrey et al. [24] and Jin et al. [25] adopt an argument-based approach [26] under which validation is understood as the process of constructing an argument in support of the proposed learning progression-based interpretation and subsequent decisions. An argument-based approach typically consists of two forms of argument: an interpretive argument and a validity argument. The interpretive argument describes the network of inferences and assumptions leading from the construct definition to the observed performances and to the conclusions and decisions based on the performance. The validity argument is the evaluation of the interpretive argument. For example, the learning progression validity framework proposed by Jin et al. [25] consists of five stages as shown in Table 1.

1.4   Evaluation of the Validity Framework

In Stage 2: Scoring of the validity framework, content experts and researchers should evaluate the degree to which the proxies for achievement level capture salient patterns of students' reasoning in a meaningful way. A source of evidence for capturing salient patterns of students' reasoning and development is item difficulty modeling (IDM). When conducting IDM studies, researchers identify task features that are expected to predict item difficulty along a test scale. For example, Ferrara et al. [27] classified item response demands into five categories that are related to task difficulty: design demands (e.g., item type, maximum points), stimulus demands (e.g., text complexity), content demands (e.g., standard/objective), cognitive demands (e.g., depth of knowledge [DOK]), and linguistic demands (e.g., vocabulary density). The studies reviewed in Ferrara et al. [27] had observed R-squares in a range of 0.36 to 0.90 for predicting item response theory (IRT) difficulty in mathematics and quantitative reasoning tests.

RALDs incorporate task features into descriptions of each achievement level. In our study, we included item DOK code [28], RALD code [5], item type, grade, and standard. Because the item RALD level is intended to reflect the interaction of design, cognitive, and content demands of an item within the trajectory of sophistication of the measurement target, the task RALD level is expected to be a good predictor of item difficulty. Relationships between task features and item difficulty can be established for an assessment. It may be possible to then use such features to predict similar relationships in instructional systems. Therefore, it may be possible to identify task features that predict

Table 1. Five stages of the learning progression (LP) validity framework.

Stage	Description
Stage 1: Development	Researchers describe the upper anchor of the LP and create the items intended to elicit evidence of knowledge and skills found at different levels of the LP. A common approach to collecting evidence for the development stage is to consult experts
Stage 2: Scoring	The LP-based rubrics are developed and used to score students' responses for the LP levels. For the validity argument, researchers evaluate the degree to which the LP-based scoring rubrics capture salient patterns of students' reasoning and present the development in a meaningful way
Stage 3: Generalization	Researchers perform quantitative analyses to the score to infer the proficiency of students from observed scores. A common source of evidence for the generalization stage is the fit of measurement models, such as a Rasch IRT model, to the scored learner responses
Stage 4: Extrapolation	Researchers describe expected relationships between proficiency on the LP and proficiency in a larger domain. Evidence to evaluate these claims may be correlations between LP-based scores and achievement in a science discipline
Stage 5: Use	Researchers describe assumptions with regard to the usefulness of LP-based results by teachers to help students move towards the upper anchor of the LP. These assumptions include the expectation the LP-based results, when used appropriately by teachers, do not having an adverse impact on identifiable subgroups of students

item difficulty from an assessment and then apply them to another set of tasks without such corresponding difficulty data. This process is referred to as IDM. Such an approach might be feasible as a method of evaluating and connecting instructional system tasks to the different levels of student thinking that are similar in nature to the levels elicited from an assessment.

2 Purpose

Our study had two purposes. First, we wanted to determine if RALD-to-task matches were a significant predictor of task difficulty. Second, we wanted to determine if we could connect systems to develop coherent inferences about where students are in their learning in ways that do not rely on common students or common tasks. Social moderation is an approach of linking inferences across different assessments for which common definitions of student performances have been established [29]. In this context, RALDs are the common definitions. This approach is coupled with the assumptions that (1) an IRT model would also fit instructional tasks found in an instructional system, (2) available collateral information about test items found in high-stakes vendor item management systems is likely to be correlated with their IRT parameters, and (3) item parameters from summative assessments are available for such predictions [30]. These tools may provide the means of linking the systems together without exposing high-stakes items or actual student data. Metadata tagging of tasks using task features such as the Webb DOK framework [28], the item type, standards, grade of the targeted content, and RALDs may work in combination to describe items across the scale, as shown in Fig. 2.

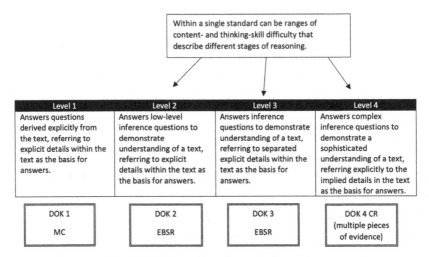

Fig. 2. RALDs and sample types of metadata.

Should RALDs support predictions of item difficulty, we believe this would support our claims of the synergies between RALDs and learning progressions that we described earlier and contribute to the learning science literature by supporting the progression of evidence collection that teachers, curriculum designers, and assessment developers need to attend to in order to better understand how students are growing to proficiency and beyond.

3   Methods

The data included in this study are items from two different mathematics assessment data sources developed for different purposes and at different times. While the study method is using two different item pools from the assessments, the intent is to understand whether RALD tagging might be useful in predicting the difficulty of instructional tasks so that the two systems can cohere. A total of 2,915 items from the first source and 3,019 items from the second source were included in this study. Table 2 shows the sample size of the items by item type from each assessment. Approximately 10% of items from Data Source 1 are polytomous items, which are treated as dichotomous items by averaging the step parameters to provide a single difficulty parameter for this study.

The data sources came from separate assessment systems. The underpinnings of each system had different samples of students, different standard alignment philosophies, and different technical steps in calibration processes. While both assessment sources used

Table 2. Number and percentage of items by item type.

Item type	Data source 1		Data source 2	
	N	%	N	%
Choice	2,040	70.0	2,773	91.9
Choice multiple	164	5.6	52	1.7
Composite	210	7.2	1	0.0
Gap match	139	4.8	158	5.2
Graphic gap match	88	3.0	32	1.1
Text entry	189	6.5	3	0.1
Hot text	85	2.9	0	0.0
Allows calculator	372	12.8	1,131	37.5
Does not allow calculator	2,543	87.2	1,888	62.5
Total	2,915	100.0	3,019	100.0

the Rasch model to calibrate items, the first source also included the use of the partial credit model (PCM) whereas the second did not.

Item difficulty parameters were calibrated based on the IRT Rasch model and PCM [31, 32]. A benefit of using IRT models to calibrate items is that student ability and item difficulty are estimated on the same continuum. The Rasch model and PCM were applied to calibrate dichotomous and polytomous items, respectively. The Rasch model estimates the probability (π_{ni}) that a student (j) with an achievement score of θ_j will correctly answer a test item (i) of difficulty δ_i. It is expressed as:

$$\pi_{ni} = \frac{e^{(\theta_n - \delta_i)}}{1 + e^{(\theta_n - \delta_i)}}$$

PCM generalizes the dichotomous Rasch model to consider multiple score points between a score of 0 and the maximum points possible for the item. The following equation shows the full PCM when more than one score point is used:

$$\pi_{nix} = \frac{e^{\left[\sum_{j=0}^{x}(\theta_n - \delta_{ij})\right]}}{\sum_{k=0}^{m_i} e^{\left[\sum_{j=0}^{k}(\theta_n - \delta_{ij})\right]}} \qquad x = 0, 1, \ldots m_i$$

where π_{ni} is the probability of person n scoring point x on the rubric to item i, qn is the ability estimate of person n, δ_{ij} is the threshold parameter for the jth category of item i, and m_i is the maximum number of score points for item i. It is based on a defined constraint shown next:

$$\sum_{j=0}^{0}(\theta_n - \delta_{ij}) = 0$$

Common to both sources were the item metadata for item type, DOK level, and whether a calculator was allowed. Items in Data Source 1 were already tagged for RALDs, standard, and grade.

Data Source 1 had three achievement levels. Panels of teachers were trained to align items from Data Source 2 during a four-day workshop using the Item-Descriptor (ID) Matching procedure [9]. During this training, teachers received training sets and validation sets of intended RALD-to-item matches so they could develop consensus on items that met the definition for each level and alignment judgment differences could be discussed. Once panels were ready to move on, they tagged items first for the RALD cell then automated the standard code and grade based on the RALD. Teachers were asked to discriminate the matching of items across roughly 90 different cells per grade. After this process was complete, data modeling of both data sources began.

The initial item difficulty model was created using Data Source 1. The item difficulty parameter was the dependent variable, and task features were the independent variables. Item difficulty parameters are on a scale set to 0 with a standard deviation of 1. An ordinary least squares linear regression model was used to model the difficulty of items. The 2,915 items were randomly split into training and validation datasets, with 80% of the items in the training dataset and 20% of the items in the validation dataset. The random splitting process was repeated 10 times. Each time, the model was built and validated using the randomly split training and validation datasets. The model evaluation results reported are the average from those 10 evaluations. After validating the model using items from Data Source 1, we applied the model to Data Source 2 as if it were a secondary validation dataset.

Task features used in the modeling included RALD code, DOK code, standard, item type, calculator required or not, and grade level of the item. The RALD, DOK, and grade-level variables were treated as ordinal variables with ordered categories from low to high. The targeted standard, item type, and calculator features were treated as dummy variables. For example, an item that measured a particular standard was coded as 1 for that standard and 0 for all the other standards.

Data Source 2 results were obtained by a special study using archival data files to locate students who had taken items from both assessment sources during the spring of the same year to support examining the proof of concept.

4   Results

When applying the model built on the training item set to the cross-validation set for Data Source 1, the average R-squared derived from the 10 cross-validation datasets was around 0.60. When applying the same model to Data Source 2 as a second validation dataset, the R-squared decreased to 0.45. These results suggest that task features included in the model explain around 60% of the item difficulty variation in Data Source 1 and 45% of the item difficulty variation in Data Source 2. When the model was applied to items from Data Source 2, it explained a smaller percentage (45%) of the item difficulty variation. The decrease in R-squared was not unexpected given that the assessments were developed for different purposes.

While implementing such an approach would not allow us to collect validity evidence on a secondary source, items from Data Source 2 had empirical item difficulty estimates that allowed us to compare the predicted item difficulty estimate based on the model and the actual item difficulty estimated formally linked to the primary source. The correlation between the predicted values and the empirical values was around 0.67. Figure 3 shows the relationship between the predicted and the actual item difficulties.

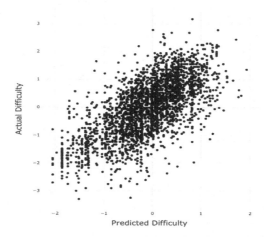

Fig. 3. Predicted difficulty vs. empirical difficulty for items.

To improve understanding of what makes task features easy or difficult, we examined how the predictors affected item difficulties in the model. Table 2 shows the coefficient of the predictors and whether they were statistically significant. The predictors of targeted grade level, RALD, DOK, multiple-choice item status, and calculator allowed are statistically significant; the p-values were less than 0.05. A number of standards were significant predictors; however, they contributed just 0.06 of the overall R-square value and are not included due to the density of the information. Five features related to item types were not statistically significant predictors of item difficulty.

The targeted grade, RALD level, and DOK level had positive coefficients that indicate they typically increase task difficulty. As the value of these variables increased, the mean of the item difficulty also tended to increase. The item type (choice) variable had a negative coefficient, indicating this item type typically decreases item difficulty. This is the system label used for multiple-choice items that are ubiquitous across the educational ecosystem. If a task is provided in a multiple-choice format, the average item difficulty tends to be lower than if a different item type is used. The value of the coefficients signifies how much the mean of the item difficulty changes given a one-unit change in the independent variable while holding other variables in the model constant. For example, if the RALD level increases one level, the mean of the item difficulties tends to increase around 0.4 along the scale (Table 3).

Table 3. Coefficients of independent variables.

Variables	Coefficient	Std Error	t	P>|t|
Targeted grade	0.182	0.043	4.241	0.000
RALD	0.414	0.021	19.609	0.000
DOK	0.120	0.028	4.292	0.000
ItemType (Choice)	-0.608	0.071	-8.597	0.000
ItemType (Choice Multiple)	0.161	0.085	1.889	0.059
ItemType (Composite)	-0.153	0.081	-1.883	0.060
ItemType (Gap Match)	-0.026	0.087	-0.296	0.767
ItemType (Graphic Gap Match)	-0.090	0.098	-0.919	0.358
ItemType (Text Entry)	0.124	0.084	1.484	0.138
Allows Calculator	0.197	0.049	4.006	0.000
Constant	-1.564	0.238	-6.577	0.000

Note. The standard variable is not shown in this table because of the large number of standards included.

Figure 4 includes boxplots of item difficulty distribution for items at different RALD levels across all grades. As the RALD levels change from Level 1 (easiest) to Level 3 (hardest), item difficulties are generally larger. RALD is a good indicator of item difficulty, and, in general, the medians of the item difficulties increase with RALD level. Figure 5 and Fig. 6 include boxplots at each grade level. The same pattern of increasing item difficulties as teacher identified RALD level increases is observed at each grade, which shows the effect of grade and RALDs on the task difficulties.

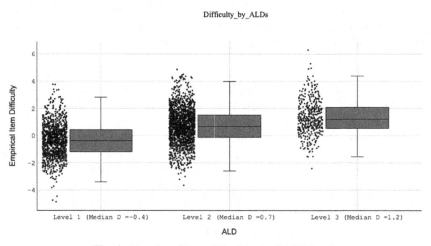

Fig. 4. Boxplot of item difficulties by RALD level.

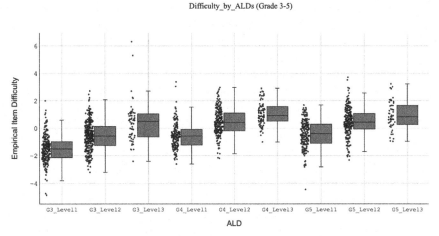

Fig. 5. Boxplot of item difficulties by RALD level and grade (Grades 3–5).

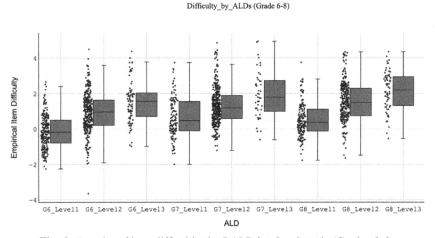

Fig. 6. Boxplot of item difficulties by RALD level and grade (Grades 6–8).

5   Conclusion and Discussion

The multiple linear regression model produced acceptable predictions of item difficulty. The R-squared value was around 0.60 for items from the primary source and around 0.45 for the secondary source. Beyond the multiple-choice item type that decreased an item's predicted difficulty, the RALD level had the most impact on predictions for increasing an item's difficulty. It is relevant to note that DOK was also a significant predictor because this feature is often viewed by content developers as not being related to item difficulty. Overall, the model supports that these item features can be used in combination to better understand where an item is likely to be on IRT scale and which students are likely to benefit from which items in an adaptive context to support student learning. Borrowing collateral information from a summative assessment could support instructional and assessment designers in predicting if tasks embedded in a secondary source, such as an instructional system, may target notions of proficiency in a manner similar to state technical buyer expectations.

Predicting task difficulties for different stages of sophistication can assist both instructional and assessment designers in creating learning and measurement opportunities using theories of learning about how thinking in the content area becomes more complex. This sets the stage of personalizing opportunities for students at different stages of learning in the same class and provides increased opportunities for students to have access to challenging problem solving and complexity that they need to become college and career ready. It also opens the door to using Enhanced ID Matching [33] to support common ways to identify proficiency across systems.

Should instructional and assessment task designers want to increase the likelihood of providing learning opportunities that are more similar to summative proficiency and beyond expectations, they may consider targeting item types that are more varied than multiple-choice only, at higher DOK levels, and targeting the evidence in Level 2 and Level 3 RALD statements. The conscious choices of creating tasks to such features are what make the evidence collection processes principled. That is, task features are strategically included by design to present students opportunities to learn based on evidence on how students are likely to increase in sophistication across time. This, in turn, supports teachers in having more robust interpretations about where students are in their learning. These learning pathways could be especially useful in an instructional system during early product deployment phases when information about task functioning is limited, but there is a desire to adapt to students. Predicted task difficulties can be compared to RALD levels in advance of task deployment as a quality control check. Task developers can obtain early evidence that a task is not expected to empirically function at the level of rigor desired. In future studies, with the inclusion of additional predictive task features and the application of more advanced models, the prediction of item difficulty is likely to improve to explain additional variance and allow more sophisticated approaches of uniting information from assessment and instructional systems.

The design and validation of systems intended for both formative and summative purposes both for classroom and high-stakes uses require careful development processes based in evidence when systems are intended to support interpretations regarding how student learning grows more sophisticated over time [34]. This is an element of learning science, and because of the kinship of LPs and RALDs, we followed the approach and process recommended by Jin et al. [25] to create a validity framework for the RALDs as shown in Table 4. We used the stages and applied them to the work from this process.

Under a principled approach to assessment design, the evidence needed to draw a conclusion is made explicit in the RALDs and items are developed specifically to those evidence pieces [5, 7, 35]. This design process is intended to support the validity of inferences about the stage of learning and the content validity of the assessment as a measure of student achievement over the course of a year. It is possible for such assessments that instructional utility can be increased by leveraging the common interpretations of proficiency across assessment and instructional systems to provide more coherent progress

Table 4. Five stages of the RALD validity framework.

Stage	Description
Stage 1: Development	We used RALDs from an assessment that were created to represent different stages of development within the standards. This is the first step in social moderation [29]
Stage 2: Scoring	Items were matched to the RALDs and coded in the original data source, thereby categorizing items to achievement levels. Students were scored on each item they took
Stage 3: Generalization	Researchers performed quantitative analyses with the individual items to infer the proficiency of students from observed scores. A common source of evidence for the generalization stage is the fit of measurement models, such as a Rasch IRT model, to the scored learner responses. Item difficulties established from two different data sources were used in this process
Stage 4: Extrapolation	For the validity argument, we used IDM to capture salient patterns of evidence and item difficulty. We described expected relationships between RALDs and task difficulty and used those assumptions to improve precision in linking inferences across data sources using a methodology to link scores that do not require exposing actual items or student-level data [30]. Evidence to evaluate our claims were predictions of item difficulty from salient features applied to two different data sources in mathematics
Stage 5: Use	We described our assumptions regarding the usefulness of RALDs to help solve teacher problems. Teachers want support and tools that allow them to challenge more students and diagnose where students are in their learning in ways that are manageable. This proof of concept includes the expectation that RALD-based results, when used appropriately by teachers as a part of an instructional and learning management system, do not having an adverse impact on identifiable subgroups of students

monitoring systems for students within a state. Thinking about the task types and characteristics of tasks needed to elicit evidence of student development with respect to RALDs provides a common formative lens regarding within-grade curriculum and instruction and allows more sophisticated, connected proficiency models to be developed.

We argue improved coherence between instructional systems and assessment systems can be established for students and support the teacher's job to be done, as shown in our theory of action depicted in Fig. 7. By developing and coding item metadata using a common learning framework across systems, we can better align interpretations of student performance using tasks that elicit evidence about what students understand using both RALDs and predictions of item difficulty from an assessment system to an instructional system. This ensures that teachers and students across a state have common interpretations of what proficiency represents. This, in turn, leads to equitable opportunities to learn and helps ensure that students get equal access to the degree of challenge the state wants for its students. This process supports systemically valid instructional and assessment systems even when one provider does not develop both systems.

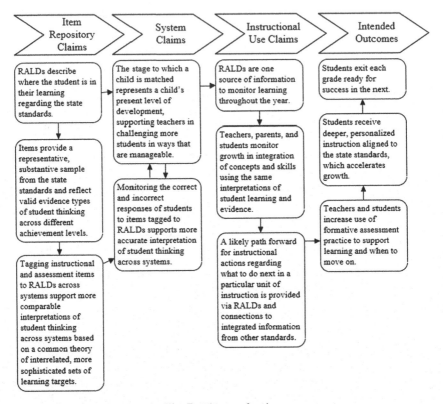

Fig. 7. Theory of action.

Predicting the achievement level classification of a student or the content the student answers correctly is not intended to be a stopping point for decision making. It is a call to administer more difficult, complex tasks that represent the next stage until a match cannot be made. This is the starting point for opportunities to grow and where teachers can provide supports. It is a call to move deeper within the standards to determine if students need more opportunities to practice the next stage of the trajectory or if the student needs support in a precursor standard, which may need additional support because proficiency requires integration across standards. This in an area ripe for additional research by applying this proof of concept with an instructional system. The support of personalization to the student also supports the teacher by serving as a manageable tool for continuing to provide students opportunities for more challenging content at just the right moment to encourage growth. Instructional tasks that are predicted to be too easy for a student in a unit or practice session can be omitted to support efficient use of student time and maximize student engagement.

References

1. Sadler, D.R.: Formative assessment and the design of instructional systems. Instr. Sci. **18**, 119–144 (1989). https://doi.org/10.1007/BF00117714
2. Llosa, L.: Assessing english learners' language proficiency: a qualitative investigation of teachers' interpretations of the California ELD standards. CATSOEL J. **17**(1), 7–18 (2005)
3. Heritage, M., Kim, J., Vendlinski, T., Herman, J.: From evidence to action: a seamless process in formative classroom assessment? Educ. Meas. Issues Pract. **28**(3), 24–31 (2009)
4. Schneider, M.C., Gowan, P.: Investigating teachers' skills in interpreting evidence of student learning. Appl. Measur. Educ. **26**(3), 191–204 (2013)
5. Egan, K.L., Schneider, M.C., Ferrara, S.: Performance level descriptors: history, practice and a proposed framework. In: Cizek, G. (ed.) Setting Performance Standards: Foundations, Methods, and Innovations, 2nd edn., pp. 79–106. Routledge, London (2012)
6. Schneider, M.C., Egan, K.: A handbook for creating range and target performance level descriptors. The National Center for the Improvement of Educational Assessment (2014)
7. Schneider, M.C., Johnson, R.L.: Creating and Implementing Student Learning Objectives to Support Student Learning and Teacher Evaluation. Taylor and Francis, London (2019)
8. Lewis, D.M., Mitzel, H.C., Mercado, R.L., Schulz, E.M.: The bookmark standard setting procedure. In: Cizek, G. (ed.) Setting Performance Standards: Foundations, Methods, and Innovations, 2nd edn., pp. 225–253. Routledge, London (2012)
9. Ferrara, S., Lewis, D.: The item-descriptor (ID) matching method. In: Cizek, G. (ed.) Setting Performance Standards: Foundations, Methods, and Innovations, 2nd edn., pp. 255–282. Routledge, London (2012)
10. Phillips, G.W.: The benchmark method of standard setting. In Cizek, G. (ed.) Setting Performance Standards: Foundations, Methods, and Innovations, 2nd ed. Routledge, London (2012)
11. Arnett, T., Moesta, B., Horn, M.B.: The teacher's quest for progress: How school leaders can motivate instructional innovation. Christensen Institute (2018)
12. Xie, H., Chu, H.-C., Hwang, G.-J., Wang, C.-C.: Trends and development in technology-enhanced adaptive/personalized learning: a systematic review of journal publications from 2007 to 2017. Comput. Educ. **140**, 103599 (2019). https://doi.org/10.1016/j.compedu.2019.103599
13. Koretz, D., Hamilton, L.S.: Testing for accountability in K–12. In: Brennan, R.L. (ed.) Educational Measurement, 4th edn., pp. 531–578. Praeger, Westport (2006)
14. Baird, J.-A., Andrich, D., Hopfenbeck, T.N., Stobart, G.: Assessment and learning: fields apart? Assess. Educ. Princip. Policy Pract. **24**(3), 317–350 (2017). https://doi.org/10.1080/0969594X.2017.1319337
15. Daro, P., Mosher, F.A., Corcoran, T.B:. Learning trajectories in mathematics: A foundation for standards, curriculum, assessment, and instruction. Consortium for Policy Research in Education (CPRE) Research Report (2011)
16. Schneider, M.C., Smith, J., Davidson, A.: Measuring teacher skill in formative assessment. Paper presented at the annual meeting of the National Council on Measurement in Education, Philadelphia, PA (2014)
17. Florida Department of Education (FDOE). Florida Standards Assessments achievement level descriptors. Author (2015)
18. Huff. K., Nichols, P., Schneider. M.C.: Designing and developing educational assessments. In: Cook, L., Pitoniak, M. (eds.) Educational Measurement, 5th ed. NCME (in press)
19. Wiggins, G., McTighe, J.: Understanding by Design, 2nd ed. Association for Supervision and Curriculum Development (ASCD) (2005)

20. Clements, D.H., Sarama, J.: Learning trajectories in mathematics education. Math. Think. Learn. **6**(2), 81–89 (2004)

21. Furtak, E.M., Morrison, D., Kroog, H.: Investigating the link between learning progressions and classroom assessment. Sci. Educ. **98**(4), 640–673 (2014)

22. Frederiksen, J.R., Collins, A.: A systems approach to educational testing. Educ. Res. **18**(9), 27–32 (1998)

23. U.S. Department of Education. Learning technology effectiveness. Author (2014)

24. Confrey, J., Toutkoushian, E., Shah, M.: A validation argument from soup to nuts: assessing progress on learning trajectories for middle-school mathematics. Appl. Measur. Educ. **32**(1), 23–42 (2019). https://doi.org/10.1080/08957347.2018.1544135

25. Jin, H., van Rijn, P., Moore, J.C., Bauer, M.I., Pressler, Y., Yestness, N.: A validation framework for science learning progression research. Int. J. Sci. Educ. **41**(10), 1324–1346 (2019). https://doi.org/10.1080/09500693.2019.1606471

26. Kane, M.T.: Validation. In: Brennan, R.L. (ed.) Educational Measurement, 4th ed., pp.17–64. American Council on Education/Praeger, Washington (2006)

27. Ferrara, S., Steedle, J.T., Frantz, R.S.: Item response demands, predicting item difficulty, and validity of inferences from test scores. In: Paper Presented at the Annual Meeting of the National Council on Measurement in Education, New York, NY (2018).

28. Webb, N.L.: Web alignment tool (WAT) training manual, draft version 1.1. Wisconsin Center for Education Research (2005)

29. Linn, R.L.: Linking results of distinct assessments. Appl. Measur. Educ. **6**, 83–102 (1993)

30. Mislevy, R.J., Sheehan, K.M., Wingersky, M.: How to equate tests with little or no data. J. Educ. Meas. **1**(30), 55–78 (1993)

31. Rasch, G.: Probabilistic models for some intelligence and attainment tests. Danmarks Paedagogiske Institute (1960)

32. Masters, G.: A Rasch model for partial credit scoring. Psychometrika **47**, 149–174 (1982)

33. Schneider, M.C., Lewis D.: Embedded ID matching: ESS-enhancements to ID matching to reduce panelists' cognitive load. In: Paper to be presented at the 2021 annual meeting of the National Council on Measurement in Education (virtual) (2021)

34. Pellegrino, J.W., DiBello, L.V., Goldman, S.R.: A framework for conceptualizing and evaluating the validity of instructionally relevant assessments. Educ. Psychol. **51**(1), 59–81 (2016)

35. Huff, K., Warner, Z., Schweid, J.: Large-scale standards based assessments of educational achievement. In: Rupp, A.A., Leighton, J.P. (eds.) The Handbook of Cognition Assessment: Frameworks, Methodologies, and Applications, pp. 399–426 (2016)

Dynamic Cognitive Modeling
for Adaptive Serious Games

Alexander Streicher[1]([✉]), Julius Busch[2], and Wolfgang Roller[1]

[1] Fraunhofer IOSB, Karlsruhe, Germany
{alexander.streicher,wolfgang.roller}@iosb.fraunhofer.de
[2] KIT, Karlsruhe, Germany
julius.busch@accenture.com

Abstract. Cognitive modeling can be a viable tool to assess the cognitive state of the users and to determine their current learning needs. For instance, adaptive educational systems must match the learning needs by estimating the level of memorization or forgetting. The research question is, how to model latent cognitive variables such as memory degradation and how to make use of it for adaptivity scenarios in the e-learning context. Tools like cognitive architectures with established psychological underpinnings can help here. However, development of cognitive architecture models is often complex, domain- and application-specific and its transfer or general applicability is not evident. We present an innovative dynamic modeling approach which automatically creates declarative rules from interoperable activity stream observations to form models for the cognitive architecture ACT-R. The developed framework uses those models to analyze user actions according to their frequency, temporal occurrence and memory activation levels. An adaptive e-learning system can use the chunks' activation levels to assess which concepts need repeated user attention. A prototype implementation for a serious game for process training demonstrates the feasibility of the approach.

Keywords: User modeling · Learner state · Cognitive modeling · Adaptivity

1 Introduction

User modeling is key for adaptive e-learning or assistance systems which aim to react to the users' (learning) needs. Adaptivity here means to personalize the usage experience to the individual needs of the users and their current working context. The quality of adaptive systems directly depends on their understanding of the users, i.e., on their user models. The more realistic these models represent the mental states and cognitive processes, the more precise the approximation of needs can be, and the better is the automatic parametrization of assistance functions. That is of particular interest for the e-learning domain, where Intelligent Tutoring Systems (ITS) target an optimal support for the learners [29].

© Springer Nature Switzerland AG 2021
R. A. Sottilare and J. Schwarz (Eds.): HCII 2021, LNCS 12793, pp. 167–184, 2021.
https://doi.org/10.1007/978-3-030-77873-6_12

A central active research question for adaptive e-learning systems addresses the correct timing of adaptive educational systems, i.e., the issue of when to actually adapt. The question when to react or adapt is especially important for digital game-based learning systems, e.g., for educational serious games, because we want to keep the users immersed in their gaming experience, not disturbing their game flow. Serious games are games which should entertain but have at least one additional characterizing goal [10]. In the case of educational serious games this goal is learning whereas the learning objectives should be aligned at the gaming experience and its objectives [18]. To achieve high learning outcomes, the game design should foster immersion and flow [13]. High immersion comes along with high intrinsic motivation to (continue) playing – and, hence, to continue to learn [13]. The very essence of digital game-based learning is to allow the users to play, to make mistakes, and to immerse themselves in a virtual environment [10]. Misdirected automatic reactions, at the wrong time, can have an extremely negative effect on immersion. For optimal efficacy and high user acceptance, the correct point in time is of fundamental importance. For example, an adaptive educational system could react when attention decreases, cognitive load increases, or when the user seems to be in a repetitive cycle with no real observable progress, or when there are signs of forgetting. Cognitive modelling addresses such kind of issues.

The research question is how cognitive modeling can contribute to "intelligent user models" and how it can be used for adaptivity in digital learning games. More specifically, how to use a data-driven approach to dynamically generate cognitive models which include latent cognitive variables such as cognitive load or memory decay.

The contribution of this work is a concept for cognitive user models for digital learning games by means of cognitive modelling and its application to adaptivity.

In comparison to cognitive models for general assistance systems, educational serious games come with additional training and learning aspects such as learning styles, achievement of learning goals, gameplay instruments such as trial and error, gamification, etc. This has to be considered when selecting a cognitive modeling tool. Our concept shows how to apply the cognitive architecture ACT-R to educational serious games, and how to control adaptivity by using memory activation levels from learned activity concepts. We have chosen ACT-R based on a subjective value-benefit study. The main criteria were its established psychological underpinnings and maturity, availability of implementation frameworks and community support, and its suitability to dynamically modify the declarative and procedural models. Key aspects of our approach are the dynamic generation of the ACT-R model based on observations, as well as its use of standardized activity stream data as a general scheme for the observed input data. This allows to apply the approach to other application domains. In our e-learning domain we make use of the tracking standard *Experience API* (xAPI) which is an established method to track learning, also in serious games [21]. Our work is embedded in research on frameworks for adaptive assistance systems [24].

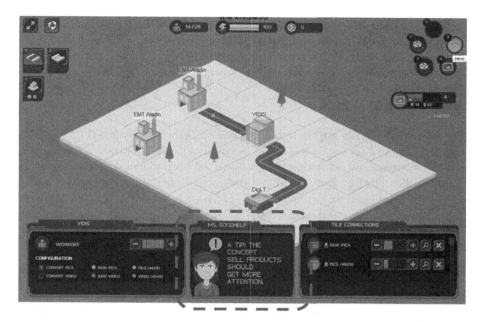

Fig. 1. Example for adaptive hints (bottom, dashed rectangle) in the serious game Exercise Trainer (EXTRA) [25]. The virtual agent recommends considering an activity that was estimated to receive too little attention.

A major challenge in the use of cognitive architectures is the required extensive modeling effort. Expert knowledge is needed for both the cognitive architectures and the application domain. Taatgen and Anderson (2010) discuss that it takes "substantial intellectual commitment to learn to understand models of a particular architecture and to learn to construct models" [26]. We address this issue by following a data-driven modeling approach. Our ACT-R model is designed as a combined user and domain model. User interactions are captured via xAPI and stored in a *Learning Record Store* (LRS) [1]. This interaction data together with the data in the declarative and procedural module of ACT-R forms the user models. A special feature of our approach is the dynamic modeling of the production rules. At runtime, interaction data is translated into ACT-R production rules for the virtual procedural ACT-R memory. Based on this model, cognitive processes can be simulated and analyzed. We make use of this to query the cognitive architecture which concept the user probably has "forgotten" – ACT-R allows to query the activation energy of the model's concepts. This activation energy – based on the Memory Decay Theory and Spreading Activation – is mapped to a continuous, real number and it is determined by the cognitive architecture at each simulation time step. Important game concepts, which are neglected by the user, can be identified by looking at their decreasing activation levels. A threshold function on the memory decay curve and ACT-R activation levels indicates "forgetting", and an adaptive system can react to this situation and offer appropriate assistance [24]. In our implementation the adaptive system offers hints on the next recommended or expected activities. This recommendation is aligned at the simulated cognitive user model. Figure 1 depicts an example for the serious game *Exercise Trainer* (EXTRA) [25].

2   Related Work

Adaptive serious games are related to *Intelligent Tutoring Systems* (ITS) [28,29]. Central to many ITS implementations is the monitoring of student interaction with the systems and to maintain a student or user model of knowledge and activity [9,29]. The literature shows multiple approaches of using cognitive architectures for Intelligent Tutoring Systems (ITS), such as the ACT-R based *Pump Algebra Tutor* by Anderson et al. (2001) [5] or the *Cognitive Tutoring Authoring Tools* (CTAT) by Aleven et al. (2006) [2]. Many ITS approaches utilize cognitive architectures for modeling [5,16]. At the core of this modeling is the division of knowledge into declarative and procedural units. Declarative knowledge represents atomic facts, while productions represent abstract individual goal-oriented problem-solving steps of a larger task. The modeling goal is to realistically represent human problem-solving thinking [16]. In this context, production rules comprise all possible solution paths that a student can undergo. A basic technique of cognitive tutors is called *model tracing* [5], which we follow for our solution approach. In model tracing, each action of the student is simulated simultaneously in the cognitive architecture. Subsequently the student's action can be classified as correct or incorrect by comparing it with this simulation. This allows the cognitive tutor to interact with the student in real time. Developers of adaptive learning systems based on cognitive architectures are confronted with complex modeling tasks, e.g., for the domain model. It requires expert knowledge and experience [20,26]. To deal with this problem, systems are developed that start from a higher level of abstraction and automatically design the more complex model from it. Examples of this are ACT-Simple and G2A, which are based on the Framework GOMS (Goals, Operators, Methods and Selection) [3,20]. The framework was conceptualized to make predictions about which methods and operations users apply in digital systems to complete known tasks. ACT-Simple uses a simple scripting language that compiles to ACT-R models [20]. Compared to our approach, here, the modeling effort should also be reduced and simplified, but our concept tries to simplify it by moving the modeling to the data observation level and to the activities to be observed. Several derivatives have evolved from GOMS, such as KLM-GOMS, CMN-GOMS, NGOMSL or CPM-GOMS. KLM-GOMS is a simple framework for the sequential description of expert behavior. ACT-Simple builds on this and combines it with the power of ACT-R. A similar work is the G2A system, which automatically GOMSL-Models transformed to ACT-R [3]. GOMSL is an abstract modeling language of the GOMS family that is more powerful than KLM-GOMS, for example, and supports several of ACT-R features features, e.g., representation of mental objects, working memory, primitive internal and external operators, composition methods, or even various flow-of-control constructs [3].

Combining serious gaming and cognitive architectures is not a new concept [11,28]. Gentile et al. (2019) provide an analysis on the potential role of cognitive architectures for serious games, with focus on A.I. and non-player characters (NPC). Such kind of virtual agents are often realized with Soar, for example in the work by Wray et al. (2013) [30]. Mills and Dalgarno (2007) present a conceptual architecture for game-based learning ITS implementations [17]. The authors discuss the role ACT-R for various modeling tasks and how to build declarative and procedural rules. In the context of serious games, we see a further relation to the *Player Experience Modeling* (PEM) by Yannakakis (2012): for personalization, adaptivity engines should be able to recognize and model the learning style and detect the cognitive state of the users [31]. This very detection of the cognitive states is the central aspect of our work and corresponds to the user modeling efforts, as stated in the introduction. ACT-R has been used to develop a virtual agent for use in training simulations for military operations in urban areas [7]. A complex production set was modeled in order to achieve autonomous action by the agent.

Although all these studies are similar in terms of modeling and use cases for serious gaming, we did not find any literature that resembles our approach.

3   Cognitive Architectures and E-Learning

Our cognitive modeling approach for adaptivity is related to modeling for intelligent tutoring systems (ITS). Generally, an ITS architecture includes various models, mainly the user interface model, a student model, a domain model, and a tutor model, all of them with varying interconnections (Fig. 2). In our work we focus on the student model and the domain model since we need information on the cognitive state of the user, and to which concepts or activities in the computer application these states are linked to.

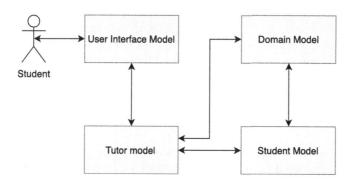

Fig. 2. General scheme of the models in an intelligent tutoring system.

In the context of e-learning, the formal modelling of the cognitive learning state is of particular interest. This includes modelling the cognitive abilities of humans, including memory, language, perception and problem solving. We focus on approaches to model forgetting or attention. The focus for adaptive knowledge transfer concentrates on the possibility of forgetting: a cognitive architecture can provide the adaptive system with information about content or activities that a user may have forgotten or that are highly likely to be forgotten. One possible adaptation strategy could be to remind and draw attention to these activities. From a neurological point of view this means that the experience and their underlying neuronal ensembles are consolidated (in the long-term memory). Cognitive architectures largely consider such psychological and neuro-scientific principles.

However, there is no precise definition of a "cognitive architecture" and it is often unclear when a concrete (software) instance belongs to the class of cognitive architectures [14]. Cognitive architectures attempt to recreate Artificial General Intelligence (AGI), i.e., computer systems that correspond to human intelligence [19]. According to Russel and Norvig (2009) there are four categories for the realization of AGI [19] that are aimed at replicating:

- systems which think like humans – here we make use of a cognitive architecture with its psychological underpinnings to simulate thinking.
- systems which act like humans – our simulation of the users' thought processes enables an approximation of a human behavior.
- systems which think rationally – since we base our modeling approach only on observations, we depend on a rational behavior by the users.
- systems which act rationally – the simulation process typically is deterministic, therefore the adaptive decision-making processes appear rational.

Cognitive architectures are typically classified according to how they represent and process information. Three paradigms have emerged:

- symbolic, also called cognitivistic: use of explicit symbolic representations to represent information. Cognitivist architectures are also referred to as symbolic architectures and A.I. approaches. Although they are quite successful, they lack generality to be applicable across domains [12].
- emergent, in the sense of connectionism: information is processed in a network of connected computing units that communicate in parallel. The units receive stimuli through their incoming connections, perform nonlinear computation and influence other units through their outgoing connections.
- hybrid, a combination of both.

The most recent overview of the last 40 years of research on cognitive architectures was conducted by Kotseruba and Tsotsos (2018) [14]. They analyzed a set of 84 architectures, of which 49 are still actively developed. They estimate the number of existing cognitive architectures to be around 300. Other comparative reviews have been conducted by Asselman et al. (2015) [6] and Thórisson and Helgasson (2012) [27]. The most prominent representatives of cognitive architectures are the "classical" candidates that have existed since the time of the emergence of cognitive architecture in the 1970 s. Most widely used are the two hybrid architectures ACT-R [4] and Soar [15].

We conducted a subjective value-benefit analysis to select a suitable cognitive architecture for our dynamic cognitive modeling approach. Criteria for the selection process included:

- general applicability and modeling flexibility.
- support for programming languages, maturity of implementing frameworks.
- complexity and learning curve.
- available documentation and community support.
- licensing costs, whereby free, open-source tools are favored.
- number of available scientific publications, indexed by Google Scholar, Web of Science and Scopus.

From our applied research perspective, we focused on the implementation aspects. The result (*cf.* Fig. 3) of our analysis indicated ACT-R as the most versatile and for our approach of dynamic modeling suitable cognitive architecture. The decisive factor for the result was above all the comprehensible code examples of Python ACT-R.

	Subjective Rating of **Cognitive Architectures** (Subjective Measures 1-10 increasing)	Weighting (1-10)	ACT-R	LEABRA	SOAR	CLARION	LIDA	ICARUS	ART
Features	Hybrid Character	6	10	2	10	10	10	3	2
	Psychological Foundation	7	10	7	3	7	6	0	3
	Relevance to Image Interpret.	3	0	4	0	0	0	0	10
	AGI	4	9	4	9	3	5	8	7
	Weighted Category Sum	7	8,3	4,5	5,9	6,1	6,1	2,5	4,6
Implemen-tation	Complexity	4	2	4	3	3	1	3	1
	Programming Languages	9	7	5	5	5	7	4	5
	Weighted Category Sum	4	5,5	4,7	4,4	4,4	5,2	3,7	3,8
Score (weighted)			7,3	4,5	5,3	5,4	5,8	2,9	4,3

Fig. 3. Results of our subjective value-benefit analysis.

ACT-R tries to implement the formal abstraction of human behavior with a module concept. At its core is the procedural module. The information generated in the surrounding modules flows into this module and is then processed so that the next action step of an agent can be determined. Production rules in ACT-R thus serve as circuit functions that map certain information patterns in the modules' memories, called buffers, to changes in buffer contents [4]. We make use of these declarative and goal modules. In the declarative module, knowledge is stored in the form of chunks. These chunks can be retrieved using productions if the goal buffer is set to a specific chunk. Therefore, the goal module serves as a state manager to determine which productions will be run in each simulation step. Based on ACT-R theory, various calculations are performed to find out which actions in the other modules, which are involved in a particular production, should be performed to fulfill the currently set goal. Section 5 explains the dynamic generation of production rules and declarative chunks.

4   Concept for User Modeling and Artificial Intelligence (UMAI)

We developed a concept for user modeling with A.I., named *User Modeling and Artificial Intelligence* (UMAI). The A.I. part is the cognitive modeling by integrating cognitive architectures for the modeling process. As stated before, our concept targets applied research and therefore the direct applicability of cognitive architectures for assistance systems. We make use of triple-structured activity data streams which can be used to track almost every user interaction event. In this article we focus on the cognitive architecture ACT-R for educational serious games. A key aspect is the dynamic generation of the ACT-R model based on observed user interaction data. The output contains estimated memory or chunk activation levels which an adaptive system can incorporate in its decision processes.

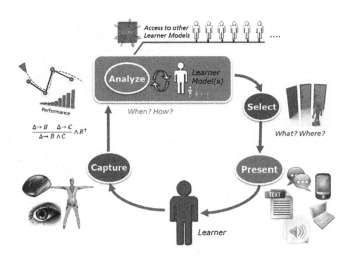

Fig. 4. Extended 4-phased adaptivity cycle (based on [22]) with combined analysis-learner-models-phase.

Our view on adaptive systems follows the 4-phased adaptivity cycle by Shute et al. (2012) [22]. The cycle depicted in Fig. 4 structures an adaptivity process in four consecutive phases or stages where each new run depends upon the previous run, hence forming a cycle. Its main components are the four phases (1) capture, (2) analysis, (3) select and (4) present, plus an additional user or learner model after the analysis phase. However, we incorporate the user models into the analysis phase (2). The argumentation is that the select phase (3) not only builds upon and uses the user models but also incorporates additional analysis results, such as usage pathways models. UMAI is located in the analysis phase (second phase) and it contributes to the formation of the user or learner models. A special feature of our approach is the dynamic modeling of the production rules. At runtime, an ACT-R user model is generated based on interaction data which is captured using the standard protocol xAPI. The interaction data is translated into ACT-R production rules for the virtual procedural ACT-R memory. Based on this model, cognitive processes can be simulated and analyzed. We make use of this to query the cognitive architecture which concept the user probably has "forgotten". ACT-R allows to query the activation energy of the modelled concepts. This activation energy, which is based on the Memory Decay Theory, can be mapped to a continuous, real number and determined by the cognitive architecture per simulation time step. Important game concepts, which are neglected by the user, can be determined by the decreasing activation energy. A threshold function is used to model "forgetting" and an adaptivity system can react to this situation and offer appropriate assistance [24].

The general process is as follows (*cf.* Fig. 5):

1. The main UMAI program is started. The start request includes a user identifier for which the cognitive modeling and simulation should take place.
2. Retrieve xAPI statements from an xAPI Learning Record Store (LRS). The query typically includes filtering on the active user and on his latest usage session. This is achieved through recording an *initialized*-statement for events like a beginning a new level or starting a session.
3. Execute the model generator which takes the recorded activities (from xAPI) and generates a simulation program. This dynamic generation of an ACT-R program containing a user model depicts our dynamic modeling approach (implementation details in Sect. 5).
4. The simulation program is started and simulates the various steps the user has undertaken. In accordance with classical cognitive modeling the simulation builds a cognitive model on the sequence of user actions. By using a cognitive architecture such as ACT-R for storing and processing the events we can determine cognitive variables such as chunk activation levels (e.g., memorization level of an activity).
5. For each observed activity a chunk is generated, and an activation value is computed using ACT-R.
6. Thresholding on the activation levels produce those chunks for which repeated attention is recommended.
7. The main program returns the selected activities and their activation levels.

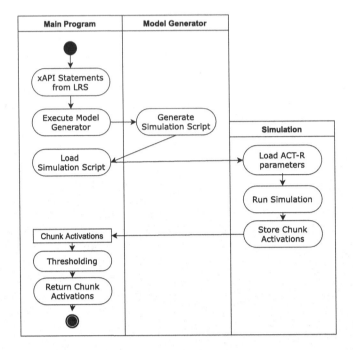

Fig. 5. Model generation process for one simulation request to the UMAI system.

5   Software Architecture, Implementation

Interactions with the game are transferred via xAPI to an LRS. This interaction data together with the data in the declarative and procedural module of ACT-R forms the learner model or student model.

The Experience API (xAPI) standard [1] allows to monitor a user's varying experiences in learning systems, ideally in a consistent format [1,21]. For general application the related W3C activity stream standard [23] works similarly, from a technical point of view, but with conceptual differences [8]. For implementation, one needs to build an activity stream or xAPI adapter which tracks selected events (many libraries for different programming languages exist). The choice of events should be aligned at the overall analysis goal or the overall research question [21].

In the designed software architecture (Fig. 6) the "intelligent user model" is implemented as a micro service, and the communication with connected assistance systems is done via HTTP RESTful services.

After each user action, the xAPI adapter generates an event statement and sends it to the LRS. On request from the user (student or tutor) UMAI retrieves all recorded statements from the beginning of the session. Subsequently, a retroactive simulation is started in the cognitive architecture.

This simulation can be repeated as often as desired to model different configuration variants, e.g., individualized memory decay and threshold parameters.

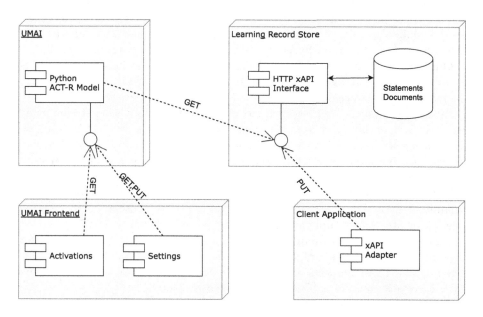

Fig. 6. System Architecture for the UMAI concept and implementation.

```
1    def action_i(focus='action_i'):
2        if (action_stream[counter] in new_actions):
3            new_actions.remove(action_stream[counter])
4            dmstring = 'action_i:' + action_stream[counter]
5            DM.add(dmstring)
6            focus.set('action_' + str(conuter+1))
7        else :
8            DM.request(dmstring)
9            focus.set('action_' + current_chunk_number + '_')
10
11   def forgot_i(focus='action_i_', DMBuffer=None, DM='error:True'):
12       print ("I forgot something")
13       if len(action_stream) == counter :
14           focus.set('stop')
15       else :
16           fired_actions[str(counter)]= action_stream[counter]
17           focus.set('action_' + str(counter+1))
18
19   def remember_i(focus='action_i_', DMBuffer="action_i:?action"):
20       print ("I remember action_i:",action)
21       if len(action_stream) == counter :
22           focus.set('stop')
23       else :
24           DM.add('action_0:?action')
25           DMBuffer.clear()
26           focus.set('action ' + str(counter+1))
```

Fig. 7. Python ACT-R code for dynamically creating production rules.

After each simulation, data accumulated in the cognitive architecture can be used for subsequent adaptivity decisions, e.g., offering recommendations or for dynamic difficulty adjustment. For learning analytics purposes, we can visualize the chunk activation values for each observation step (line diagram Fig. 9).

Once the activity stream from the session start to the last fired action is retrieved, an ACT-R agent is run on a production set which is dynamically generated from the stream.

In the first step the xAPI statements are parsed into an action stream array where the sequential order is maintained. Our modeling in ACT-R is based on the resulting stream and is independent of the domain of the underlying learning system. The methodology analyzes the occurrence and frequency of action steps as time series. As described in Sect. 3, in ACT-R each chunk is assigned an activity rate which degenerates over time. Chunks of declarative memory are dynamically created for each of these action descriptions by dynamically creating code fragments. An example for the code template is shown in Fig. 7.

If actions occur more than once and chunks have already been created for them during the processing of the action stream, queries are made to the declarative module. These requests may fail if the activity rate of the respective chunk of the correlating action is below a pre-defined threshold.

The processing logic is as follows (*cf.* Fig. 7):

- For each action, a base production is first generated.
- If an action has been executed for the first time it is added to the declarative memory as a chunk. Also, an identifying number is stored in a `chunk_numbers` array and the focus buffer is set to the subsequent action.
- If an action occurred previously its chunk is retrieved from the declarative memory and the focus buffer is set to the current chunk number.
- For each action, the production is called only once and a chunk of the form `action_0:action_descriptor` is created. In Python ACT-R, a request is made to a declarative chunk by passing `DM.request()` to the function `action_0:?action`. Before this request can be sent, the chunk number is determined when the particular action first occurred.
- Afterwards, the focus is not set to the next action, but to the production that matches the chunk number. This is therefore the production at the point where the action occurred for the first time. The focus is not set on the base production, but on the productions `forget` and `remember`, which are also generated for each action (Fig. 7).
- In case the declarative action-chunks have an activation less than or equal to the `threshold` and the action is called, the forget-production is called. Here, within the production rule, only the focus is set on the serial action. If the activation is greater than the `threshold`, the `remember` production is called. In case of calling the forget-production, the respective chunk cannot be reactivated.

– In the **remember** production it is first checked whether all actions have been processed. If this is the case, the focus is set to **stop** so that the simulation of the agent can be ended in the next step with the **stop** production. If the processing status of the action stream has not yet reached the end, the focus is set on the next action. In contrast to the original implementation, in Python ACT-R it is necessary to add the called action to the declarative memory again in order to increase the activation of the respective called chunk.

6   Application and Results

For technical verification of the UMAI concept we implemented it for our serious game *Exercise Trainer* (EXTRA) [25] (Fig. 1 and 8). An adaptive assistance system [24] linked to EXTRA is meant to point out little noticed – but essential – concepts to the user. The UMAI concept can provide the necessary modeling for the adaptivity response model.

In the following section, we briefly explain EXTRA, then we describe how EXTRA relates to the UMAI concept and its application.

6.1   Serious Game: Exercise Trainer (EXTRA)

The game concept of EXTRA is designed as an isometric, turn-based simulation game (Fig. 8). The general form of the game is geared towards process training games which are related to logistics or business processes. The learning objective is to learn the actors and relationships involved in complex processes. The application background is technically complex IT scenarios with different subsystems, inputs and outputs. In EXTRA, the complex roles, activities and processes as well as the technical system-of-systems structure are abstracted into a flexible game world and described by metaphors. For this purpose, the player must build logistics chains with factories and infrastructure (*cf.* Fig. 8). The learning objects are interwoven with the gameplay so as not to compromise immersion. The terminology and the properties of the factories or connections are therefore based on real systems, and the game supports training and receptive knowledge transfer in a transparent way. The didactic goal is that essential components and relationships of complex system-to-system structures are being learned. An application example is the training of a process for image-based intelligence in which the users experience the varying activities of tasking, collection, processing, exploitation and information dissemination. The actual game goal is to satisfy demanding "customers" with changing product desires (metaphor for tasks) by constructing optimal logistic chains (metaphor for data or information links) to optimally distribute products to markets. Gamification approaches such as high-scores help to motivate players to compete with others and to repeat playing the game. The score reflects the degree of success in satisfying customer needs. If the requirements are not met in time, the score decreases; if the score drops to zero, the game is lost.

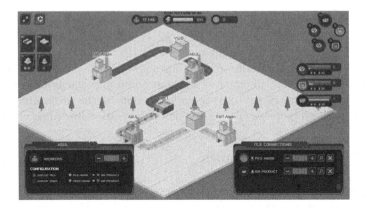

Fig. 8. The serious game Exercise Trainer (EXTRA) [25] for playful learning and training of complex processes.

6.2   Application of UMAI

To verify the UMAI concept we focused on four essential EXTRA activities (*cf.* Fig. 8) which the user can perform, and the sequence and timing of which can be arbitrary:

- place street road: the user connects two stations in the supply chain with a street. Either a street or a waterway must be placed, the type depends on the player's strategy.
- place waterway: like streets but with higher capacity although slower.
- increase workforce: the user increases the workforce at a factory in the supply chain to speed up the production and decrease the time to fulfil the customers' needs. To successfully master a level this activity should be used.
- sell images: once the user has established a fully functioning supply chain, he is able to sell fabricated products, in this case imagery products. To sell products he must click on an icon to place them in the distribution center (the market). This is a required activity.

Each of these activities or events trigger sending of corresponding xAPI statements which are used by UMAI as input data in order to build the ACT-R agent.

As shown in Fig. 5 the dynamic modelling is based on a file generator which makes use of a Python template. From this template a simulation script is generated and run to calculate and return chunk activation values to an API endpoint. This enables not only reporting use cases but also adaptive tutoring if the activity rates are sent back to a tutoring model.

Figure 9 shows a report of activity rates which was recorded in EXTRA. In this session the player started a level by connecting a factory to a market with a street. This allows to bring products from the factory to the market. In the next step he sold products at the market. In UMAI a chunk in the declarative module is generated for each of the actions, the user has performed. After each iteration the activation level of these chunks is stored. The spikes in the diagram represent an initial performing of an action or a memory retrieval. A good example would be the tracking of the chunk which represents selling of products (bottom green line in Fig. 9). If the threshold would be set to 0.75 the chunk would be forgotten in the simulation and the corresponding production would have been set by the goal buffer as described in Sect. 5.

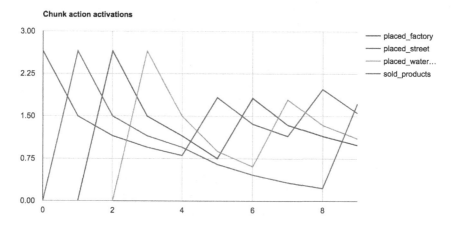

Fig. 9. Chunk activation values for 4 selected activities in the EXTRA game. The bottom green line shows the memory degradation computed by ACT-R for the neglected activity "sell products". In step 7 an adaptive hint was displayed which refreshed the chunk and its activation value.

The implemented architecture has been extended to provide adaptive hints, as shown in Fig. 1. To accomplish this, the tutoring model was extended to send a request to UMAI after certain events or in a time interval. After every request UMAI will simulate the current session and returns the corresponding activity values. The computation of the simulation in our case took less than one second. Based on thresholding the tutoring model uses these results to offer preemptive hints to support the user.

Although the concept has been applied successfully, the technical study revealed some limitations in respect to the power of the resulting model. As stated, the complex and time-consuming modelling of declarative memory (factual knowledge) or production rules (action knowledge) makes direct application unattractive. Whilst our solution approach addresses this issue by the dynamic generation of procedural rules, real "intelligence" is not obvious. The intelligence lies in the underlying mechanisms of cognitive architecture and its implementation. The presented modelling of "forgetting" by means of ACT-R can, considered on its own, be realized more easily without a cognitive architecture. However, this is only one aspect and ACT-R offers many more features that can be used for adaptivity decision making, such as cognitive load measurement or semantic cognitive association tracking.

7   Conclusion

We developed a concept for data-driven user modeling with the cognitive architecture ACT-R. The concept targets applied research and the direct applicability of cognitive architectures for assistance systems. We make use of triple-structured activity data streams which can be used to track user interaction events.

The research question is how cognitive modeling can contribute to "intelligent user models" and how it can be made operational for adaptivity.

The contribution of this work is a concept for data-driven, cognitive user models for digital learning games by means of dynamic cognitive modelling and its application to adaptivity.

We focus on the cognitive architecture ACT-R and its application for adaptive serious games. A key aspect is the data-driven, dynamic generation of the ACT-R model based on observed user interaction data. The output contains estimated memory or chunk activation levels which an adaptivity system can incorporate in its decision processes, e.g., to find the right point in time to offer context-sensitive recommendations.

The concept has been applied to a turn-based serious game in which an adaptivity component in form of a virtual agent giving hints is controlled by the cognitive model. Although the concept has been applied successfully, the technical study will be developed further to incorporate the full potential of the cognitive architecture.

Future work aims at the application to other serious games and assistance systems. Further research looks at Hierarchical Bayesian Models for cognitive models to estimate latent cognitive variables such as workload, attention, planing, perceived difficulty or forgetfulness.

Acknowledgments. The underlying project to this article is funded by the Federal Office of Bundeswehr Equipment, Information Technology and In-Service Support under promotional references.

References

1. ADL.net: Experience API (xAPI) specification 1.0.3. https://github.com/adlnet/xAPI-Spec/blob/xAPI-1.0.3/xAPI-Data.md. publisher: ADL
2. Aleven, V., McLaren, B.M., Sewall, J., Koedinger, K.R.: The cognitive tutor authoring tools (CTAT): preliminary evaluation of efficiency gains. In: Ikeda, M., Ashley, K.D., Chan, T.-W. (eds.) ITS 2006. LNCS, vol. 4053, pp. 61–70. Springer, Heidelberg (2006). https://doi.org/10.1007/11774303_7
3. Amant, R., Ritter, F.: Automated GOMS-to-ACT-r model generation. In: Proceedings of the 6. ICCM, Mahway, NJ:. p. 6 (2004)
4. Anderson, J., Christian, L., Taatgen, N., Sun, R.: Modeling Paradigms in ACT-r. In: Cognition and Multi-Agent Interaction: From Cognitive Modeling to Social Simulation, pp. 29–52. Cambridge University Press, Cambridge (2006)
5. Anderson, J.R., Gluck, K.: What Role do Cognitive Architectures Play in Intelligent Tutoring Systems. Cognition & Instruction: Twenty-five years of progress, pp. 227–262. Lawrence Erlbaum Associates, Inc., New Jersey (2001)

6. Asselman, A., Aammou, S., Nasseh, A.E.: Comparative study of cognitive architectures. Int. Res. J. Comput. Sci. (IRJCS) **9**(2), 8–13 (2015)
7. Best, B.J., Lebiere, C., Scarpinatto, K.C.: Modeling synthetic opponents in MOUT training simulations using the ACT-R cognitive architecture. In: Proceedings of the 11th Computer Generated Forces Conference, pp. 2–56, 505–516 (2002)
8. Bowe, M.: Tin Can vs. Activity Streams (2013). https://tincanapi.com/tin-can-vs-activity-streams/
9. Brusilovsky, P., Millán, E.: User models for adaptive hypermedia and adaptive educational systems. In: Brusilovsky, P., Kobsa, A., Nejdl, W. (eds.) The Adaptive Web. LNCS, vol. 4321, pp. 3–53. Springer, Heidelberg (2007). https://doi.org/10.1007/978-3-540-72079-9_1
10. Dörner, R., Göbel, S., Effelsberg, W., Wiemeyer, J. (eds.): Serious Games. Springer, Cham (2016). https://doi.org/10.1007/978-3-319-40612-1
11. Gentile, M., Città, G., Lieto, A., Allegra, M.: Some notes on the possibile role of cognitive architectures in serious games. In: Liapis, A., Yannakakis, G.N., Gentile, M., Ninaus, M. (eds.) GALA 2019. LNCS, vol. 11899, pp. 231–241. Springer, Cham (2019). https://doi.org/10.1007/978-3-030-34350-7_23
12. Gudivada, V.N.: Cognitive computing: Concepts, architectures, systems, and applications. In: Gudivada, V.N., Raghavan, V.V., Govindaraju, V., Rao, C.R. (eds.) Handbook of Statistics, Cognitive Computing: Theory and Applications, vol. 35, pp. 3–38. Elsevier (2016). https://doi.org/10.1016/bs.host.2016.07.004
13. Kiili, K., de Freitas, S., Arnab, S., Lainema, T.: The design principles for flow experience in educational games. Procedia Comput. Sci. **15**, 78–91 (2012). https://doi.org/10.1016/j.procs.2012.10.060
14. Kotseruba, I., Tsotsos, J.K.: 40 years of cognitive architectures: Core cognitive abilities and practical applications. Artif. Intell. Rev. (2018). https://doi.org/10.1007/s10462-018-9646-y
15. Laird, J.E., et al.: SOAR: An architecture for general intelligence. Artif. Intell. **33**, 1–64 (1987) https://doi.org/10.1016/0004-3702(87)90050-6
16. Ma, W., Adesope, O.O., Nesbit, J.C., Liu, Q.: Intelligent tutoring systems and learning outcomes: a meta-analysis. J. Educ. Psychol. **106**(4), 901–918 (2014). https://doi.org/10.1037/a0037123
17. Mills, C., Dalgarno, B.: A conceptual model for game based intelligent tutoring systems. In: Proceedings of ASCILITE - Australian Society for Computers in Learning in Tertiary Education Annual Conference 2007, pp. 692–702. Australasian Society for Computers in Learning in Tertiary Education (2007)
18. Prensky, M.: Digital game-based learning. Comput. Entertainment (CIE) **1**(1), p. 21 (2003). https://doi.org/10.1145/950566.950596
19. Russell, S.J., Norvig, P.: Artificial Intelligence: A Modern Approach (3rd Edition). Prentice Hall (2009)
20. Salvucci, D.D., Lee, F.J.: Simple cognitive modeling in a complex cognitive architecture. In: Proceedings of the conference on Human factors in computing systems, CHI 2003, p. 265. ACM Press (2003). https://doi.org/10.1145/642611.642658
21. Serrano-Laguna, A., Martínez-Ortiz, I., Haag, J., Regan, D., Johnson, A., Fernández-Manjón, B.: Applying standards to systematize learning analytics in serious games. Comput. Stand. Interfaces **50**, 116–123 (2017)
22. Shute, V., Zapata-Rivera, D.: Adaptive educational systems. Adapt. Technol. Training Educ. **7**(1), 1–35 (2012). https://doi.org/10.1017/CBO9781139049580.004
23. Snell, J., Prodromou, E.: Activity streams 2.0 (2017). https://www.w3.org/TR/2017/REC-activitystreams-core-20170523/

24. Streicher, A., Roller, W.: Interoperable adaptivity and learning analytics for serious games in image interpretation. In: Lavoué, É., Drachsler, H., Verbert, K., Broisin, J., Pérez-Sanagustín, M. (eds.) EC-TEL 2017. LNCS, vol. 10474, pp. 598–601. Springer, Cham (2017). https://doi.org/10.1007/978-3-319-66610-5_71

25. Streicher, A., Szentes, D., Gundermann, A.: Game-based training for complex multi-institutional exercises of joint forces. In: Verbert, K., Sharples, M., Klobučar, T. (eds.) EC-TEL 2016. LNCS, vol. 9891, pp. 497–502. Springer, Cham (2016). https://doi.org/10.1007/978-3-319-45153-4_49

26. Taatgen, N., Anderson, J.R.: The past, present, and future of cognitive architectures. Topics Cogn. Sci. **2**(4), 693–704 (2010). https://doi.org/10.1111/j.1756-8765.2009.01063.x

27. Thórisson, K., Helgasson, H.: Cognitive architectures and autonomy: a comparative review. J. Artif. Gen. Intell. **3**(2), 1–30 (2012)

28. Van Eck, R.: Building artificially intelligent learning games. In: Gibson, D., Aldrich, C., Prensky, M. (eds.) Games and Simulations in Online Learning: Research and Development Frameworks, pp. 271–307. IGI Global (2007). https://doi.org/10.4018/978-1-59904-304-3.ch014

29. Woolf, B.P.: Building Intelligent Interactive Tutors. Morgan Kaufmann, Burlington (2009)

30. Wray, R.E., Woods, A.: A cognitive systems approach to tailoring learner practice. In: Proceedings of the Second Annual Conference on Advances in Cognitive Systems ACS, vol. 21, p. 18 (2013)

31. Yannakakis, G.N.: Game AI revisited. In: Proceedings of the 9th Conference on Computing Frontiers, CF 2012, p. 285. ACM Press, Cagliari, Italy (2012). https://doi.org/10.1145/2212908.2212954

Staying Ahead of the Curve: Selecting Students for Newly Arising Tasks

Armon Toubman$^{(\boxtimes)}$ ⓘ, Maxim van Oldenbeek, and Olivier Claessen

Royal Netherlands Aerospace Centre NLR, Anthony Fokkerweg 2, 1059 CM
Amsterdam, The Netherlands
{Armon.Toubman,Maxim.van.Oldenbeek,Olivier.Claessen}@nlr.nl

Abstract. Adaptive instructional systems (AISs) usually involve some form of task selection. By selecting certain tasks for a student, the AIS aims to improve the student's skills and performance. In this paper, we explore the opposite of this concept, namely *student selection*: given (a) the past performance of a set of students on a set of tasks, and (b) a newly arising (and perhaps previously unseen) task, we aim to select the student that is expected to reach the best performance on this task. We investigate three methods for selecting students: (1) matrix factorization and (2) a neighborhood model, both collaborative filtering methods commonly found in recommender systems, and (3) random forest regression, a content-based filtering method that aims to predict the exact score of a given student on a certain task. For a proof-of-concept, we construct a data set of the performance data of various machine learning algorithms (i.e., virtual students) on a set of video games (i.e., virtual tasks), and apply the three methods to this data set. We present the results of the application, and then conclude the paper by discussing the potential and the limitations of our research.

Keywords: Adaptive instructional systems · Recommender systems · Prediction

1 Introduction

In high-pressure, time-critical situations, new tasks may arise that must be dealt with appropriately and in a timely manner. In the future, this may involve quickly selecting a student (whether a person or an algorithm) to learn to master the task at hand and present a solution. Having an early indication of which student will produce the most optimal learning curve on a particular task may decrease the time needed for experimentation, and thereby increase the rate by which real-world problems are solved successfully. The indication may be provided by an adaptive instructional system (AIS). However, whereas an AIS usually performs *task selection* (i.e., selecting the next task for a student, in order for the student to learn from the task), here we consider the opposite, namely *student selection*: given (a) the past performance of a set of students on a set of tasks, and (b) a newly arising (and perhaps previously unseen) task, we aim to select the student that is expected to reach the best performance on this task.

For instance, consider a small population of human settlers on Mars. The settlers have limited physical resources available, and also limited expertise shared between the

© Springer Nature Switzerland AG 2021
R. A. Sottilare and J. Schwarz (Eds.): HCII 2021, LNCS 12793, pp. 185–198, 2021.
https://doi.org/10.1007/978-3-030-77873-6_13

settlers. However, they have brought vast knowledge bases complete with study materials with them to Mars. The unknown environment may pose novel problems to the settlers, and formulating solutions to the problems may require the settlers to quickly develop new skills. Given a novel time-critical problem, out of the available settlers, who can be expected to learn the required skills the fastest, and to develop the solution? In such a situation, a traditional AIS would offer adaptive instruction to each individual student, in a student-centric manner (cf. [1]). By contrast, in this paper, we envision a system that uses the combined past performance of all potential students to select a student for the task at hand.

We approach student selection as described above as a recommendation problem. The main idea behind this paper is that a recommender system may be able to propose a suitable student for a newly arising task, based on historical data on similar tasks performed by similar students. In the remainder of the paper, we investigate the construction of such a system. The two contributions of the paper are the following.

1. For a proof-of-concept, we construct a data set consisting of task performance data (see Sect. 2). The data is generated by applying machine learning algorithms to a selection of Atari 2600 video games. We add features to the data set by labelling the tasks (based on the game elements that have to be learned to perform the tasks successfully).
2. We select three techniques to build a recommender system upon the data set (see Sect. 3), namely matrix factorization, a neighborhood model, and random forest regression, and apply the techniques to the data set (see Sect. 4). The results show that the three techniques provide better-than-random recommendations (see Sect. 5). However, since the results are highly task-specific, it is challenging to generalize the results (see Sect. 6). We conclude the paper by discussing what the results mean with regard to human students and real-world tasks.

2 Constructing a Data Set

For our proof-of-concept of a recommender system for student selection, we construct a synthetic data set. The data set consists of performance measurements that are generated by machine learning algorithms that learn to perform virtual tasks. Ideally, we would prove the concept with a data set consisting of learning curves produced by human students on actual tasks. Such a data set would reflect real-world conditions, but would therefore also be quite costly to create. However, we see added value in the use of the synthetic data set as well, as the use of a recommender system on the data set may provide insight into the selection of algorithms to perform particular tasks. The synthetic data set thus serves two purposes. First, we use the data set as a stand-in for a data set of the learning curves of human students. Second, we use the data set to study the differences in the performance of machine learning algorithms on the same tasks.

In the remainder of the section, we describe the machine learning algorithms that act as our students (see Sect. 2.1), and the tasks that the students learn to perform (see Sect. 2.2). Next, we discuss our method of generating data (see Sect. 2.3), and our method of enriching the data set by labelling the students and the tasks (see Sect. 2.4).

2.1 The Students

In our data set, the students are four different machine learning algorithms, each used with four different parameter configurations (see below). Thus, 16 different students were used in total. However, machine learning is a broad research field that provides many different learning algorithms. Therefore, below, we first introduce the specific algorithms that were used.

The subfield of machine learning called reinforcement learning concerns itself with algorithms that enable software agents to learn the behavior that is required to perform particular tasks. The general goal of any reinforcement learning algorithm is to find a policy for an agent that leads to desirable behavior in some environment. The agent *observes* the state of the environment, and based on its policy decides what *action* to take given its observations. Feedback from the environment tells the agent how desirable that agent's actions are. However, the agent might not immediately receive feedback on whether its actions were desirable. This is usually decided when a particular task is completely solved (or failed), e.g., whether a game is won or lost. As a result, it usually takes many tries before the agent behaves in a desirable manner. The feedback to the agent is used by the reinforcement learning algorithm to refine the agent's policy, thereby gradually steering the agent towards producing more desirable behavior.

A particular class of reinforcement learning algorithms are the *deep* reinforcement learning algorithms. This class of algorithms constructs neural networks to use as the policy of agents. The neural networks take as input image data (e.g., a still frame of a video game), or other data vectors, and produce as output a singular action. Deep reinforcement learning algorithms are able to automatically detect which features are important in the data, which makes it relatively straightforward to apply the same algorithms to various virtual tasks, as limited to no feature engineering is required.

As the basis for our students, we have selected four deep reinforcement learning algorithms. The four algorithms are as follows.

1. PPO1, the first version of Proximate Policy Optimization;
2. PPO2, the second version of Proximate Policy Optimization;
3. ACER, Actor Critic with Experience Replay;
4. A2C, the synchronous and deterministic version of the Asynchronous Advantage Actor Critic (A3C).

The implementations of the algorithms were provided by the *Stable Baselines* library [2] for the Python programming language. This library offers many more reinforcement learning algorithms. We selected the four algorithms for their technical compatibility with our tasks (see Sect. 2.2).

The four algorithms share three hyperparameters (namely, the learning rate, the entropy, and the discount), which are parameters that control the entire learning process. A specific instantiation of a machine learning algorithm is thus defined by the algorithm that is used, together with the hyperparameters that are set. However, since the data set that is constructed here is intended as a sample of the performance of each of the algorithms, it is important that we refrain from tuning the hyperparameters to a specific task in advance. Rather, to enlarge our sample, we create four separate hyperparameter configurations to use with each algorithm. Table 1 shows the four configurations. Each of the four algorithms set up with one of the four configurations thus constitutes one student. For completeness, Table 2 shows the resulting 16 students.

Table 1. The four hyperparameter configurations.

Configuration	Learning rate	Entropy	Discount
C0	.0001	.01	.99
C1	.0001	.05	.99
C2	.0007	.01	.99
C3	.0001	.01	.95

Table 2. An algorithm paired with a hyperparameter configuration constitutes a student. In total, we have 16 students.

Algorithm	C0	C1	C2	C3
PPO1	PPO1, C0	PPO1, C1	PPO1, C2	PPO1, C3
PPO2	PPO2, C0	PPO2, C1	PPO2, C2	PPO2, C3
ACER	ACER, C0	ACER, C1	ACER, C2	ACER, C3
A2C	A2C, C0	A2C, C1	A2C, C2	A2C, C3

2.2 The Tasks

We use a subset of the Atari 2600 video games as our tasks. The Atari games have been a popular machine learning task since 2013 (cf. [3–5]), and have since been published by OpenAI Gym [6] for research purposes. The game mechanics and the graphics of the game are relatively simple compared to modern standards, while the games still require various competencies to complete. The limited complexity has made the games the preferred benchmark tasks for deep reinforcement learning algorithms, which use either (a) the pixels of the game screen or (b) the RAM state of the emulated Atari computer to determine the game state.

We have selected 11 games to use in our research. The 11 games are listed in Table 3. Our selection is based on the relative difficulty of each game, so that games that are both easy and difficult to learn by machine learning are represented in our data set. Table 3 also shows for each game the average score obtained by human players, and the score obtained by an agent that performs random actions [5].

2.3 Data Generation

Each of the students (see Sect. 2.1) learns to perform each of the tasks (see Sect. 2.2) for two million frames (viz., each algorithm receives as input the information of two

Table 3. The selected Atari games, along with the average human score and the score obtained by a randomly playing agent (both scores from [5]).

Game	Average human score	Random score
Alien	7127.70	227.80
Asterix	8503.30	210.00
BattleZone	37187.50	2360.00
Bowling	160.70	23.10
Boxing	12.10	0.10
Breakout	30.50	1.70
Enduro	860.50	0.00
MsPacman	6951.60	307.30
Pong	14.60	−20.70
Seaquest	42054.70	68.40
SpaceInvaders	1668.70	148.00

million game states, determines an action per game state, and receives feedback for the action). The algorithms are evaluated after learning by performing each complete game 10 times and taking the average score.

Next, because each game uses a different method of scoring, the scores are normalized. The different scorekeeping methods of different games mean that the scores on that the scores that an agent achieves on two games are inherently incomparable. For example, in Pong the standard method of play is "first to 21", with a score of +1 when the player scores a point, and a score of −1 when the opponent scores a point. The total score for a game of *Pong* thus lies in the range $[-21,21]$. In Space Invaders the scores are calculated differently. Here, the player receives points for each ship that the player destroys. The total score of a game of *Space Invaders* thus lies in a totally different range than that of Pong. So, to be able to compare the different game we need to normalize the scores between the different games. We do so by calculating the human normalized score (HNS). In the reinforcement learning literature the performance of the agent is compared against the random and human performance, and is then scaled accordingly. The HNS is calculated as shown in Eq. 1. An HNS of 0 means that the algorithm performs randomly, and a score of higher than 1 means the algorithm performs above human level.

$$HNS(s) = \frac{s - s_{rand}}{s_{human} - s_{rand}} \tag{1}$$

The HNSs achieved by the students on the tasks are shown in Table 4. Due to computational issues, not all of the tasks were completed by the students. However, since our student selection methods (see Sect. 3) are based on recommender systems that often deal with incomplete data, the gaps in our data should not affect our analyses.

Table 4. The human normalized score of each student on each task.

Student	Alien	Asterix	BattleZone	Bowling	Boxing	Breakout	Enduro	MsPacman	Pong	Seaquest	SpaceInvaders
PPO1, C0	.018	−.001	.028	.246	.125	.366	.052	−.017	.564	.003	.038
PPO1, C1	.005	.052	.018	.254		.392	.589	.005	.014	.004	.069
PPO1, C2	−.003	.014	−.068	.450	.067			.004		.004	.089
PPO1, C3			.093		−.125			−.020		−.001	.127
PPO2, C0	.065	.047	.047	.217	.121	.182	.152	.045	.515	.007	.125
PPO2, C1	.042	.043	.326	.230		.201		.040	.105		.154
PPO2, C2	.022	.030	.176	.272	−.292			.039		.004	.094
PPO2, C3					−.083			.007		.006	.059
ACER, C0	.067	.093	.015	.055	.092	.223	0	.065	.353	.004	.124
ACER, C1	.016	.078	.155	.064	−.017	.271	0	.063	.365	.003	.080
ACER, C2	.060	.016	.061	.020	.017			.085		.005	.108
ACER, C3					−.033			.083		.005	.129
A2C, C0	.095	.548	.525	.313	.250	.444	0	.292	.839	.049	.250
A2C, C1	.320	.572	.531	.329			0	.279			.179
A2C, C2	.175	.244	.532	.547	.625			.284		.036	.160
A2C, C3								.194			.171

2.4 Labelling the Students and Tasks

So far, the data set consists of the scores achieved by the reinforcement learning algorithms on the Atari games. Although a recommender system can certainly provide recommendations using only this data, we may be able to obtain better recommendations by providing more context on the data. A straightforward manner of enriching the data set is to label the students and the tasks with their properties.

Compare our proposed recommender system with e.g., a film recommender system as described by Bennett & Lanning [7] and by Goel [8]. The data set for such a system would contain flags indicating whether a certain user has viewed a certain film (or perhaps even contain a rating of the film by the user). However, what enables the system to provide accurate recommendations is the labelling of the users and the films. The users might be labelled with their demographics and viewing behavior, whereas the films are likely labelled with their genres. Essentially, the more features available in the data set, the more intersections the recommender system can find between the existing data points and a newly presented data point for which a recommendation should be made.

Labels for the Students. After analysis of the deep learning algorithms, we deemed the differences between the students too abstract to create meaningful labels. Therefore, we did not label the students, and focused on labelling the tasks.

Labels for the Tasks. We formulated 34 labels for the tasks. the labels and the label assignments are shown in Table 5. The labels were developed manually, by referencing the player manual [9] of each game, and noting (a) distinctive game elements and (b) game rules that were mentioned.

3   Student Selection Methods

In this section, we describe the three methods we used to build the student selection system upon the data set described in Sect. 2. The methods can be divided into two categories, which we explain discuss below.

First, we consider two *collaborative filtering* methods. These methods are widely used in recommender systems. The collaborative filtering methods used in this paper are *matrix factorization* (Sect. 3.1) and a *neighborhood model* (Sect. 3.2).

The student selection problem discussed in this paper has parallels to the prediction of the rating of a user on some item (e.g., a movie rating), for which recommender systems have been developed. To align our terminology with the recommender system literature, in the remainder of this section we will discuss users that rate items, which in our case refer to algorithms that reach scores on games. The data can be represented in a rating matrix. This is a matrix, $R \in \mathbb{R}^{d_u \times d_i}$, that has a row per user and a column per item. The entries are the ratings of the user on the items. Collaborative filtering algorithms try to find new recommendations based on ratings of similar users. The underlying idea of these methods is that they only use the user-item interaction, such as ratings [10]. Often, the rating matrix is sparse with a long-tailed distribution, which are difficult properties for collaborative filtering methods. Since our data set is relatively small and evenly distributed over the algorithms and games, we do not expect data sparsity to play a role in our research.

Second, we consider a content-based filtering method, namely a random forest regressor (see Sect. 3.3). Content-based filtering uses property descriptions (in the form of a feature vector) of items and users in order to predict whether a user will give an item a high or low rating.

Finally, we compare the results of the three methods to the results of two simple recommenders based on the mean and median scores found in the data set (Sect. 3.4), which provide us with baseline performance measurements.

3.1 Matrix Factorization

Matrix factorization is a family of linear algebra methods. In our research, we use the singular value decomposition (SVD) variant as described by Aggarwal [10]. Consider the rating matrix R, where some of the entries are empty. Predicting new ratings can be seen as a matrix completion problem, viz. the problem of finding the right rating that will complete the matrix. Matrix factorization aims to solve the matrix completion problem by approaching it as a factorization problem.

Matrix factorization assumes that there are latent variables that explain the behavior of users. Intuitively, this method finds an embedding of users, p_u, and items, q_i, so that the inner product gives the rating. For added expressivity, we add biases to the model, items, and users. The predicted rating would then become as shown in Eq. 2.

$$\hat{r}_{ui} = b_{ui} + p_u^T q_i. \tag{2}$$

Here, $b_{ui} = \mu + b_i + b_u$ is the sum of the bias of the model, item and user.

The goal becomes to find the best biases and embeddings for the user and the items. This can be solved using a stochastic gradient descent approach. With this approach one tries to minimize the mean squared error between the known entries and the predictions over the training set D, as shown in Eq. 3.

$$L(D) = \frac{1}{|D|} \sum_{\{(i,j) \in D\}} \left(r_{ij} - \hat{r}_{ij} \right)^2 \tag{3}$$

Since the minimization of the mean squared error is a convex problem, it will converge to the global minimum (cf. [11]).

In the implementation of the matrix factorization model, whenever the model has to predict a rating for user u and item i, and it previously did not know of the existence of i, it will return $\mu + b_u$ as a prediction. The model will always give a prediction, even if the training data does not contain any relevant items.

3.2 Neighborhood Model

We use a generic neighborhood model. The formulas below are adapted from Aggarwal [10]. Like matrix factorization, the neighborhood model also takes the rating matrix into account. However, unlike matrix factorization, the neighborhood model gives a

Table 5. Each task is labelled based on distinctive game elements and game rules.

Label	Alien	Asterix	BattleZone	Bowling	Boxing	Breakout	Enduro	MsPacman	Pong	Seaquest	SpaceInvaders
1-D navigation				1		1				1	
2-D navigation	1	1	1		1		1	1	1		1
Enemies move in 1-D		1						1		1	
Enemies move in 2-D	1		1						1		1
3-D perspective			1								
Additional world view			1								
Enemies move predictably		1	1				1	1			1
Enemies move unpredictably									1	1	
Dynamic background			1								
First person view			1								
Friendly fire among enemies			1								
Physics				1		1					
Non-grid navigation			1								
Evade objects							1	1			
Collect non-moving objects	1	1							1		
Collect moving objects											1
Destroy objects				1		1					
Evade projectiles			1								1
Aiming				1						1	1
Tank-like navigation			1								
Time-bound navigation	1						1				
Hitting enemies (shooting)			1	1							1
Static background	1	1		1	1	1	1	1	1		1
Colliding with enemies	1								1		
Disarming enemies							1				
Evading enemies					1			1	1		
Hitting enemies (melee)					1						
Destroying enemies											1
Destroy objects for points				1	1	1					
Collect non-moving objects for points	1	1								1	
Collect moving objects for points											1
Destroy enemies for points			1							1	1
Complete levels for points							1	1	1		
Opponent blocks scoring										1	

prediction based on user (or item) similarities. The calculation of the similarity of two users u, v is shown in Eq. 4.

$$sim(u, v) = \frac{\sum_{i \in I_u \cap I_v}(r_v - \mu_v)(r_u - \mu_u)}{\sqrt{\sum_{i \in I_v \cap I_u}(r_u - \mu_u)^2}\sqrt{\sum_{i \in I_v \cap I_u}(r_v - \mu_v)^2}} \tag{4}$$

In Eq. 4, I_u are the items rated by user u, and the cosine similarity is calculated on the rated items that user u and v have in common. If the union is the empty set, then the similarity is not defined. In that case, the rating for an item i can be calculated as shown in Eq. 5.

$$\hat{r}_{vi} = \frac{\sum_{u \in P_v(i)} sim(u, v)(r_{ui} - \mu_u)}{\sum_{u \in P_v(i)} |sim(u, v)|} + \mu_v \tag{5}$$

The neighborhood model takes a weighted average of the ratings of the users that are similar to the user v and that have rated item i. The set $P_v(i)$ contains these similar users. A disadvantage of the neighborhood model is that it might be possible that the rating cannot be predicted. This occurs when the union is always empty.

3.3 Random Forest Regression

A random forest is a collection of decision trees trained on a random subset of features in the data (cf. [12, 13]). The decision trees each vote on the outcome and the mean of the outcome is returned as the prediction of the random forest. Because of their effectiveness, random forests have become a popular regression technique (see, e.g., [14]). A well-known drawback of decision trees is that they tend to overfit on the training data, especially when there is no limit on the tree depth yielding a high variance. This tendency can be reduced by bootstrap aggregating, also called bagging [15], thus increasing the accuracy of the prediction. Bagging is a sampling method whereby a random subset of the training data is sampled with replacement. Like the deep reinforcement learning algorithms used as students (see Sect. 2.1), random forests have a number of hyperparameters that can be tuned in order to observe the effect on the predictions and evaluation metrics. These hyperparameters include, e.g., the number of trees that is generated, the maximum depth of each tree, and the cost criterion. For our research, we generated a random forest using the *scikit-learn* library for Python [16], with 100 trees, no maximum tree depth, and the mean squared error as the cost criterion.

3.4 Baseline Recommenders

In order to establish a baseline for the performance of our student selection methods, we construct two baseline recommenders. The first baseline recommender uses the data set to calculate the mean score, and then always predicts the score on a given task to be that mean score. The second baseline recommender functions in a similar manner, but uses the median score instead.

4   Method

The student selection methods (see Sect. 3) were applied to build models upon the data set (see Sect. 2) by means of repeated k-fold cross-validation. Cross-validation entails splitting the data into equally sized splits. One of the splits becomes the validation set, whereas the remaining splits together become the training set. This allows training and validating each model multiple times, using different samples from a single data set. Repeatedly splitting, training, and validating models gives a better estimate of the performance of each method in comparison to one-shot training and validation (see, e.g., [17]).

In our experiment we consider two different ways of splitting the data set: (1) a global split and (2) an item split. The split affects the amount of data that each student selection method may use to base their score predictions on, and thus influences the selection of students. We briefly explain the two splits below.

The global split divides the elements of the data set into a training set and a test set, regardless of the columns and rows. This corresponds to a scenario in which there is a lack of skill in an already known task, and we want to find a student who might fulfil this task. The item split aggregates the data per column (i.e., per task), so that the columns are divided into a training set and a test set. This corresponds to having completely new, previously unseen tasks for which we need to find a suitable student.

The item split presents a problem for collaborative filtering methods (viz. matrix factorization and the neighborhood model), since they are unable to relate *completely unseen* tasks (i.e., when an item does not occur in the training set), to known tasks. For recommender systems, this problem is known as the *cold start problem* (cf. [18]). In these cases, we used the labels presented in Sect. 2.4 to compute a cosine similarity. This allows us to select items in the training set that are most similar to the newly presented item. From these similar items we can make a prediction, namely a weighted average of the predictions of the similar items.

Since our dataset is relatively small we can permit ourselves to do many repeats. Therefore, we performed 5 splits and 10 repeats for the cross-validation. As the performance metrics for the student selection methods, we use the root mean squared error (RMSE), and the mean absolute error (MAE). Here, the RMSE is the standard deviation of the prediction errors. The MAE indicates the absolute difference between predictions and the true values.

5   Results

In this section, we present the results of training and validating the models using the global split (see Sect. 5.1) and using the item split (see Sect. 5.2).

5.1   Global Split Results

The results of the global split are shown in Table 6. The three methods of interest (matrix factorization, the neighborhood model, and the random forest) all perform significantly better ($p < 0.01$) than the two baseline recommenders, on both performance metrics. The random forest shows the lowest error rates overall.

5.2   Item Split Results

The results of the item split are shown in Table 7. None of the three methods of interest (matrix factorization, the neighborhood model, and the random forest) perform better than the two baseline recommenders, on either performance metric.

Table 6. Global split results.

Method	RMSE		MAE	
	μ	σ	μ	σ
Matrix factorization	.155	.029	.111	.019
Neighborhood model	.148	.032	.105	.022
Random forest	.134	.031	.087	.020
Baseline (mean)	.180	.034	.141	.023
Baseline (median)	.191	.040	.130	.026

Table 7. Item split results.

Method	RMSE		MAE	
	μ	σ	μ	σ
Matrix factorization	.184	.051	.147	.039
Neighborhood model	.189	.051	.148	.041
Random forest	.181	.047	.142	.038
Baseline (mean)	.187	.054	.151	.041
Baseline (median)	.196	.066	.142	.052

6   Discussion and Related Work

The results presented in Sect. 5 show the methods that we have selected (matrix factorization, a neighborhood model, and random forest regression) provide us with favorable predictions of the scores achieved by students on tasks, compared to simple mean- and median-based recommenders (see Table 6). Based on the results, we may conclude that it is possible to make somewhat informed decisions regarding the selection of students for upcoming tasks, in the case of the global split of the data. However, there is great difficulty in selecting students for tasks that bear no resemblance at all to the tasks that are known (see Table 7), and upon which the decisions thus must be based (viz. the cold start problem). Our effort to remediate this problem in the collaborative filtering methods, using the cosine similarity of tasks (see Sect. 4), was unsuccessful. However, it is encouraging to see the content-based filtering method (viz. the random forest) outperform the collaborative filtering methods (viz. matrix factorization and the neighborhood model) without special optimizations. Still, without a "gold standard" benchmark, the interpretation of the improvement remains open.

In related work, Sweeney, Lester, Rangwala & Johri framed the problem of score prediction in the context of student retention [19]. The successful prediction of student scores may enable timely interventions in course-following behavior, and thereby improve the retention of students. Like us, Sweeney et al. employed both a matrix factorization variant (in their case, factorization machines [20]) and a random forest. For their study, they also developed a hybrid model that was able to overcome the cold start problem, and provide the best overall result in their experiments. Applying this hybrid model to our data set presents an interesting avenue for future work.

A second topic for future work may be the inclusion of learning curves in the data set. Intermediate testing of the students on the task provides data points by which a learning curve can be constructed for each student. In our research, during the learning processes of the algorithms, we stored a "snapshot" of each model after every 500.000 frames. By applying the snapshot models to the tasks, we are able to review and measure the performance of the models at set points during the learning process, thereby forming rough learning curves. The shape of the learning curve may then provide us with additional features on which the prediction of the final performance can be based. The ability to store these snapshots is one of the benefits of working with machine learning algorithms in the study of instructional systems. However, the most interesting case remains to be the prediction of the performance of human students, as there is still much to discover about the learning process of humans.

Working with human data exposes us to two interesting properties of human learning, namely (a) skill transfer (cf. [21]) and (b) the retention of skills (cf. [22]). Skill transfer entails the application of skills learned previously for one task, to another, related task. In other words, in contrast to the machine learning algorithms used as students in this paper, a human student builds up a history of learned tasks, and is able to identify relations between the tasks. However, this brings along with it the factor of skill retention, which is the problem of "keeping up" various skills. Therefore, we will next investigate the possibility of applying our methods to publicly available human performance data, e.g., massive open online course (MOOC) data sets (see, e.g., [23]).

References

1. Roessingh, J.J., Poppinga, G., van Oijen, J., Toubman, A.: Application of artificial intelligence to adaptive instruction - combining the concepts. In: Sottilare, R.A., Schwarz, J. (eds.) HCII 2019. LNCS, vol. 11597, pp. 542–556. Springer, Cham (2019). https://doi.org/10.1007/978-3-030-22341-0_43
2. Hill, A., et al.: Stable Baselines. GitHub (2018)
3. Mnih, V., et al.: Playing Atari with Deep Reinforcement Learning. arXiv:1312.5602 [cs]. (2013)
4. Fedus, W., Ghosh, D., Martin, J.D., Bellemare, M.G., Bengio, Y., Larochelle, H.: On Catastrophic Interference in Atari 2600 Games. arXiv:2002.12499 [cs, stat] (2020)

5. Badia, A.P., et al.: Agent57: outperforming the atari human benchmark. In: III, H.D., Singh, A. (eds.) Proceedings of the 37th International Conference on Machine Learning, pp. 507–517. PMLR (2020)
6. Brockman, G., et al.: OpenAI Gym. arXiv:1606.01540 [cs] (2016)
7. Bennett, J., Lanning, S., Netflix, N.: The Netflix prize. In: In KDD Cup and Workshop in conjunction with KDD (2007)
8. Goel, H., Melnyk, I., Banerjee, A.: R2N2: Residual Recurrent Neural Networks for Multivariate Time Series Forecasting. arXiv:1709.03159 [cs, stat] (2017)
9. AtariAge - Atari 2600 Manuals. https://www.atariage.com/system_items.php?SystemID=2600&itemTypeID=MANUAL. Accessed 25 Jan 2021
10. Aggarwal, C.C.: Recommender Systems. Springer International Publishing, Cham (2016). https://doi.org/10.1007/978-3-319-29659-3.
11. Mnih, A., Salakhutdinov, R.R.: Probabilistic matrix factorization. Adv. Neural. Inf. Process. Syst. **20**, 1257–1264 (2007)
12. Breiman, L.: Random forests. Mach. Learn. **45**, 5–32 (2001). https://doi.org/10.1023/A:1010933404324
13. Denisko, D., Hoffman, M.M.: Classification and interaction in random forests. PNAS **115**, 1690–1692 (2018). https://doi.org/10.1073/pnas.1800256115
14. Couronné, R., Probst, P., Boulesteix, A.-L.: Random forest versus logistic regression: a large-scale benchmark experiment. BMC Bioinf. **19**, 270 (2018). https://doi.org/10.1186/s12859-018-2264-5
15. Liaw, A., Wiener, M.: Classification and regression by randomForest. R news. **2**(3), 18–22 (2002)
16. Pedregosa, F., et al.: Scikit-learn: machine learning in Python. J. Mach. Learn. Res. **12**, 2825–2830 (2011)
17. Wong, T., Yeh, P.: Reliable accuracy estimates from k-fold cross validation. IEEE Trans. Knowl. Data Eng. **32**, 1586–1594 (2020). https://doi.org/10.1109/TKDE.2019.2912815
18. Wei, J., He, J., Chen, K., Zhou, Y., Tang, Z.: Collaborative filtering and deep learning based recommendation system for cold start items. Expert Syst. Appl. **69**, 29–39 (2017). https://doi.org/10.1016/j.eswa.2016.09.040
19. Sweeney, M., Lester, J., Rangwala, H., Johri, A.: Next-term student performance prediction: a recommender systems approach. J. Educ. Data Mining. **8**, 22–51 (2016). https://doi.org/10.5281/zenodo.3554604
20. Rendle, S.: Factorization Machines with libFM. ACM Trans. Intell. Syst. Technol. **3**, 57:1–57:22 (2012). https://doi.org/10.1145/2168752.2168771.
21. Suzuki, Y., Sunada, M.: Dynamic interplay between practice type and practice schedule in a second language: the potential and limits of skill transfer and practice schedule. Stud. Second. Lang. Acquis. **42**, 169–197 (2020). https://doi.org/10.1017/S0272263119000470
22. van der Pal, J., Toubman, A.: An adaptive instructional system for the retention of complex skills. In: Sottilare, R.A., Schwarz, J. (eds.) HCII 2020. LNCS, vol. 12214, pp. 411–421. Springer, Cham (2020). https://doi.org/10.1007/978-3-030-50788-6_30
23. Lohse, J.J., McManus, C.A., Joyner, D.A.: Surveying the MOOC data set universe. In: 2019 IEEE Learning With MOOCS (LWMOOCS), pp. 159–164 (2019). https://doi.org/10.1109/LWMOOCS47620.2019.8939594.

Designing a Learner Model for Use in Training Analysts in a Social Media Practice Environment

Elizabeth T. Whitaker[1]([⊠]) [iD], Ethan B. Trewhitt[1] [iD], Lauren Massey[2],
Robert Wray[2] [iD], and Laura Hamel[2]

[1] Georgia Tech Research Institute, Atlanta, GA 30332, USA
elizabeth.whitaker@gtri.gatech.edu
[2] Soar Technology, Inc., Ann Arbor, MI 48105, USA

Abstract. This paper describes the characteristics, design and architecture of a learner model, the GTRI Learner Assessment Engine (GLAsE), that is designed to operate within a practice environment for teaching the analysis of social media feeds. The purpose of GLAsE in the practice environment is to provide a state of the learner's competency or proficiency for the information and use by the learner and instructor to guide the learning activities, e.g., the experience of the learner in the practice environment. The Learner Model is represented as a curriculum overlay model with additional annotations and background information. The contents of the Learner Model consist of items represented in the Curriculum Model as learning objectives: Concepts, Skills, and Problem-solving approaches. This Learner Model is called an overlay model because the Learner Model has the same representation as the expert domain knowledge, i.e., the Curriculum Model—it is overlaid on that representation. The Learner Model will provide mastery or proficiency scores for each of the learning objectives that represent the model's best estimate of the state of the learner proficiency for that objective. The learner assessment process will identify and prioritize any concepts in which the learner has deficiency and will, whenever it is appropriate in a learning or practice system, provide information to other system components that could be used to direct the learner to particular activities to help increase proficiency in those concepts. Results of the learner assessment will be used to update the Learner Model.

Keywords: Learner model · Intelligent tutoring · Curriculum model

1 Introduction

The GTRI Learner Assessment Engine, or GLAsE, Learner Model is designed to apply and extend learner modeling methodologies to the specialized needs of supporting a learning system consisting of a practice environment built to support training of analysts in analyzing information from social media data streams. In intelligent tutoring, a learner model is a component of an intelligent tutoring system with the purpose of providing a representation of the state of the learner's competency for information and use by the learner and the instructor for guiding the learning activities and experience of the learner in the practice environment [1]. The GLAsE Learner Model is represented as a

© Springer Nature Switzerland AG 2021
R. A. Sottilare and J. Schwarz (Eds.): HCII 2021, LNCS 12793, pp. 199–208, 2021.
https://doi.org/10.1007/978-3-030-77873-6_14

curriculum overlay model (see Sect. 3.1) with additional annotations and background information. Items in the Learner Model are represented in the Curriculum Model as learning objectives, also called curriculum elements. The contents of the Learner Model include proficiency scores for each of the learning objectives that represent the model's best estimate of the state of the learner competency for that objective. It also includes background information on the learner which is valuable for understanding what learning experiences the user might need, both by a human and by a computer-based tutor.

2   Learner Modeling Background

A learner model overlay representation is an approach to learner modeling in which the student model is built on top of a curriculum model, i.e., using the same representation as the curriculum model [2]. The curriculum is a form of the domain model and is a representation, enumeration, or indexing of the concepts being taught by the learning system. The learner model uses student performance and behaviors in the learning system to provide evidence of mastery levels associated with elements in the curriculum. The mastery levels are increased or decreased, depending on the student's behaviors. This approach uses both the identification of the learner's *missing* information and the identification of the learner's *incorrect* information (bugs) to assess the learner's state of mastery–see [3].

The **Curriculum Model** consists of an explicit representation of the concepts and skills in the domain. In the practice environment for analyzing social media, these concepts and skills are related to recognizing patterns or anomalies in the data, analyzing the situation and drawing conclusions, and they are represented in the curriculum model as curriculum elements. The Curriculum Model will also contain representations of the relationships and interconnections among the concepts and skills. The Curriculum Elements include the concepts that are to be taught or experienced through the student's interaction with the practice environment through experiencing learning activities. The learning activities will be stored as content in the catalog of **Learning Activities** and indexed by the learning concepts, represented as curriculum elements, which are experienced through interaction with each Learning Activity within the practice environment.

2.1   Learner Assessment Characteristics

The Learner Assessment is designed based on a set of desirable characteristics that enable integration with the practice environment functionality. The assessment will be enabled by a mapping of low-level user events or actions to tasks represented by Curriculum Elements. The Learner Assessment will estimate learner ability or proficiency for individual learning objectives based on observations of the user actions while performing the learning tasks.

The system curriculum model represents a hierarchical collection of curriculum elements which describe domain-specific concepts, skills, elements of workflows, and problem-solving approaches. In support of Learner Assessment, the curriculum model will "weight" contributions of sub-skills to skills as defined by experts. The Learner Model **will** maintain an estimate of learner proficiency based on the demonstrated skills of learners, and it will record the assessments that are mapped to identified curriculum elements and compute and update proficiency estimates for the indicated curriculum elements, storing them in the Learner Model.

The Learner Model will support learning by being available to other system components which are responsible for guiding the choices of learning activities, and by being available to the human learner and other users who need to be aware of the proficiency states of the learner. The learner model **will** be able to accept queries for and retrieve a proficiency estimate of a given learner for each leaf node/element in the curriculum model and each higher-level node in the curriculum model.

3 GLAsE Component Overview

GLAsE is integrated with an intelligent learning system that will provide a practice environment to support a learner in analysis and interpretation of an ongoing, evolving situation which includes communications through social media. The learning system includes a **Practice environment** augmented by a set of modular components for facilitating training. The GLAsE components as shown in Fig. 1 interact with this practice environment to update the Learner Model. The **Learner Model** will provide the current state of the learner's domain competency. The **Curriculum Model** represents the concepts, activities, and skills of an expert analyst in this domain.

The **Analysis Products Comparator** provides a mechanism for comparing the user's approach, set of steps, or solution to an expected or expert solution. The **Scoring Mechanism** uses the results of the Analysis Products Comparator to calculate a score to be included in the student model based on how the user's solution matches the expected or expert solution. There is a **Blame Assignment** component which will be used to reason about the student's knowledge based on evaluation of their online activities and comparing them to the **Expert Solution.** We use the term **Learner Model** for the database that provides a snapshot of the learner's competency and **Learner Modeler** for the software module that reasons about the data and updates the **Learner Model.**

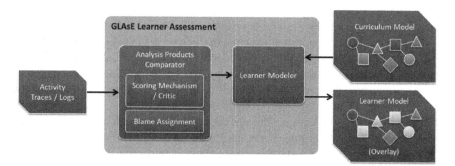

Fig. 1. GLAsE system architecture

3.1   Curriculum Model

The Curriculum Model is an explicit representation of the concepts and skills related to recognizing patterns or anomalies in the data, analyzing the situation and drawing conclusions. It contains representations of the hierarchical relationships among the concepts and skills. This includes the concepts that are to be learned or experienced through the learner's interaction with the practice environment through a set of learning activities, tasks, or games. The learning activities will be stored as content in the **Catalog of Learning Activities** and indexed by the learning concepts which are experienced through interaction with this Learning Activity. Figure 2 shows a set of example curriculum elements associated with a social media analysis scenario.

- Recognizing hidden relationships among actors
- Identifying which actors are pushing deceptive content or influence campaigns
- Understanding how deceptive content is being received
- Understanding how deceptive content is being countered
- Pinpointing where the actors are
- Identifying who is supporting or working against particular actors
- Recognizing what problems this activity poses

Fig. 2. A few curriculum elements for sample social media scenario

The Curriculum Model is built from curriculum elements, where each element is either a topic, concept, or skill. Every curriculum element is indexed with the learning objectives that it supports, and the curriculum elements are hierarchically arranged as a tree structure. The highest level of the hierarchy specifies the type of learning that is taking place when that learning objective is being satisfied. There are four highest level categories of curriculum elements: Analysis Approach, Tool Training, Understand Important Concepts (Concepts), Compound Tasks (Skills). This hierarchical representation is anchored by an abstract root node, with a set of children that represent the high-level topics covered by the entire system. All nodes may have children of their own, which represent the conceptual structure of those other topics/concepts/skills. Each topic/concept/skill contains the following properties: Name, Curriculum element group, Prerequisites (list of other curriculum elements). The system has access to a catalog that has information about the LAs that teach or evaluate each concept. Learning Objectives are organized into a Curriculum Hierarchy (see Fig. 3).

Each of these types of learning has several sub-components and each of those sub-components has a set of sub-objectives until after several levels, every branch of the hierarchy has reached a leaf node. Since we are using an overlay representation of the learner model, the learner model will use this same representation and each node in the learner model will contain a value which represents the proficiency of the student in the curriculum element or learner objective represented by that node.

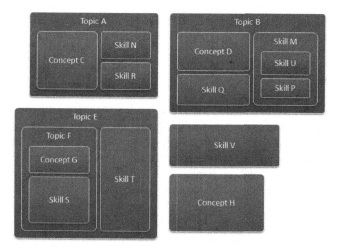

Fig. 3. Curriculum model hierarchy example

3.2 Analysis Products Comparator

The Analysis Products Comparator is a primary enabler of the **Learner Modeler** (the component used to build the Learner Model). It observes learner activity while the learner performs analyses, measuring proficiency in one or more concepts by comparing it to expert-generated analysis products by evaluating characteristics of the product and comparing them to the characteristics of the expert product. Each learning objective that is addressed in the learner's latest activities will be scored on the performance level of the results. Concept proficiency scores will be logged as part of the Learner Model for reading by other components or by humans.

The **Scoring Mechanism** or **Critic** will make use of expert problem-solving knowledge to be used in evaluating the student's performance and identifying the level of mastery exhibited for skills and concepts used in the activities, and will make use of the catalog of evaluation metrics, which is organized by concept. This information will be made available to the **Learner Modeler** and used to update the **Learner Model**.

One enabler of the Analysis Products Comparator is the Blame Assignment attribution mechanism. Its purpose is to identify the source of shortcomings in the user's output or products (the user's solution). It monitors for missing information or buggy information (indexed to curriculum concepts) and identifies steps, or approaches that may be the source of the errors or shortcomings. If there are subcomponents or intermediate products of the learner's output product, this mechanism examines them tow see where the errors may have occurred.

3.3 Learner Modeler

The Learner Modeler is a component responsible for updating the Learner Model in response to new information about the learner's proficiency in one or more curriculum elements. It infers and models the learner's strengths and weaknesses by analysis of logged activities, then updates the *Learner Model* to represent the current state of the learner's knowledge and skills.

4 Proficiency Scoring

The GLAsE Proficiency Calculation is designed to enable the tracking and estimation of the proficiency level for each curriculum element. We have chosen to use five proficiency levels: novice, advanced beginner, competent, proficient, and expert. In order to support this more user-friendly use of qualitative proficiency values, the internal quantitative calculations of proficiency will be transformed and displayed to human users as qualitative values. The proficiency is based on the activities and experiences that the user has had with each curriculum element. The Proficiency Calculation requires that there be an estimate of the space of activities related to the curriculum element. As we build the curriculum we will characterize the space of activities that it takes to learn and show proficiency. This will be part of the indexing of activities and will be used to provide a more detailed mapping from the activities to the curriculum elements. The system will be provided with a number that represents the fraction of each curriculum element that is provided for each activity. The proficiency will be represented across all of the user's interactions with the system, that is, it will include interactions with multiple scenarios, across multiple days, and multiple interaction systems.

In this discussion the term Learning Activity (LA) refers to a simple aggregation or a collection of the most basic commands or actions that represents a meaningful intent or plan of the user. The Learner Assessment for GLAsE will have access to a **Catalog of Concepts** in which students should demonstrate competence/proficiency and a **Catalog of Learning Activities** provide experience which can lead to proficiency. In order to enable the updating of the student model there must be a mapping of which learning activities evaluate which concepts. The LA is associated with a **Fraction of the Curriculum Element** that is experienced in that activity. This provides the capability for the system to require multiple experiences with a particular curriculum element in order to develop total proficiency.

The learner assessment process in GLAsE is based on a set of clearly defined steps. Whenever it is possible to evaluate student proficiency in the concepts being experienced by the student, the proficiency will be evaluated and used to populate and update the Learner Model. This evaluation will identify deficient concepts and prioritize them for suggesting engagement with appropriate Las. When possible, given the constraints of the practice environment, this information should be used to direct the attention of the learner in the practice environment to an LA that provides experience in one or more deficient concepts and adheres to learning activity constraints. After completing an LA, the evaluation metrics will be use to update the Learner Model.

The proficiency algorithm used to evaluate the curriculum element is based on several items. The seed value (the estimated level of proficiency before interaction with the system) is used to initialize the Student Model elements. It is desirable that the proficiency calculation recognizes the recency of the learner's performance, that is, items that the user has performed more recently should be weighted more highly than performance on activities that were performed longer ago. This is based on the assumption that the user has learned, and that more recent activities more accurately reflect what the user knows. The user may have learned or forgotten. The percentage of the space related to a particular curriculum element that has been experienced by the user is used to prorate the proficiency. The proficiency calculation for a given curriculum element folds into previous calculations for that element. The user's proficiency for a curriculum element will reflect the score on each activity in which the user was evaluated for that curriculum element, as shown in Fig. 4.

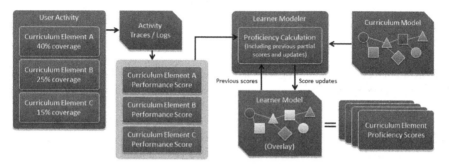

Fig. 4. Cumulative weighted proficiency scoring (CWPS)

In order to set the stage for the proficiency calculations example below, we describe the details of the proficiency algorithm. Proficiency score algorithm for a single leaf-node curriculum element (CE) in the curriculum hierarchy uses an activity-to-curriculum element mapping which uses a percent coverage with a value between 0 and 100. The learner model is initialized with a seed score which has an initial coverage percentage. The most recent 100 points' worth of Curriculum Element coverage are used for evaluation. For each activity, the user's trace score for that activity is scaled by the percentage coverage of that activity. If the oldest included activity exceeds the 100-point recency cutoff, the coverage of that activity *prior to* the cutoff is used to scale the user's score for that activity. If a user has not yet experienced activities totaling 100% coverage, their greatest possible score is the total % coverage so far.

4.1 Proficiency Example

A user has a seed score and has completed 3 activities, but the total % coverage of the seed score and all activities does not yet reach 100%, therefore the user cannot reach a perfect score yet even with perfect trace scores. In the example in Table 1, the user has reached a score of 70.25% out of 80% possible (sum of all seed and activity coverage so far).

This proficiency calculation accounts for the decay of learner information if it is not used over time and the possible need for review or practice. If the user has performed well on a given curriculum element on some activities and then shows lower performance, the most recent scores will take precedent once enough activities have been evaluated. GLAsE Learner Model will collect and represent mis-learnings or bugs that can be used to identify the need for a correction message or example. GLAsE will flag a bug that is

Table 1. Example proficiency score calculation

Activity	Activity coverage	User's trace score	Net effect on CE score (coverage * trace)
Seed	25%	89%	22.25%
Activity 1	10%	60%	6.0%
Activity 2	15%	90%	13.5%
Activity 3	30%	95%	28.5%
User's current CE proficiency score (sum of column):			**70.25% (80.0% possible)**

recognized in a curriculum element. It will lower the proficiency level and add the flag. The user only knows part of the material (proficiency level), but in addition the user can know some things incorrectly (bug).

The hierarchical representation provided for the curriculum allows a read-out of the leaf node concepts as well as a proficiency calculation for the parent nodes, including intermediate nodes. Leaf node proficiency scores are calculated using the algorithm above. Intermediate node scores are the weighted average of direct descendants and so on up the tree.

5 Mapping User Actions to Expert Plans

The Mapping Component needs to map sequences of low-level user events or actions to tasks represented by Curriculum Elements and support a scoring (an evaluation of the action sequence) and an associated coverage percentage for the Curriculum Element. The coverage percentage along with the score defines how the proficiency level will be updated. The mapping and related scoring information is to be used by the Learner Modeler to update the estimated proficiency of the appropriate Curriculum Elements in the Learner Model. Figure 5 shows an overview of this process.

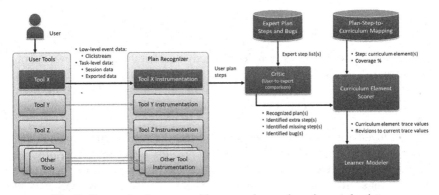

Fig. 5. Expert plan/bug recognition, mapping, and scoring mechanisms

In order for the Learner Modeler to function, there must be a mechanism for inferring or being told the user intent or user task from a sequence of low-level user events and actions. The inference mechanism must be able to determine when a task transition occurs – That is it must be able to tell when, in the sequence of steps, the user has completed the task at hand and has started a new one. A sequence of these events or actions can be thought of as a plan to accomplish some higher-level goal or intent which will be represented in the Curriculum Model as a Curriculum Element also called a Learner Objective. These plan step sequences must be separated to account for task transitions.

The set of plan steps will be compared to a library of plans so that the mapping component will be able to determine which stored plan is most similar to the sequence of activities performed by the user and thereby determine the user intent or user task and its associated Curriculum Element. From this comparison, the mechanism should be able to tell, in addition to the user intent or task, If the user performed the task correctly, If the user was missing steps in performance of the task, and, If the user performed a buggy plan that indicates a misunderstanding.

In order to complete this mapping, the Mapping Component will use the **Curriculum**, and a **Catalog of learning activities that is indexed by curriculum elements that they support**. In addition to the mappings of which learning activities evaluate which curriculum elements there must be a **Fraction of the curriculum element which is experienced in each activity (the coverage percentage)**. This provides the capability for the system to require multiple experiences with a particular curriculum element in order to develop total proficiency.

The GLAsE Mapping Component is based on the concept of a library of plans which the sequence of user actions can be compared to. This library will include expert plans, plans which are correct but not expert, and buggy plans which contain actions based on a user misunderstanding.

A similarity measure is used to determine which plan or plans in the library most closely match the user sequence. The similarity metric will be able to **compare any two plans** to determine **which steps match, to hypothesize that there might be missing step(s), to hypothesize that there might be extra step(s), or to hypothesize that there might be incorrect step(s).**

There are number of complicating factors likely to exist in a set of actions resulting from a user performing a task in the practice environment. The Similarity Measure must be able to handle the partially ordered plan steps. The user may not always execute plan steps in the same sequence, in contrast this with a totally ordered plan where there is only one sequence of plan steps. The system may also need to be able to recognize multiple concurrent goals resulting when a user may have several goals that are being pursued in parallel. The steps to complete one goal may be interleaved with steps to complete another. Simply having observations that support one goal hypothesis doesn't mean there might not be another goal for which some of the same actions provide support. This could result in steps for two goals that are intermingled. In addition, actions can have multiple effects: One action could be used to support two concurrent goal. Because of the above considerations, the system reasoning mechanisms need to be able to carry several interpretations of the user's actions and a way to make a final determination for updating the student model.

In the GLAsE current design, the similarity measure acts as the Analysis Products Comparator, as it provides a mechanism for comparing the user's approach, set of steps, or solution to an expected or expert solution. The Blame Assignment function is currently accomplished by the plan recognition steps done by the similarity measure and related reasoning as well, through the plan library descriptions of plans as expert, correct or buggy and their associated annotations. We envision that in future versions, GLAsE would require a more fine-grained blame assignment mechanism.

6 Conclusion and Next Steps

This paper describes a design for a learner modeling architecture, GLAsE. The design incorporates a number of intelligent tutoring student modeling and assessment approaches specialized for integration into a practice environment for social media analysis. The ability to train analysts of multiple domains to recognize, make connections, and identify patterns or anomalies in social media has applications in economic, political, terrorism, insurgency, gray zone analysis, criminal investigation, and market analysis. The desire to support a practice environment that allows the user to choose to perform tasks that may be open-ended, and that may not be known in advance by the system presents a challenge for the evaluation of the sequence of steps or plans, and we address this challenge through the functionality and design of the expert plan mapping concept of operations.

GLAsE is designed and extended from the Heuristica Student Model [4, 5] which the GTRI team designed and implemented to support learning in a video game. We are unit-testing the GLAsE components and have performed a preliminary integration of early an early GLAsE prototype with the practice environment.

References

1. Woolf, B.P.: Building Intelligent Interactive Tutors Student-Centered Strategies for Revolutionizing e-learning. Morgan Kaufmann, Burlington (2010)
2. Goldstein, I., Carr, B.: The computer as coach as athletic paradigm for intellectual education. In: Proceedings of the 1977 Annual Conference. ACM 1977 (1977)
3. VanLehn, K.: Bugs are not enough: empirical studies of bugs, impasses and repairs in procedural skills. J. Math. Behav. (1982)
4. Whitaker, E.T., Trewhitt, E.B., Hale, C.R., Veinott, E.S., Argenta, C., Catrambone, R.: The effectiveness of intelligent tutoring on training in a video game. In: Proceedings of IGIC 2013, the IEEE International Games Innovation Conference, pp. 267–274 (2013)
5. Whitaker, E., Trewhitt, E., Veinott, E.S.: Intelligent tutoring design alternatives in a serious game. In: Sottilare, R.A., Schwarz, J. (eds.) HCII 2019. LNCS, vol. 11597, pp. 151–165. Springer, Cham (2019). https://doi.org/10.1007/978-3-030-22341-0_13

Measuring Cognitive Load for Adaptive Instructional Systems by Using a Pressure Sensitive Computer Mouse

Thomas E. F. Witte[1]([⊠]) (iD), Henrike Haase[2], and Jessica Schwarz[1]

[1] Fraunhofer FKIE, Fraunhoferstr. 20, 53343 Wachtberg, Germany
{thomas.witte,jessica.schwarz}@fkie.fraunhofer.de
[2] Karlsruhe Institute of Technology (ifab), Engler-Bunte-Ring 4, 76131 Karlsruhe, Germany
Henrike.Haase@kit.edu

Abstract. Adaptive instructional systems need to understand the trainee's mental state to be effective and efficient. The measurement method that assesses the mental state has to fulfill several requirements to be useful for such a system. It has to be valid, reliable, as unobtrusive as possible, processable by technical systems, and cost-efficient. The parameters of a pressure-sensitive computer mouse *duration of a mouse click, click frequency,* and *applied pressure during clicking* are promising candidates to fulfill these requirements. To assess the parameters' sensitivity to variations in cognitive load, we conducted a repeated measures experiment with N = 16 subjects using the Warship Commander Task as a quasi-realistic simulation of command and control tasks. Results indicate that the mouse parameters could differentiate between different levels of cognitive workload. In addition, it showed similar outcomes as the NASA-TLX which was used for comparison as a subjective measure of workload. The results of the experiment, therefore, suggest that a pressure-sensitive computer mouse can be a useful user state analysis tool in adaptive instructional systems.

Keywords: Cognitive load · Workload · User state analysis · Pressure-sensitive mouse · Adaptive instructional system

1 Introduction

Crucial factors of training success are the well-orchestrated interdependencies of the trainee and the tutor. According to Vygotskij's zone of proximal development, the main task of an individual training program is to keep the trainee in the zone, where they can do things with the help of guidance [1]. Therefore, the trainee's abilities, diligence, and mental state should be considered when a trainee program or system is developed. The tutor's task is to consider the mental state and to support the trainee's needs accordingly [2]. For example, if the workload of the trainee is already high, the tutor should not increase the amount and complexity of tasks. However, when the trainee is bored the tutor could assign tasks that are more demanding to the trainee in order to keep the trainee in the zone of proximal development. Instead of human tutors, there is a growing demand

© Springer Nature Switzerland AG 2021
R. A. Sottilare and J. Schwarz (Eds.): HCII 2021, LNCS 12793, pp. 209–218, 2021.
https://doi.org/10.1007/978-3-030-77873-6_15

for alternative computer-based support, which can increase training effectiveness while reducing the strain on training support resources [3].

Adaptive instructional systems (AIS), that intend to deliver personalized support, have the potential to improve the effectiveness of training programs [2]. For a widespread adoption of AIS, the training effectiveness of the system needs to be better than the two opposing alternatives. First, the AIS training effectiveness should outperform non-adaptive training, and second, it needs to match or outperform the effectiveness of human tutors to substantiate the development and use of such training systems. However, a literature review performed by Carrol et al. [2] indicated why human tutor-based training outperforms computer-based tutoring systems, stating that "a significant share of the performance gap between computer-based tutoring and human tutors lies in the ability of the humans to be aware of and responsive to the learner's cognitive/affective states" [1, p. 1]. Therefore, AIS needs to be able to consider the learner's cognitive and affective states to increase effectiveness and to outperform human tutor-based training. This poses two challenges. First, the system needs to be able to detect the state of the learner with high validity and reliability. Second, the state of the learner needs to be formally describable in terms that algorithms can process and compute. An example of a computable user state analysis is the multidimensional, multifactorial user state assessment tool "RASMUS" by Schwarz et al. [4]. Additionally, the measurements need to be as nonintrusive as possible for the learner. The usability of the AIS would otherwise suffer significantly and the user acceptance could be low.

Examples of user states that influence learning can be both affective and cognitive. Changes in cognitive states like workload and engagement can affect the learning process. For example, high engagement leads to an increase of attentional focus [2]. However, if mental workload increases too much and exceeds the available resources, less efficient performance, higher error rates, and slower information processing are the consequences [5]. Similar effects can be observed if the workload is too low [6]. Both extremes of workload hinder during training and should be detected and addressed by AIS.

Affective states, like feelings of high arousal and negative valence or stress, can also have an impact on training success, as emotions impact numerous learning processes, e.g. attention, encoding, and recall [2]. Compared to its informal use, literature uses "stress" with quite different annotations and diverse concepts describing it. Some researchers subdivide stress into different types, e.g. positive and negative stress [7]. On the one hand, positive stress is perceived as a challenge; it can be stimulating towards achieving a goal. Negative stress, on the other hand, is perceived as a strain and results in a feeling of overload and frustration. Other affective states that influence learning are boredom, which "leads to lower retention and less ability to apply information" [1, p. 4], or joy, which increases performance. Generally, user states are highly personal [8] and should be kept at a well-balanced level [5, 8].

There are numerous methods to detect user state. Typical measurements of user states are questionnaires, psychophysiological measures, facial expressions, speech recognition, or eye-tracking [9, 10]. The downsides of these measures include discomfort, obtrusiveness, high costs, or interruptions for administering questionnaires. Physiological measures, e.g. electrodermal activity, heart rate, or EEG, have the advantage of continuous measurements in real time [4]. However, they often require wearing a wristband, chest straps, or EEG-equipment including a cap and multiple cables. The equipment can be irritating or even disturbing to the user [11], which might bias the detection of affective states [10].

Instead of physiological measures, behavioral data has a great potential to detect user states [12]. Behavior can be the interaction with input devices such as keyboard, mouse, or touch screen [13]. The keyboard and computer mouse are common input devices and do not distract the user. Next to their unobtrusiveness, their ease of use is another advantage. There is no additional equipment or costs and once the devices are fully set up and connected to the computer, only little expertise is needed to employ them for user state assessment. These input devices do not require specific conditions and are less sensitive to the movements of the user, compared to physiological measures [12]. Additionally, user states can also be measured continuously and in real-time. Research on keyboard behavior has shown that interaction with the devices changed when participants experienced more workload [10].

While there has been some research on the keyboard, there is less research on the mouse as an input device. In previous studies, mostly overall grip or mouse dynamics such as speed or acceleration have been analyzed. Only a few studies have used it as an input device showing that there is a relation between affect and mouse pressure (e.g. [14]). A mouse is an unobtrusive input device and can be used relatively irrespective of the environment, which makes it worthwhile to investigate the ability of a mouse as a potential input device. Similar to studies by Hernandez et al. [10] or Schaaff et al. [14] on mouse pressure, this study will take the pressure intensification and the duration of clicks on the left mouse button into account. Measuring affect with a computer mouse is a promising unobtrusive method to feed an AIS with user state information [14]. For our purpose, integrating such a measure into a multifactorial user state analysis, we aimed to demonstrate that parameters of a pressure-sensitive mouse are valid indicators of cognitive load for a quasi-realistic task. In an experimental study, we evaluated whether parameters of a pressure-sensitive mouse can indicate changes in task load and whether they correspond with subjective measures of cognitive load and stress.

2 Materials and Methods

2.1 Participants

The experiment was conducted at the usability laboratory of Fraunhofer FKIE. A total of $N = 16$ subjects (nine female, M = 29.7; SD = 6.6) performed the Warship Commander Task (WCT) [15], (see Fig. 1). All subjects were employees of the Fraunhofer FKIE. They had no prior knowledge, that the mouse click pressure was measured during the experiment but were informed afterwards.

2.2 Materials

The WCT is a simulated quasi-realistic naval command and control task, in which the subject has the role of a commander of a Navy ship that escorts a ship formation. The job is to identify all approaching aircraft, react appropriately to the presented aircraft (tracks) and thereby earn points. There are three groups of tracks: blue (friendly), red (hostile), and yellow (ambiguous). The subject should warn threatening tracks to leave, and will eliminate hostile ones if they do not turn away. Possibly threatening aircraft may not pass the ship that is located at the bottom of the screen (see Fig. 1). Tracks appear at frequent intervals, always coming from the top of the screen. During the experiment, participants had to complete four scenarios in total, which differed in terms of difficulty. The level of difficulty was manipulated by the number of tracks per wave and by the number of tracks that were yellow, thus ambiguous, and required more consideration. Additionally, each wave had a time constraint and a clock was visible on the lower-left corner of the interface once the scenario started (see Fig. 1). Earlier research has shown, that the WCT is indeed able to systematically manipulate the cognitive load of a subject, resulting in performance differences [15].

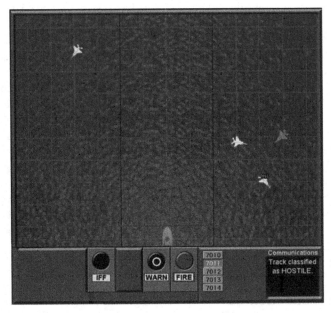

Fig. 1. The Interface of the warship commander task

Cognitive load was measured twofold, with parameters of a computer mouse as an objective, and the NASA-TLX as a subjective measurement. The mouse parameters were clicking duration, clicking frequency, and left mouse-button pressure when clicking.

The mouse was a commercially available gaming mouse from Swiftpoint (see Fig. 2). It can detect and record the frequency, duration, and pressure intensification of the left mouse button click. Pressure applied on the left mouse button is measured on a scale of −1 to 0, with −0.5 being the neutral value when no pressure is applied. The higher the pressure is, the higher the value gets, thus moving closer towards zero. The duration of the left button mouse click is measured in milliseconds.

Fig. 2. Pressure-sensitive mouse Swiftpoint Z

The NASA-TLX measures subjective workload with six questions, which were answered on a 15-point Likert scale. The NASA-TLX was administered after every scenario, four times in total. This questionnaire can detect small changes in workload [5] and has already been used in similar studies regarding air traffic control [7].

2.3 Experimental Design

The experiment was run in a two-factor repeated measures design [see Table 1]. Factor one varied the number of tracks to be processed, with either six or 24 tracks per wave. Factor two varied the complexity of the situation with low (33%) versus high (66%) numbers of unidentified radar contacts (yellow tracks), which required more actions. Every subject performed each task of every condition in a randomized order. The variation of task load is based on the Cognitive Task Load (CTL) Model, which states that cognitive load depends on the volume of information processed, the complexity of the situation, and the number of task-set switching [16]. The number of tracks that are displayed per wave represents the volume of information processed, while task switching occurs as attention shifts between objects and the required actions. This leads to the third factor, complexity, which occurs through a more advanced identification process for yellow tracks. By varying these factors, the different scenarios should induce different levels of workload. DeGreef and Arciszewski [16] used this model as a basis for modeling operator cognition in their research on adaptive automation using a similar task.

Table 1. Overview of scenarios in the WCT

	Number of tracks per wave		
		6	24
Percentage of ambiguous yellow tracks	33%	Low/Low	Low/High
	66%	High/Low	High/High

2.4 Hypotheses

For evaluating whether the parameters of the pressure-sensitive computer mouse serve as indicators of cognitive load the following hypotheses were tested:

H1: Pressure applied to the mouse differs depending on the cognitive load (track volume (H1a) and complexity of the situation (H1b)).

H2: The duration of mouse clicks differs depending on the cognitive load (track volume (H2a) and complexity of the situation (H2b)).

H3: The frequency of mouse clicks differs depending on the cognitive load (track volume (H3a) and complexity of the situation (H3b)).

H4: The NASA-TLX score differs depending on the cognitive load (track volume (H4a) and complexity of the situation (H4b)).

2.5 Procedure

Upon arrival, participants were informed about the general purpose of the study to assess mental states of the user during a computer task. Participants then received the instructions of the WCT and were informed about the steps they needed to take to complete the task and earn points. They trained the WCT, with six waves of differing sizes (from 6 to 12 tracks). The practice scenario took about 7.5 min to complete. Participants could freely stop the training session or ask questions in the meantime. After completion of the training and sufficient discussion of possible questions, participants were given the first of four scenarios, each lasting about 4 min. After each scenario, they answered the NASA-TLX. After the last questionnaire, participants were debriefed about the purpose of the study to measure workload with the pressure sensitive computer mouse.

2.6 Data Analysis

The hypotheses one to four were tested by calculating repeated measures analysis of variance (ANOVA). According to Bortz [17], ANOVA can be considered robust to violations of the assumptions (e.g., assumption of normal distribution) if the groups are of equal size, as is the case in the repeated measures design. For repeated measures ANOVA, there is also the assumption of variance homogeneity or homogeneity of correlations between factor levels. However, this assumption is negligible when testing only two levels per factor [17].

For calculation of the ANOVA's the two experimental factors track volume (number of tracks) and complexity of the situation (percentage of yellow tracks) served as within-subject factors. Mouse pressure, click duration, click frequency, and the NASA-TLX total score were used as dependent factors. All calculations were performed with the statistical software SPSS 20 (IBM Corp., 2011).

Alpha value was set to .05 for all statistical tests. To avoid an accumulation of the alpha error when conducting several statistical tests on the same data set, we applied the Bonferroni-Holm correction [18].

3   Results

The results of the repeated measures ANOVAs are summarized in Table 2. Additionally, Fig. 3 shows the mean values per experimental condition for the mouse parameters and the NASA-TLX total score as separate charts (a–d).

Table 2. Results of repeated measures ANOVAs for the mouse parameters and NASA-TLX total score

Metric	F1: Track volume			F2: Complexity			Interaction F1xF2		
	$F(1,15)$	p	Eta^2	$F(1,15)$	p	Eta^2	$F(1,15)$	p	Eta^2
Mouse pressure	10.32	<.01	.41	6.7	<.05	.31	0.43	ns	.03
Click duration	52.06	<.001	.78	8.37	<.05	.36	1.2	ns	.07
Click frequency	437.42	<.001	.97	68.68	<.001	.82	20.76	<.001	.58
Nasa-TLX	123,33	<.001	.89	15.52	.001	.51	1.57	ns	.1

Note: all effects with p < .05 remain significant when applying the Bonferroni-Holm correction.

3.1   Pressure

Concerning the pressure applied to the computer mouse, the ANOVA revealed a significant main effect for the factor track volume (p < .01; see Table 2). Figure 3a shows that the pressure was higher during the conditions of high track volume (high task load) than in the conditions of low track volume (low task load) in both, low and high complexity conditions. There is also a significant main effect for the factor complexity (p < .05). Figure 3a indicates that according to expectations the conditions of high complexity were associated with higher pressure than the conditions of low complexity. This applies to both low and high track volume conditions. Thus, the interaction effect did not turn out to be significant.

3.2   Click Duration

According to Table 2 there are also significant main effects for track volume and complexity concerning click frequency. As for the parameter of pressure, the interaction effect is not significant. However, it appears that click duration is affected differently by track volume than by complexity. As Fig. 3b reveals, the duration of mouse clicks decreased in conditions of high track volume compared to low track volume. With Eta^2 = .78 this can be considered as a large effect. In contrast, click duration increased in conditions of high complexity compared to the low complexity conditions.

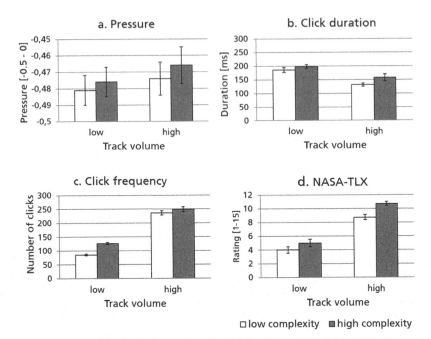

Fig. 3. Mean values with standard error (error bars) of each experimental condition for pressure, click duration, click frequency, and the NASA-TLX total score.

3.3 Click Frequency

For click frequency, the ANOVA revealed significant main effects for track volume and complexity as well as a significant interaction effect (see Table 2). According to Fig. 3c, click frequency increased considerably with a higher volume of tracks. This is reflected in a large effect size of $Eta^2 = .97$. Click frequency also increased when the complexity was higher. However, as indicated by the interaction effect, the difference in click frequency between low and high complexity conditions is higher for conditions of low track volume than for high track volume conditions.

3.4 NASA-TLX

Similar to the parameters of the computer mouse, the NASA-TLX total score also showed significant main effects for track volume and complexity (see Table 2). A higher number of air contacts resulted in a statistically significant higher subjective cognitive load for the NASA-TLX (see Fig. 3d). Also, the higher complexity of the situation resulted in a higher subjective workload rating. Compared to the track volume this effect is a bit smaller but still large.

3.5 Summary and Discussion

In sum, results confirm the hypotheses for the assessed parameters: The increase in cognitive load by higher track volume is reflected in all three parameters of the computer mouse: increase in pressure, decrease in click duration, and increase in click frequency. It also affects the perceived level of workload, as shown by an increase in the NASA-TLX total score. The effect size is highest for click frequency, which is not surprising as higher track volume implicates that more tracks have to be processed, and thus, more clicks are necessary to complete the tasks. The effect size of pressure applied to the computer mouse is the lowest but still significant. This is an interesting outcome, as this parameter is not directly affected by the number of tasks (you could also complete all tasks correctly and in time by applying less pressure). Hence, higher pressure rather seems to be an outcome of a higher cognitive stress level than an outcome of the characteristics of the task.

The complexity of the situation also affects all parameters significantly. Higher complexity is reflected, similar to higher track volume, in an increase of pressure and click frequency. However, in contrast to track volume, a higher complexity is associated with an increase in click duration. This finding might reflect the higher level of cognitive processing that is necessary to process the ambiguous yellow tracks in the higher complexity situation.

Overall, a comparison with the outcomes of the subjective rating reveals that the parameters of the pressure-sensitive computer mouse indicate changes in cognitive load in a similar way to the NASA-TLX total score.

4   Conclusion

The experiment has shown that the mouse parameters pressure and click duration are unintrusive, valid, and sensitive parameters to measure cognitive workload. An aggregated scoring of mouse parameters could be a key ingredient to overcome the two earlier described challenges of AIS. Firstly, mouse parameters could be used to detect the trainee's user states. Secondly, the properties of the mouse parameters are symbolic in nature, thus understandable for a technical system, such as an AIS.

Future research could determine the reliability of the mouse-parameters, by replicating the experiment. Further, experiments could focus on a more realistic task, which elicits different user states more accurately, to find more fine-grained differences in clicking behavior. Additionally, eye-tracking or psychophysiological data could be used to further validate mouse usage with respect to its incremental validity. In this regard, it could be examined whether a mouse in combination with other physiological parameters can enhance the user states detection. If the validity and reliability of mouse parameters can be further confirmed in future studies the detection of workload with a computer mouse would be a cost efficient way to help the AIS's understanding of the trainee's mental state. Hence, an AIS could use this information to keep the trainee in the zone of proximal development by adjusting task characteristics, such as task volume and task complexity.

References

1. Matusov, E.: Vygotskij's theory of human development and new approaches to education. In: International Encyclopedia of the Social & Behavioral Sciences, pp 16339–16343. Elsevier (2001)

2. Carroll, M., Kokini, C., Champney, R., Sottilare, R., Goldberg, B.: Modeling trainee affective and cognitive state using low cost sensors. In: Proceedings of the Interservice/Industry Training, Simulation, and Edu-cation Conference, pp. 1–12 (2011)

3. Self, J.: The defining characteristics of intelligent tutoring systems research: ITSs care, precisely. Int. J. Artif. Intell. Educ. **10**, 350–364 (1998)

4. Schwarz, J., Fuchs, S., Flemisch, F.: Towards a more holistic view on user state assessment in adaptive human-computer interaction. In: 2014 IEEE International Conference on Systems, Man, and Cybernetics (SMC), pp. 1228–1234. IEEE (2014)

5. Galy, E., Cariou, M., Mélan, C.: What is the relationship between mental workload factors and cognitive load types? Int. J. Psychophysiol. **83**, 269–275 (2012). https://doi.org/10.1016/j.ijpsycho.2011.09.023

6. Parasuraman, R., Bahri, T., Deaton, J.E., Morrison, J.G., Barnes, M.: Theory and design of adaptive automation in aviation systems. Washington, DC, USA (1992)

7. Collet, C., Averty, P., Dittmar, A.: Autonomic nervous system and subjective ratings of strain in air-traffic control. Appl. Ergon. **40**, 23–32 (2009). https://doi.org/10.1016/j.apergo.2008.01.019

8. Charles, R.L., Nixon, J.: Measuring mental workload using physiological measures: a systematic review. Appl. Ergon. **74**, 221–232 (2019). https://doi.org/10.1016/j.apergo.2018.08.028

9. Rowe, D.W., Sibert, J., Irwin, D.: Heart rate variability: indicator of user state as an aid to human-computer interaction. In: Proceedings of the SIGCHI Conference on Human Factors in Computing Systems, pp. 480–487 (1998)

10. Hernandez, J., Paredes, P., Roseway, A., Czerwinski, M.: Under pressure: sensing stress of computer users. In: Proceedings of the SIGCHI Conference on Human Factors in Computing Systems, pp. 51–60 (2014)

11. Schwarz, J.: Benutzerzustandserfassung zur Regelung Kognitiver Assistenz an Bord von Marineschiffen. 2 Interdiszip Work Kognitive Syst Mensch, Teams, Syst und Autom (2013)

12. Bixler, R., D'Mello, S.: Detecting boredom and engagement during writing with keystroke analysis, task appraisals, and stable traits. In: Proceedings of the 2013 International Conference on Intelligent User Interfaces - IUI 2013, ACM Press, New York, USA, pp. 225–234 (2013)

13. Kolakowska, A.: A review of emotion recognition methods based on keystroke dynamics and mouse movements. In: 2013 6th International Conference on Human System Interactions (HSI), pp. 548–555. IEEE (2013)

14. Schaaff, K., Degen, R., Adler, N., Adam, M.T.P.: Measuring affect using a standard mouse device. Biomed. Eng./Biomed. Tech. **57**, 761–764 (2012). https://doi.org/10.1515/bmt-2012-4013

15. St. John, M., Kobus, D.A., Morrison, J.G., Schmorrow, D.: Overview of the DARPA Augmented Cognition Technical Integration Experiment. Int. J. Hum. Comput. Interact. **17**, 131–149 (2004). https://doi.org/10.1207/s15327590ijhc1702_2

16. De Greef, T., Arciszewski, H.: Triggering adaptive automation in naval command and control. In: Frontiers in Adaptive Control. InTech (2009)

17. Bortz, J.: Statistik. Springer, Heidelberg (2005)

18. Holm, S.: A simple sequentially rejective multiple test procedure. Scand. J. Stat. **6**, 65–70 (1979)

Measuring and Integrating Facial Expressions and Head Pose as Indicators of Engagement and Affect in Tutoring Systems

Hao Yu[1], Ankit Gupta[2], Will Lee[3], Ivon Arroyo[3(✉)], Margrit Betke[1], Danielle Allesio[3], Tom Murray[3], John Magee[4], and Beverly P. Woolf[3]

[1] Boston University, Boston, MA 02215, USA
{haoyu,betke}@bu.edu
[2] Worcester Polytechnic Institute, Worcester, MA 01609, USA
[3] University of Massachusetts-Amherst, Amherst, MA 01003, USA
{williamlee,ivon,allessio,tmurray,bev}@cs.umass.edu
[4] Clark University, Worcester, MA 01610, USA
jmagee@clarku.edu

Abstract. While using online learning software, students demonstrate many reactions, various levels of engagement, and emotions (e.g. confusion, boredom, excitement). Having such information automatically accessible to teachers (or digital tutors) can aid in understanding how students are progressing, and suggest who and when needs further assistance. As part of this work, we conducted two studies using computer vision techniques to measure students' engagement and affective states from their head pose and facial expressions, as they use an online tutoring system, MathSpring.org, designed to aid students' practice of mathematics problem-solving. We present a Head Pose Tutor, which estimates the real-time head direction of students and responds to potential disengagement, and a Facial Expression-Augmented Teacher Dashboard, that identifies students' affective states and provides this information to teachers. We collected video data of undergraduate students interacting with MathSpring. Preliminary results on MathSpring videos were encouraging indicating accuracy in detecting head orientation. A usability study was conducted with actual teachers to start to evaluate the possible impact of the proposed Teacher Dashboard software.

Keywords: Computer vision · Engagement · Emotions · Gaze · Intelligent tutoring systems

1 Introduction

As students engage with online learning technologies, they often demonstrate a wide variety of reactions, dependent on a combination of their motivation,

© Springer Nature Switzerland AG 2021
R. A. Sottilare and J. Schwarz (Eds.): HCII 2021, LNCS 12793, pp. 219–233, 2021.
https://doi.org/10.1007/978-3-030-77873-6_16

mood, and background knowledge. Students experience various levels of engagement and might express emotions such as confusion, boredom, excitement, and anxiety. The engagement and different affective states of students can be tightly correlated with their learning gains on many learning tasks, such as problem solving and concept understanding [2,9]. Having such engagement and affective information accessible to teachers (or digital tutors) can aid in understanding students' progress, and suggest who and when needs further assistance, which has the potential to improve students' learning outcomes.

MathSpring.org is a web-based tutoring system, designed to aid middle school students' practice of mathematics problem-solving [1]. We developed computer vision software to detect students' engagement and emotional expressions, as they use MathSpring.org, with two main goals: a) to respond "just-in-time" to students' states as they work; b) to provide teachers with real-time information to gauge the "pulse" of their students, so as to better assist them. Ultimately, teachers would gain insights into their students' motivation, interests, attention, and effort. By monitoring and capturing students' affective states, and engagement, these constructs could help teachers realize whether their lesson plans are helping the students to engage with the material and learn (Fig. 1).

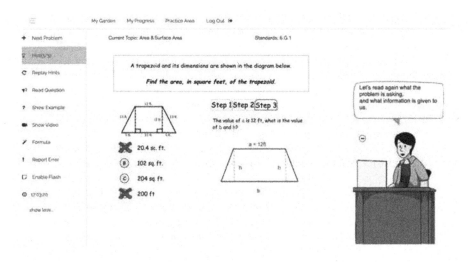

Fig. 1. The existing tutor, MathSpring.org., showing the practice area. Several hints are available from the "Hints" button on the left, which are supplemented with audio for any text displayed. Worked-out examples, tutorial videos, and formulas are also accessible. Jake (right) is a learning companion who talks to students about the importance of effort and perseverance, in the precise moment that they make mistakes.

This paper describes two efforts of using computer vision to benefit students and teachers in MathSpring as indicators of affective states and engagement. First, we present a Head Pose Detector, a deep learning based system that estimates the head pose of students and responds to potential disengagement and off-task behavior. In our studies with undergraduate students in the United States, video data of students interacting with MathSpring was collected, which includes 2822 recorded problem-solving interaction samples. We describe encouraging preliminary results, indicating the initial accurate estimations of head poses. We present valuable information which results from the analysis of the Head Pose Detector on MathSpring videos of students. Second, we present a Facial Expression-Augmented Teacher Dashboard, to identify students' affective states and provide enhanced information to teachers. We present results from a usability study with teachers, which revealed promising results. Finally, we discuss our planned experiments for the next phase of this research. We summarize our contributions as follows:

- Move beyond traditional log data to demonstrate the use of computer vision with live video data to infer affect as one indicator of students' motivation.
- Develop a deep learning based computer vision model to identify head pose as an indicator of engagement vs. distraction, as each student in a math class works on MathSpring.
- Develop a deep learning based computer vision detector of facial expressions, which feeds a Teacher Dashboard that shows facial expressions and other information of a full class of students working on MathSpring.

2   Related Work

2.1   Affect-Aware and Gaze-Reactive Intelligent Tutoring System

A growing body of literature has analyzed user affect and expressions during interacting with online learning systems [2,3,6,15,30–32,34]. Student affect is measured and modeled using techniques such as self-report [31], human rating [2], log data [6], facial expression recognition [34], and a combination of them [15]. As facial expression recognition advances in computer vision and machine learning, a subset of literature has analyzed student affect using various facial expression analysis techniques [3,7,15,30]. For example, Bosch et al. [3] analyzed videos of students interacting with an educational physics game and used computer vision techniques to detect students' affect from facial expressions and body movements. Whitehill et al. [30] developed machine-learning based detectors of engagement from students' facial expressions. While various studies have been conducted on estimating students' knowledge and affect, little research has been done to transform this collected (Raw) data into meaningful information that is more relatable to teachers, parents and other stakeholders, i.e. Non- Researchers. We conducted research that captures student performance and detects students' facial expressions to generate a live dashboard for teachers to use in the classroom, as their students are using MathSpring.

Prior research has shown a tight coupling between gaze and attention [16,26]. Researchers hence have focused on measuring and analyzing gaze to identify disengagement and model attentional states of learners in intelligent tutoring systems [8, 18, 29]. For example, Gaze tutor [8] used eye gaze to detect students' boredom and disengagement, and then attempted to redirect attention with gaze-reactive dialogue moves. Hutt et al. [18] integrated commercial eye tracker to monitor attention when students were interacting with an ITS, GuruTutor. They detected mind wandering by analyzing the recorded eye gaze data using machine learning methods. All these works used special hardware (e.g. an eye tracker) to measure gaze. By contrast, we operationalize gaze as head poses [19] and utilize state-of-the-art computer vision techniques for head pose estimation using visuals captured by a built-in camera or a connected webcam only, which is readily available in most common learning platforms (e.g. laptops, phones), which allow for scale up and use by real students in their math classes.

2.2 Facial Expression Recognition

Automatic facial expressions recognition has been widely studied in the field of computer vision and machine learning. Given a facial image or a sequence of facial images, a facial expression recognition (FER) system aims to analyze and encode the expression information from facial behaviors. Existing methods either recognize the occurrence of facial actions relying on the Facial Action Coding System (FACS) [11], or the emotions conveyed by facial actions, such as happy, sad, angry, and fear [12].

Generally, a FER system includes two stages, namely feature extraction and expression recognition. For feature extraction, traditional methods use hand-crafted features such as local binary patterns (LBP) [28], sparse coding [37], and non-negative matrix factorization (NMF) [36]. These engineered features often lack generalizability when applied to images with large variations, such as illumination, pose, and resolution. Alternatively, recent advancements of deep neural networks have shown the ability to learn and extract highly discriminative features, and deep-learning based approaches have achieved state-of-the-art performance for both lab-controlled and in-the-wild facial expression datasets. For example, Khorrami [20] trained a zero-bias CNN and achieved state-of-the-art results on the extended Cohn-Kanade dataset (CK+) and the Toronto Face Dataset (TFD). Meng [23] proposed an identity-aware CNN (IA-CNN) which used identity- and expression-sensitive contrastive losses to alleviate variations introduced by personal attributes. Zhang presented a generative adversarial network (GAN) based model that jointly exploits poses and expressions [35]. For the last stage, the extracted features are used to train a classifier or regressor, e.g. Support Vector Machines (SVMs), multilayer perceptrons (MLPs), for the target expressions.

2.3 Head Pose Estimation

In the context of computer vision, head pose estimation aims at identifying human head orientation from digital images. Early landmark-based methods [14, 17, 22] first predict geometric facial features (e.g. landmarks) and estimate head poses from these features by 3D head model fitting. As the development of face alignment [4,39], landmark-based methods have become increasingly popular for head pose estimation. However, facial landmark detection often incurs unnecessary computation. Instead, landmark-free methods [5,27,33] directly predict head poses from facial images. For example, Ruiz et al. [27] presented a multi-loss convolutional neural network (CNN) and performed joint binned pose classification and regression. Yang et al. [33] proposed a compact CNN model based on regression and feature aggregation, which achieved state-of-the-art accuracy.

In addition, multitask learning has been widely adopted for pose estimation recently, where head pose estimation is jointly learned with other closely related tasks, such as gender estimation, and facial landmark detection. HyperFace [25] simultaneously performed face detection, landmarks localization, pose estimation and gender recognition using deep convolutional neural networks. Kumar et al. [21] proposed to use Heatmap-CNN regressors for keypoint estimation and pose estimation. Finally, some methods utilize depth data which provide 3D information of images [13,24]. Though they achieved accurate estimation, the depth information is not always available in real-word applications as special cameras are needed.

3   Tutoring System's Response to Students' Head Pose

The first effort to leverage Computer Vision to measure student engagement and affective state is a Head Pose Detector. As students use MathSpring.org, the Head Pose Tutor will recognize the real-time head pose and infer potential disengagement. When disengagement is detected, it will then perform interventions to redirect students' attention. The real-time detection and automatic responses help students sustain and effectively allocate attentional resources to learning tasks, which is critical for effective learning [10]. We created a deep neural network-based system that recognizes the direction of students' heads from students' face images. To keep the level of invasiveness as low as possible, the face images are captured using a built-in/mounted camera, which is often readily available in most common learning platforms (e.g. laptops, phones).

3.1   Method to Detect Student Head Pose

The procedure includes three stages, i.e. face extraction, head pose estimation, and off-screen pose detection. Given a video of a student using MathSpring, we perform frame-wise estimation and analysis of head poses. For each frame, we first detect the face using face-api.js, a JavaScript face detection/recognition API implemented on top of Tensorflow.js. The face with the highest confidence score will be cropped and resized as the input of the head pose estimation network.

We predict head pose angles (i.e., yaw, pitch and roll) using the deep neural network FSA-Net [33]. The network learns a discriminative representation of the face by generating and combining the feature maps from different layers of the network through fine-grained structure feature aggregation. This representation is then used to perform soft stagewise regression to predict the head pose angles. The head pose estimation model is trained on the 300W-LP synthetic dataset [38] containing 122,450 images with labelled head poses and facial landmarks. The dataset synthesized large-scale faces across large poses (above 45°) so that the trained model is robust to self-occlusion in large poses. This is important because we observed in our data that students have large poses variations when using MathSpring. The trained Python model is then converted into a JavaScript model using Tensorflow.js for estimation in the browser where MathSpring is run.

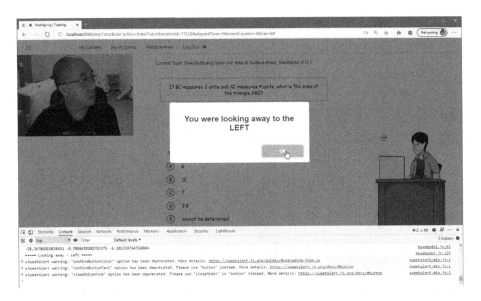

Fig. 2. The head position detector has detected that the user is looking left, and is ready to intervene. A pedagogical Agent will talk to the student attempting to bring the student back on task. Note that due to the mirror image of the recording of the web cam, the user was shown looking to the right when the user was actually looking to the left.

Finally, the system detects whether the student is looking off-screen by analyzing the pose angle values. Specifically, we consider a student facing straight at the screen as that student's neutral state (i.e. the pose angle would be 0°) and infer off-screen poses when the angle values exceed certain thresholds. Though the prediction is already accurate, the performance could be further improved by a simple calibration step. Since students may have different hardware setups that could affect the corresponding thresholds (e.g. the webcam could be placed either above or below the screen), the thresholds could be further personalized by requesting the student to stare at multiple calibration points on the screen. The system will record the head pose angles and compute the thresholds based on the recorded angles for the specific user.

The Head Pose Tutor was integrated into MathSpring as a front-end application, see Fig. 2. Given the real-time image captured by a webcam as a student is using MathSpring, the system will identify the user's head pose. If the system detects that the user is looking off-screen for certain time, it will deliver real-time interventions (e.g. messages, animations) to reengage the student (see Fig. 2 for an example).

3.2   Experiment to Measure Student Head Pose

Fifty-four (54) undergraduate students used MathSpring.org, and their faces were videotaped via laptop webcam. The data was collected in a classroom setting where students were asked to solve math problems for approximately one hour, which yielded 68 student sessions. Each student session is segmented into shorter video clips using the system log data, where each clip is associated with an individual math problem, resulting in 2822 recorded problem-solving interaction samples.

In order to assess our model detection accuracy, we ran our Head Pose Detector on the above MathSpring videos. We chose to downsample the videos from 30 frame per second to 3 frame per second in order to reduce storage and computation cost while not affecting the performance much. For each of 68 student sessions in the dataset, we generated random samples of images showing that the target student is facing up, down, left, right or facing straight at the screen predicted by the model. Overall 340 images were generated. Two human coders labeled the images indicating the head position with 99% inter-rater accuracy. The detector achieved 97.94% accuracy when comparing the human annotations and system predictions, an accurate estimation.

By analyzing the estimation results of Head Pose Detector on MathSpring videos, we found invaluable information in the juxtaposition of head position and the logs of problem-solving activity. For example, Fig. 3 juxtaposes both (e.g., hints requested, time to solve and attempting an answer to the math problem are shown, and it appears that a "head tilt" is a sign of concentration, cognitive engagement.

4   Teacher Dashboard to Inform Teachers

The second effort is a Facial Expression-Augmented Teacher Dashboard, seeking to enhance information provided to teachers through MathSpring's "Teacher Tools", while students are using the MathSpring Tutoring system. The dashboard captures student performance and detects students' facial expressions (smiles, nose wrinkles and frowns), which highlight students' emotion and engagement, using a deep learning model for facial expression detection. Instead of the intelligent tutor performing an intervention (e.g., provide an empathetic message to the student) this information is shown to teachers, in hopes that it will support them to understand and juxtapose the state of knowledge and corresponding affect of students. This should help teachers understand students'

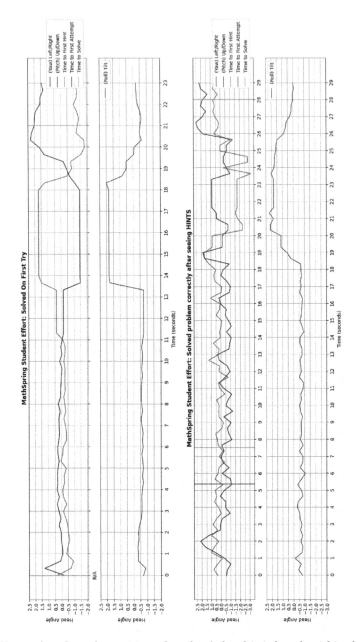

Fig. 3. Charts show how the position of student's head is inferred, within the lapse of time of a student solving a math problem. The Head Position is neutral around 0 of Y-Axis, and is pronounced when outside of the interval [−1, 1]. Lines indicate left/right head position (Blue), up/down (Orange). The second chart shows head tilt (Green). Top two graphs correspond to a problem "solved on first attempt" ant the bottom two graphs correspond to a student who "asks for a Hint" pretty quickly (NOTR is for first action without even reading the problem), but never solved the problem (moved on to the next problem). (Color figure online)

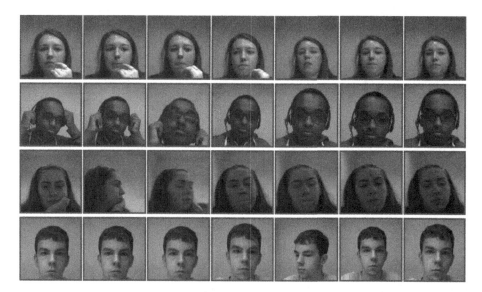

Fig. 4. Example face-cropped images from the collected MathSpring dataset showing the evolution of student expressions.

states of mind, and feed this information back to act and alter their instruction or interaction with each student in a personalized way. Figure 4 shows the Teacher Dashboard highlighting students' smiles, nose wrinkles and frowns, expressions of emotions.

4.1 Method to Develop the Teacher Dashboard

A fully connected neural network was trained to detect the presence and intensity of three action units for smile, nose wrinkle and frown (AU4, AU9, and AU12, respectively). Face detection, face extraction, and facial landmark detection are all performed using face-api.js with Tensorflow.js. The model was trained on a dataset of 35K face images labeled with 68 face landmark points. The input of the model consists of facial landmarks of eyebrows, eyes, nose, and mouth. The output contains the confidence predictions of the 3 facial action units.

The AU detector was deployed in the front-end of MathSpring (Fig. 5). As teachers click on a student card, they can see further detail (Fig. 7). Facial Action Unit Prediction count comparison chart provides the concentration or counts of the three action units (AU4, AU9, and AU12 or facial expression, Frown, Nose wrinkle, and Smile) during the student's live session. The student effort pie chart provides the concentration for the different levels of effort excerpted on problems, behaviors of the students on various mathematics problems, which are combinations of a variety of actions and their timing (e.g. GIVEUP, SKIPPED, SOLVED ON FIRST attempt, etc.). It provides an analysis of the students'

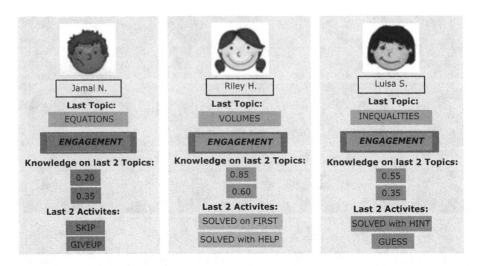

Fig. 5. The Teachers' Dashboard provides a snapshot of the class. Student cards display student expressions, recent topic visited, engagement, along with recent knowledge and effort on problems (e.g. GIVEUP means a student has moved on without answering the problem, SOLVED on FIRST means the student has correctly solved a question on the first attempt. Jamal shows a frown, Riley a smile, and Luisa a nose wrinke.

performance during each session, in real time. The student detail page also provides estimations of knowledge for the last problems and the effort in the form of behaviors excerpted on problems, depicting the student's performance during the last problems. Additionally, it provides teachers with information about which topics students are currently working on.

4.2   Usability Study for the Teacher Dashboard

A live video of the dashboard, as it was being used by MathSpring students simultaneously as part of a class, was shown to four (4) senior math teachers who were users of MathSpring, and had experience with its use in the classroom. The teachers completed a qualitative and quantitative 11-question survey that captured teachers' critical view, suggestions regarding the new development, and perceptions of usefulness, after seeing the Dashboard while a class of actual students was using MathSpring. The survey contains questions that capture teachers' view about various aspect of the dashboard, the facial gestures component in particular, and the impact of it in their understanding of students' current states while they solve problems on MathSpring platform. For instance, the two first questions were : "Do you think this dashboard could be useful for you as a teacher in the classroom, as students use MathSpring?" and "Does the facial expression in the dashboard seem to provide useful information or not? Please explain."

Mastery Range	Grade & Color Code for 2 or more problems	Grade/Color Code for 10 or more problems
0.75 or Greater	Grade A (Excellent)	Grade A (Excellent)
Between 0.5 and 0.75	Grade B (Good)	Grade B (Good))
Between 0.25 and 0.5	Grade C (Needs Improvement)	Grade C (Needs Improvement)
0.25 or Less	Grade D (Unsatisfactory)	Grade D (Unsatisfactory)

Fig. 6. MathSpring masteries chart displays the mastery range, grades and color codes.

The usability study showed promising results from teachers, rating the information as very useful in general, with a majority of positive answers for all questions. Most of the teachers found the information on the student details informative and meaningful. On being asked about how valuable they think it is on a scale of zero to five (zero being least valuable and 5 being most valuable), they responded with three and above (3+). In general, teachers liked the new live dashboard included in the Teachers Tool. Given the history of teachers not being able to monitor the students in live sessions, and the situation of studying from home, teachers expressed that the live dashboard seems to be a great way to monitor the classroom. The tile representation of all the live students together in one place is liked by all the teachers (Fig. 6).

The new facial expression depiction on the live dashboard was also considered as a "nice and quick" way of understanding the students' comfort level while they solved problems. The participant teachers also described it as a "useful tool" to highlight students who express a lack of confidence and could put more focus on them. In general, the feedback received from teachers was encouraging and we believe the new enhancements recommended by them, would help teachers understand their students better, and personalize their response to their students as well.

5 Discussion and Future Work

We are evolving the head pose detector's intervention as a learning companion for maintaining students' level of engagement. For the next phase of the research, we plan to evaluate the head pose detector's performance and students' subjective feedback, as it is used live, in real classrooms.

While the head pose detection system provides a coarse estimation of where students are looking, the intelligent tutor will acquire more information when the gaze direction of students can be detected and engagement inferred. During learning or solving problems, it is quite common that a student keeps a relatively

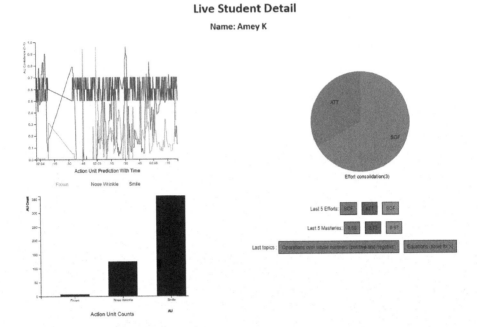

Fig. 7. When clicking on a student tile in Fig. 5, further detail on the student comes up. The left charts show that this student has smiled very frequently (appears relaxed). The charts to the right show student performance on math problems. The "student effort" pie chart shows the frequency of recent behaviors by the students during problem-solving (This student has 65% of the time, solved on first attempt (SOF). About 35% of the time attempted a problem incorrectly and then self-corrected their mistake, ATT).

fixed head position but the gaze direction moves frequently, which makes it insufficient to detect head poses only. Therefore, we plan to further develop a system for inferring gaze direction when students are interacting with the digital tutor.

6   Conclusion

Computer Vision can be combined with tutoring systems to detect head pose and expression while providing real-time information to teachers or tutoring systems, and helping to address students' disengagement and affective states. Student privacy is respected, as only expressions and head pose are detected locally, in the front-end of the web-based software. The combination of logged problem-solving activity, head position and facial expressions, can provide invaluable data to assess and address students' engagement as they learn.

References

1. Arroyo, I., Woolf, B.P., Burelson, W., Muldner, K., Rai, D., Tai, M.: A multimedia adaptive tutoring system for mathematics that addresses cognition, metacognition and affect. Int. J. Artif. Intell. Educ. **24**(4), 387–426 (2014)
2. Baker, R.S., D'Mello, S.K., Rodrigo, M.M.T., Graesser, A.C.: Better to be frustrated than bored: The incidence, persistence, and impact of learners' cognitive-affective states during interactions with three different computer-based learning environments. Int. J. Hum.-Comput. Stud. **68**(4), 223–241 (2010)
3. Bosch, N., D'mello, S.K., Ocumpaugh, J., Baker, R.S., Shute, V.: Using video to automatically detect learner affect in computer-enabled classrooms. ACM Trans. Inter. Intell. Syst. (TiiS) **6**(2), 1–26 (2016)
4. Bulat, A., Tzimiropoulos, G.: How far are we from solving the 2d & 3d face alignment problem?(and a dataset of 230,000 3D facial landmarks). In: Proceedings of the IEEE International Conference on Computer Vision, pp. 1021–1030 (2017)
5. Chang, F.J., Tuan Tran, A., Hassner, T., Masi, I., Nevatia, R., Medioni, G.: Faceposenet: making a case for landmark-free face alignment. In: Proceedings of the IEEE International Conference on Computer Vision Workshops, pp. 1599–1608 (2017)
6. Corrigan, S., Barkley, T., Pardos, Z.: Dynamic approaches to modeling student affect and its changing role in learning and performance. In: Ricci, F., Bontcheva, K., Conlan, O., Lawless, S. (eds.) UMAP 2015. LNCS, vol. 9146, pp. 92–103. Springer, Cham (2015). https://doi.org/10.1007/978-3-319-20267-9_8
7. D'Mello, S., Dieterle, E., Duckworth, A.: Advanced, analytic, automated (AAA) measurement of engagement during learning. Educ. Psychol. **52**(2), 104–123 (2017)
8. D'Mello, S., Olney, A., Williams, C., Hays, P.: Gaze tutor: a gaze-reactive intelligent tutoring system. Int. J. Hum.-Comput. Stud. **70**(5), 377–398 (2012)
9. D'Mello, S., Lehman, B., Pekrun, R., Graesser, A.: Confusion can be beneficial for learning. Learn. Instr. **29**, 153–170 (2014)
10. D'Mello, S.K.: Gaze-based attention-aware cyberlearning technologies. In: Parsons, T.D., Lin, L., Cockerham, D. (eds.) Mind, Brain and Technology. ECTII, pp. 87–105. Springer, Cham (2019). https://doi.org/10.1007/978-3-030-02631-8_6
11. Ekman, P., Friesen, W.V., Hager, J.C.: Facial action coding system. Research Nexus, Salt Lake City (2002)
12. Ekman, P., Friesen, W.V.: Constants across cultures in the face and emotion. J. Pers. Soc. Psychol. **17**(2), 124 (1971)
13. Fanelli, G., Weise, T., Gall, J., Van Gool, L.: Real time head pose estimation from consumer depth cameras. In: Mester, R., Felsberg, M. (eds.) DAGM 2011. LNCS, vol. 6835, pp. 101–110. Springer, Heidelberg (2011). https://doi.org/10.1007/978-3-642-23123-0_11
14. Gou, C., Wu, Y., Wang, F.Y., Ji, Q.: Coupled cascade regression for simultaneous facial landmark detection and head pose estimation. In: 2017 IEEE International Conference on Image Processing (ICIP), pp. 2906–2910. IEEE (2017)
15. Grafsgaard, J.F., Wiggins, J.B., Vail, A.K., Boyer, K.E., Wiebe, E.N., Lester, J.C.: The additive value of multimodal features for predicting engagement, frustration, and learning during tutoring. In: Proceedings of the 16th International Conference on Multimodal Interaction, pp. 42–49 (2014)
16. Hoffman, J.E., Subramaniam, B.: The role of visual attention in saccadic eye movements. Percept. Psychophysics. **57**(6), 787–795 (1995)

17. Hu, Y., Chen, L., Zhou, Y., Zhang, H.: Estimating face pose by facial asymmetry and geometry. In: Proceedings of Sixth IEEE International Conference on Automatic Face and Gesture Recognition, 2004, pp. 651–656. IEEE (2004)
18. Hutt, S., Mills, C., Bosch, N., Krasich, K., Brockmole, J., D'mello, S.: Out of the fr-eye-ing pan towards gaze-based models of attention during learning with technology in the classroom. In: Proceedings of the 25th Conference on User Modeling, Adaptation and Personalization, pp. 94–103 (2017)
19. Khan, A.Z., Blohm, G., McPeek, R.M., Lefevre, P.: Differential influence of attention on gaze and head movements. J. Neurophysiol. **101**(1), 198–206 (2009)
20. Khorrami, P., Paine, T., Huang, T.: Do deep neural networks learn facial action units when doing expression recognition? In: Proceedings of the IEEE International Conference on Computer Vision Workshops, pp. 19–27 (2015)
21. Kumar, A., Alavi, A., Chellappa, R.: Kepler: keypoint and pose estimation of unconstrained faces by learning efficient H-CNN regressors. In: 2017 12th IEEE International Conference on Automatic Face & Gesture Recognition (FG 2017), pp. 258–265. IEEE (2017)
22. Martins, P., Batista, J.: Accurate single view model-based head pose estimation. In: 2008 8th IEEE International Conference on Automatic Face & Gesture Recognition, pp. 1–6. IEEE (2008)
23. Meng, Z., Liu, P., Cai, J., Han, S., Tong, Y.: Identity-aware convolutional neural network for facial expression recognition. In: 2017 12th IEEE International Conference on Automatic Face & Gesture Recognition (FG 2017), pp. 558–565. IEEE (2017)
24. Mukherjee, S.S., Robertson, N.M.: Deep head pose: Gaze-direction estimation in multimodal video. IEEE Trans. Multimedia. **17**(11), 2094–2107 (2015)
25. Ranjan, R., Patel, V.M., Chellappa, R.: Hyperface: a deep multi-task learning framework for face detection, landmark localization, pose estimation, and gender recognition. IEEE Trans. Pattern Anal. Mach. Intell. **41**(1), 121–135 (2017)
26. Rayner, K.: Eye movements in reading and information processing: 20 years of research. Psychol. Bull. **124**(3), 372 (1998)
27. Ruiz, N., Chong, E., Rehg, J.M.: Fine-grained head pose estimation without keypoints. In: Proceedings of the IEEE Conference on Computer Vision and Pattern Recognition Workshops, pp. 2074–2083 (2018)
28. Shan, C., Gong, S., McOwan, P.W.: Facial expression recognition based on local binary patterns: A comprehensive study. Image Vis. Comput. **27**(6), 803–816 (2009)
29. Sharma, K., Alavi, H.S., Jermann, P., Dillenbourg, P.: A gaze-based learning analytics model: in-video visual feedback to improve learner's attention in MOOCs. In: Proceedings of the Sixth International Conference on Learning Analytics & Knowledge, pp. 417–421 (2016)
30. Whitehill, J., Serpell, Z., Lin, Y.C., Foster, A., Movellan, J.R.: The faces of engagement: automatic recognition of student engagement from facial expressions. IEEE Trans. Affect. Comput. **5**(1), 86–98 (2014)
31. Wixon, M., Arroyo, I.: When the question is part of the answer: examining the impact of emotion self-reports on student emotion. In: Dimitrova, V., Kuflik, T., Chin, D., Ricci, F., Dolog, P., Houben, G.-J. (eds.) UMAP 2014. LNCS, vol. 8538, pp. 471–477. Springer, Cham (2014). https://doi.org/10.1007/978-3-319-08786-3_42
32. Woolf, B., Burleson, W., Arroyo, I., Dragon, T., Cooper, D., Picard, R.: Affect-aware tutors: recognising and responding to student affect. Int. J. Learn. Technol. **4**(3–4), 129–164 (2009)

33. Yang, T.Y., Chen, Y.T., Lin, Y.Y., Chuang, Y.Y.: FSA-net: learning fine-grained structure aggregation for head pose estimation from a single image. In: Proceedings of the IEEE Conference on Computer Vision and Pattern Recognition, pp. 1087–1096 (2019)

34. Zatarain-Cabada, R., Barrón-Estrada, M.L., Camacho, J.L.O., Reyes-García, C.A.: Affective tutoring system for android mobiles. In: Huang, D.-S., Jo, K.-H., Wang, L. (eds.) ICIC 2014. LNCS (LNAI), vol. 8589, pp. 1–10. Springer, Cham (2014). https://doi.org/10.1007/978-3-319-09339-0_1

35. Zhang, F., Zhang, T., Mao, Q., Xu, C.: Joint pose and expression modeling for facial expression recognition. In: Proceedings of the IEEE Conference on Computer Vision and Pattern Recognition, pp. 3359–3368 (2018)

36. Zhi, R., Flierl, M., Ruan, Q., Kleijn, W.B.: Graph-preserving sparse nonnegative matrix factorization with application to facial expression recognition. IEEE Trans. Syst. Man Cybern. B Cybern. **41**(1), 38–52 (2010)

37. Zhong, L., Liu, Q., Yang, P., Liu, B., Huang, J., Metaxas, D.N.: Learning active facial patches for expression analysis. In: 2012 IEEE Conference on Computer Vision and Pattern Recognition, pp. 2562–2569. IEEE (2012)

38. Zhu, X., Lei, Z., Liu, X., Shi, H., Li, S.Z.: Face alignment across large poses: a 3D solution. In: Proceedings of the IEEE Conference on Computer Vision and Pattern Recognition, pp. 146–155 (2016)

39. Zhu, X., Liu, X., Lei, Z., Li, S.Z.: Face alignment in full pose range: a 3D total solution. IEEE Trans. Pattern Anal. Mach. Intell. **41**(1), 78–92 (2017)

Enhancing Personalization by Integrating Top-Down and Bottom-Up Approaches to Learner Modeling

Diego Zapata-Rivera[✉] and Burcu Arslan

Educational Testing Service, Princeton, NJ 08541, USA
{dzapata,barslan}@ets.org

Abstract. Learner models are representations of the learner's knowledge, skills and other attributes used by Adaptive Instructional Systems (AISs) to personalize their interactions with the learners (e.g., by implementing adaptive feedback, and recommending tasks/activities). Top-down and bottom-up approaches to learner modeling provide various affordances and challenges in terms of the need for interpretable learner models, the amount of data available, the complexity of the model, and the amount of human effort needed to implement and validate learner models. Research shows that hybrid approaches involving both top-down and bottom-up approaches are needed to effectively deal with the challenges of learner modeling in AISs. This paper describes several learner modeling approaches for integrating top-down and bottom-up approaches to gather additional evidence for supporting assessment claims and implementing personalization approaches. We elaborate on several learner modeling issues, including (a) evidence identification and aggregation in assessment systems; (b) making sense of process data aimed at supporting assessment claims related to learner cognition; and (c) approaches for improving interpretability and explainability of student models with some implications for validity and fairness of AISs.

Keywords: Learner modeling · Personalization · Hybrid approaches · Human-in-the-loop

1 Introduction

Learner models are representations of the learner's knowledge, skills and other attributes (KSAs) used by Adaptive Instructional Systems (AISs) to personalize their interactions with the learners (e.g., by implementing adaptive feedback, and recommending tasks/activities). Learner models may include cognitive, metacognitive, affective, personality, social and perceptual aspects of the learner [1, 17, 73]. Learner modeling challenges involve modeling and reasoning under uncertainty, aggregating evidence from various sources, and keeping an up-to-date representation of the learner that can be used by other modules of the AISs to implement recommendations (e.g., a pedagogical module), and by teachers and learners to examine the system's representation of the learner [14].

© Springer Nature Switzerland AG 2021
R. A. Sottilare and J. Schwarz (Eds.): HCII 2021, LNCS 12793, pp. 234–246, 2021.
https://doi.org/10.1007/978-3-030-77873-6_17

Top-down and bottom-up approaches to learner modeling have been used to implement personalization and adaptation features in AISs. These approaches include probabilistic models, computational cognitive models, machine learning (ML) models, constraint-based models, stereotype models, and overlay models [1, 17, 52, 73]. Several of these approaches have been combined in the implementation of learner models. Top-down and bottom-up approaches provide various affordances and challenges in terms of interpretability, the required amount of data and human effort to implement and validate learner models [27, 36, 67, 79]. For example, bottom-up, complex ML models (e.g., deep neural networks) require a lot of data and relatively less human effort; however, it is hard to interpret these types of models (e.g., see [66]). On the contrary, top-down learner models require a lot of human effort and less amount of data; however, they are interpretable. It has been shown that human-in-the-loop hybrid approaches that combine the strengths of both top-down and bottom-up approaches have a potential to effectively deal with the challenges of learner modeling in AISs (see [68] for details). Figure 1 shows a high-level representation of bottom-up, top-down, and human-in-the-loop hybrid approaches in terms of the required amount of data and human effort. The direction of the involvement of human and/or data in learner modeling is indicated with the dashed lines with arrows.

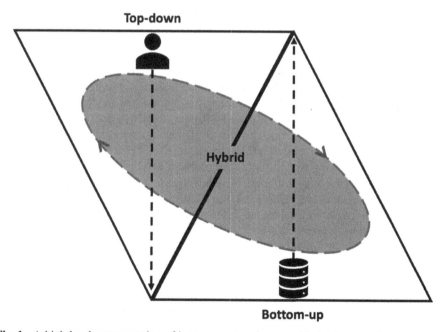

Fig. 1. A high-level representation of bottom-up, top-down, and hybrid approaches in terms of the required amount of data and human effort. The direction of the involvement of human and/or data in learner modeling is indicated with the dashed lines with arrows.

In this paper, we review several learner modeling approaches. Subsequently, we describe several approaches for integrating top-down and bottom-up learner modeling techniques to gather additional evidence for supporting assessment claims and implementing personalization approaches. The approaches examined include: (a) evidence identification and aggregation in assessment systems; (b) making sense of process data aimed at supporting assessment claims related to learner cognition; (c) improving interpretability and explainability of student models with some implications for validity and fairness of learner models. Finally, we discuss general aspects to consider for the successful design and implementation of learner models in AISs and future work in this area.

2   Learner Modeling Approaches

Several learner modeling approaches have been used in the past. These approaches varied in terms of the variables used to represent the learner's knowledge, skills and other attributes (KSAs), the techniques employed to model these KSAs, and the contexts where they have been applied and evaluated. Some learner modeling approaches include:

- *Overlay approaches* [15, 74]. These approaches represent the learner model as a subset of the expert model, usually as an overlay on the concepts or domain knowledge with a knowledge network or hierarchical tree of knowledge. This overlay shows the differences and commonalities between the learner and the expert models. Differential modeling (what learners should know and what learners could not be expected to know; [11]) and perturbation models that extend the scope of the model to include other aspects such as bugs and misconceptions [10, 35]. Overlay approaches have been implemented using various methods for modeling uncertainty (e.g., [19, 63, 90]).
- *Stereotype approaches* [31, 38, 65]. Stereotypes approaches are frequently used to assign learners to particular groups based on some characteristics (e.g., preferences, prior knowledge, types of errors) that can be available before the learning session. These stereotypes can be used to initialize the learner model. Thus, they can serve as a mechanism for dealing with the cold-start problem in AISs (i.e., not having enough information about the learner to implement adaptive features).
- *Constraint-based modeling (CBM; [53, 60]).* CBM uses constraints to represent the learner model. These constraints are associated with correct solutions/knowledge. Each constraint has a satisfaction condition, a relevant condition and associated feedback that includes information about what aspect of the solution is wrong, and an explanation indicating the correct answer or principle.
- *ACT-R cognitive modeling [3–5]. ACT-R is a hybrid (i.e., symbolic and subsymbolic) cognitive architecture that implements a unified theory of cognition that explains how all components of the mind (e.g., working memory and declarative memory, and procedural knowledge) work together to produce coherent cognition. In ACT-R theory, declarative knowledge (knowing what) and procedural knowledge (knowing how) are represented differently. While factual knowledge is represented in the form of chunks (e.g., the chunk "The capital of France is Paris.") in declarative memory which has a sub-symbolic structure, procedural knowledge is represented in the form of production rules (i.e., IF-THEN rules) which has a symbolic structure. Importantly, ACT-R learner models can make predictions about learner's response and response*

time by simulating learners' cognitive processes (e.g., retrieving factual knowledge from declarative memory and holding that information in working memory) when performing a task at a fine-grained level. These fine-grained predictions can be fit to the data from a human learner to track learner's improvement and/or update ACT-R's learner model.

- *Probabilistic learner models.* Probabilistic approaches have been used to model learners' KSAs. For example, Bayesian networks have been used to model knowledge levels and performance on activities or tasks [2, 19, 46, 48, 63, 90, 93]. Some of these approaches are based on a mapping between tasks and KSAs represented by a Q-matrix [76]. Latent trait approaches such as classical test theory [50, 60, 77], and item response theory [34] have been extensively used in assessment and some AISs [33]. Knowledge Spaces [24, 25] do not require a mapping from tasks to KSAs. Instead, the structure of the model is made of links among tasks representing precedence or prerequisite relationships. These links are learned from student performance data. Information about student performance on tasks can be used to identify the region including the tasks that students are able to solve correctly. Bayesian Knowledge Tracing (BKT) is a probabilistic approach based on the ACT-R cognitive modeling approach [21]. BKT has been used to model mastery of knowledge components. BKT has been widely studied and extended to take into account aspects such as forgetting, task difficulty, and representing the relationships among skills [36, 41, 62, 81]. Markov decision models have been used to model various aspects of the learner including cognitive and motivation aspects [45]. Fuzzy approaches offer another way to handle uncertainty in learner modeling [28]. Fuzzy learner models make use of fuzzy logic to model cognitive and noncognitive aspects of the learner [82].

- *Machine learning models.* ML models including supervised, unsupervised, and reinforcement learning have been used in learner modeling [70, 80]. Some recent cases use deep neural networks to implement predictive student models in game-based learning environments [27] as well as an approach that makes use of clustering and association rules to implement a student model in the context of Massive Open Online Courses (MOOCs; [44]).

The above-mentioned approaches have been used to infer learner KSAs as well as to predict their future performance. They have been combined in the implementation of the adaptive features of AISs in particular contexts [70]. These contexts vary in terms of the degree of data available and the existence of appropriate theoretical approaches and human experts in the area. Thus, ML approaches are expected to be used in situations where more data are available. However, insights gathered through the years designing and applying learner modeling techniques by experts should not be ignored. Instead, these insights should be used to inform ML approaches. Similarly, data patterns discovered by applying bottom-up approaches can be used to examine the theory behind these learner models and help understand the role of such new data patterns in the theory (e.g., see [42, 43]). As represented in Fig. 1, hybrid approaches can be employed to implement learner modeling solutions that build on the strengths of both bottom-up and top-down approaches.

The next section discusses approaches for identifying and aggregating evidence based on Evidence-Centered Design principles [55, 56].

3 Evidence Identification and Aggregation

Evidence-Centered Design (ECD; [55, 56]) provides a top-down, theory-driven approach to assessment design. This approach supports the design of assessments that can be used to collect high-quality evidence about learners KSAs from a limited set of student responses. ECD's approach to evidence identification and evidence aggregation provides a principled approach to identify relevant observations about learners' performance and aggregate them to use them as evidence to support assessment claims. However, relevant observed data can originate from different sources including process data on how learners arrived at a response (e.g., navigation, timing, and keystrokes). Following a principled process for integrating process data into decision-making processes used by adaptive learning systems can improve the quality of inferences supported by the system.

Zapata-Rivera et al. [92] propose a hybrid approach to integrate process and response data in assessment for learning systems designed based on ECD principles. This approach involves (a) using traditional psychometric methods to determine how current tasks measure the intended constructs, (b) determining the need for making changes to particular tasks (e.g., removing tasks that are too hard or additional tasks to achieve target reliability levels), (c) understanding how selected, construct relevant process features relate to the target construct(s), (d) refining/expanding the construct based on insights gathered from process data about underlying cognitive processes learners have exhibited. Some approaches used to implement game-based assessment also rely on ECD principles (e.g., [40, 57, 71]).

Improving evidence and aggregation processes in AISs contributes to improving their validity [37]. In general, formalizing the notion of evidence in AISs as the basis for supporting learner claims maintained in the learner model, which in turn plays an important role in the implementation of adaptive mechanisms in AISs, can benefit developers and researchers by facilitating the implementation of these systems. It also benefits teachers and learners by improving the effectiveness of the learning system and by supporting the generation of actionable instructional insights [88].

The next section discusses additional hybrid approaches that have been used to making sense of process data.

4 Making Sense of Process Data

Several hybrid approaches have been explored in making sense of process data. These approaches provide additional information about problem-solving behaviors and cognitive processes used by learners in answering questions or solving problems.

For instance, identifying profiles for learners who have similar problem-solving behaviors at various levels of proficiency is a common strategy for generating actionable feedback for instructors and learners. Bottom-up cluster analysis techniques can be applied to data that have been coded by humans or have been generated by automated scoring or classification processes. These hybrid cluster techniques can be used to create profiles by characterizing different types of learners in terms of their strengths and weaknesses on relevant skills (e.g., see [26] for application of this method for identifying different types of learners in the context of assessing Collaborative Problem-Solving skills with a methodology referred to as theoretically grounded data mining). Insights about profiles representing clusters of behaviors that characterize learner performance can potentially enhance information in score reports or dashboards for teachers and learners.

In addition to creating profiles of different problem-solving behaviors based on logged learner actions in process data, hybrid approaches have been used to infer learner cognitive states during problem solving (e.g., see [6, 75] for combining data-driven methods and ACT-R theory) by using the time elapsed between two adjacent actions, namely pauses. Insights about learner pauses can be used as descriptive models to better understand differences between learners and capture variation in skills in more detail as well as to inform task design.

Learners' actions in game-based learning environments have been used in conjunction with an underlying ECD model to assess learners' KSAs [57, 72]. These approaches usually require the input from human experts to identify the learner actions that are relevant to particular KSAs. For example, Min et al. [53] have used deep learning techniques to automatically identify sequences of actions associated with KSAs, reducing the human effort required to elicit these models.

The next section discusses issues related to improving the interpretability of learner models and their implications for improving validity and fairness.

5 Improving Interpretability of Learner Models

Together with the advances in ML algorithms and their predictive power, the trade-off between the required human effort in learner modeling and the need for interpretable models has started to be a central issue in AI and learning analytics [16, 20, 68]. Understanding the rationales behind inferences about learner knowledge, skills and other attributes (KSAs) and recommendations in intelligent systems (e.g., AISs) is crucial for *trust* in these systems [64]. Therefore, interpretability and explainability of the learner models is important for learners, teachers, parents, and decision makers for adopting AISs.

For instance, Open Learner Models (OLM) can contribute to improving trust by supporting learners' and teachers' inspection of learner models and adaptive decisions made by the system thus facilitating adoption of AISs [87]. In addition, research in the area of OLM has shown to contribute to learners' self-awareness, self-reflection, and learning [14, 18]. Moreover, OLM can provide insights for the design of dashboards and reporting systems that provide learners and teachers with information about the learner model and how it is being used to implement adaptive components. Learning and assessment systems should be able to provide information to users interested in knowing more about personalization aspects. Different types of user interfaces can be designed to respond to the needs of different types of users [89].

Different methodologies have been used to make learner models interpretable and explainable. One approach is trying to make *black box* ML models interpretable. For example, Gunning [32] describes a general approach to improving explainability of ML approaches by adding models on top of existing models with support for human inspection so they can help humans interpret these complex models. However, Rudin

[66] argues that researchers should not try to make black box ML models interpretable; instead, they should build models that are inherently interpretable.

Human-in-the-loop hybrid approaches also have implications for issues around validity and fairness of these models. For example, a common practice used to evaluate the performance of automated scoring systems is to compare the results of the scoring engine to those produced by human experts [84]. A close alignment to human ratings is usually considered as evidence of good performance. However, there are cases where machine-generated scores and human scores do not match. These cases could result from patterns in the data that are identified by applying ML approaches but are not covered by the definition of the construct. Thus, these approaches might produce consistently lower or higher scores for certain subgroups of learners, which is critical for fairness (see [51] for the details of different dimensions of algorithmic fairness and its applications in education). Some of these patterns could capture construct irrelevant aspects and can be addressed by implementing *quality-control processes* [8]. However, in some cases, these patterns may reveal interesting aspects that were not previously considered, in such cases it is possible to use information from such patterns to refine the definition of the construct to include additional cases or categories. Bauer and Zapata-Rivera [7] suggest implementing mechanisms for identifying such cases and making sure they are connected to appropriate assessment argument structures [58]. This evidence interpretation layer can improve the validity of AISs that make use of ML approaches [88].

Another case where ML approaches could benefit from approaches that rely on expert pedagogical knowledge is the creation of personalized learning paths. ML has been applied to the generation of such paths [49, 59, 69, 83]. However, prior work in the area of instructional planning has produced instructional decisions made by the system based on instructional goals, actions exhibited by learners, characteristics of the domain knowledge, and the contents of the learner model. Various pedagogical approaches including cognitive apprenticeship, tutoring and coaching have been explored [78]. This prior work on instructional planning can inform current approaches to produce personalized learning plans.

Work on interpretable and explainable learner modeling requires the input of experts with different backgrounds including human-computer interaction, cognitive and learning science, artificial intelligence and data sciences. Rosé et al. [68] recommend interdisciplinary learning engineering teams working on enhancing interpretability of learner models. The work of these interdisciplinary teams together with a close interaction with users can result in AISs that produce effective learning systems that provide users with interpretable, relevant, and actionable feedback.

The next section discusses general aspects to consider in the implementation of learner models for AISs.

6   Discussion

The selection and implementation of appropriate learner modeling techniques and related approaches are key to the successful implementation of AISs. It is through learner models that effective adaptive features, recommendations, personalized guidance and actionable feedback to teachers and learners can be possible [30]. Some general aspects to consider in designing and evaluating learner models include:

- Learner modeling approaches are characterized by different levels of integration between top-down and bottom-up techniques. Data about learners gathered from different sources should be made part of a sound chain of reasoning to be used as evidence to support personalization in AISs. This would facilitate answering questions such as how much evidence is needed before the system can intervene or provide a recommendation to the user. Also, even when enough evidence is available, additional information about the learning context would be useful in determining whether to intervene and how to intervene. For example, research on modeling emotions provides some insights in this area [22, 29, 47]. Also, broadening the learner model to include noncognitive and social aspects of the learners can provide more information about the learning context which may result in more effective AISs [13, 73, 91].
- Multidisciplinary teams with expertise in areas such as cognitive and learning science, human-computer interaction, domain knowledge, data science, learner/user modeling, learning engineering, adaptive learning systems, and assessment, should work together in identifying, implementing and evaluating learner modeling approaches for AISs. Contributions from team members with particular skillsets will be relevant at different stages of the process. Focusing on the needs from teachers and learners can help guide decisions about aspects to include in the learner models and appropriate ways to implement personalized features. Short research and development iteration cycles with the intended users are well suited to support this type of work. In addition, large-scale studies are necessary to evaluate the effectiveness of the approach under various conditions [12, 23, 73].
- Learner model interpretability can be addressed using various approaches including (a) aligning evidence of learner performance to learner KSAs, (b) implementing learner modeling techniques that can be easily inspected and used to explain adaptive features/recommendations, and (c) involving the work of humans who can help interpret results of models and assess theoretical and practical implications. By improving interpretability, it is expected to create AISs that are scrutable and can be evaluated to avoid possible fairness and bias issues [39]. Graphical interfaces and other reporting systems designed to communicate learner model information should be evaluated with the intended users to ensure they understand the information provided and make appropriate decisions based on this information [9, 86].

7 Future Work

Future work in this area includes (a) exploring additional learner modeling approaches that leverage the strengths of top-down and bottom-up hybrid approaches, (b) improving validity aspects of AISs by supporting the development of evidence arguments that integrate data from various sources to support learner model information, and (c) building on best practices and results from areas such as OLM to provide users with actionable insights that make use of learner model information to support learning.

References

1. Abyaa, A., Khalidi Idrissi, M., Bennani, S.: Learner modelling: systematic review of the literature from the last 5 years. Educ. Tech. Research Dev. **67**(5), 1105–1143 (2019). https://doi.org/10.1007/s11423-018-09644-1

2. Almond, R.G., Zapata-Rivera, J.-D.: Bayesian Networks. In: von Davier, M., Lee, Y.-S. (eds.) Handbook of diagnostic classification models. MEMA, pp. 81–106. Springer, Cham (2019). https://doi.org/10.1007/978-3-030-05584-4_4
3. Anderson, J.R.: How can the human mind occur in the physical universe? Oxford University Press, New York (2007). https://doi.org/10.1093/acprof:oso/9780195324259.001.0001
4. Anderson, J.R., Corbett, A.T., Koedinger, K.R., Pelletier, R.: Cognitive tutors: lessons learned. J. Learn. Sci. **4**, 167–207 (1995)
5. Anderson, J.R., Lebiere, C.J.: The Atomic Components of Thought. Erlbaum, Mahwah (1998)
6. Arslan, B., Jiang, Y., Keehner, M., Gong, T., Katz, I.R., Yan, F.: The effect of drag-and-drop item features on test-taker performance and response strategies. Educ. Measur. Issues Pract. **39**, 96–106 (2020)
7. Bauer, M., Zapata-Rivera, D.: Cognitive foundations of automated scoring. In: Yan, D., Rupp, A.A., Foltz, P.W. (eds.) Handbook of Automated Scoring: Theory into Practice, pp. 13–28. Taylor and Francis Group, New York (2020)
8. Bejar, I.I.: Threats to score meaning in automated scoring. In: Ercikan, K., Pellegrino, J.W. (eds.) Validation of Score Meaning for the Next Generation of Assessments, pp. 75–84. Routledge, New York (2017)
9. Bodily, R., et al.: Open learner models and learning analytics dashboards: a systematic review. In: Proceedings of the 8th International Conference on Learning Analytics and Knowledge, pp. 41–50 (2018)
10. Brown, J.S., Burton, R.: Diagnostic models for procedural bugs in basic mathematical skills. Cognitive Sci. **2**, 155–192 (1978)
11. Brown, J.S., et al.: Steps towards a theoretical foundation for complex, knowledge-based CAI. Bolt, Beranek and Newman, Cambridge (1975)
12. Brusilovsky, P., Karagiannidis, C., Sampson, D.: Layered evaluation of adaptive learning systems. Int. J. Continuing Eng. Educ. Lifelong Learn. **14**(4–5), 402–421 (2004)
13. Bull, S., Brna, P., Pain, H.: Extending the scope of the student model. User Model. User-Adap. Inter. **5**, 45–65 (1995)
14. Bull, S., Kay, J.: SMILI☺: a framework for interfaces to learning data in open learner models, learning analytics and related fields. Int. J. Artif. Intell. Educ. **26**(1), 293–331 (2016)
15. Carr, B., Goldstein, I.: Overlays: a theory of modeling for computer-aided instruction, Technical Report, AI Lab Memo 406. MIT (1977)
16. Chen, H., Tan, E., Lee, Y., Praharaj, S., Specht, M., Zhao, G.: Developing AI into explanatory supporting models: An explanation-visualized deep learning prototype. In: The International Conference of Learning Science (ICLS) (2020)
17. Chrysafiadi, K., Virvou, M.: Student modeling approaches: a literature review for the last decade. Expert Syst. Appl. **40**(11), 4715–4729 (2013)
18. Conati, C., Porayska-Pomsta, K., Mavrikis, M.: AI in education needs interpretable machine learning: lessons from open learner modelling. Arxiv. http://arxiv.org/abs/1807.00154 (2018)
19. Conati, C., Gertner, A., VanLehn, K.: Using Bayesian networks to manage uncertainly in student modeling. User Model. User-Adap. Inter. **12**(4), 371–417 (2002)
20. Confalonieri, R., Coba, L., Wagner, B., Besold, T.R.: A historical perspective of explainable artificial intelligence. WIREs Data Min. Knowl. Disc. **11**, e1391 (2021). https://doi.org/10.1002/widm.1391
21. Corbett, A.T., Anderson, J.R.: Knowledge tracing: modeling the acquisition of procedural knowledge. User Model. User-Adap. Inter. **4**, 253–278 (1995)
22. D'Mello, S., Graesser, A.: Dynamics of affective states during complex learning. Learn. Instr. **22**(2), 145–157 (2012)
23. Durlach, P.J., Ray, J.M.: Designing adaptive instructional environments: insights from empirical evidence. Technical Report 1297. U. S. Army Research Institute for the Behavioral Social Sciences, Arlington, VA (2011)

24. Falmagne, J.C., Koppen, M., Villano, M., Doignon, J.P., Johannesen, L.: Introduction to knowledge spaces: how to build, test, and search them. Psychol. Rev. **97**(2), 201–224 (1990)
25. Falmagne, J.C., Albert, D., Doble, C., Eppstein, D., Hu, X. (ed.): Knowledge Spaces: Applications in Education. Springer, Heidelberg (2013). https://doi.org/10.1007/978-3-642-353 29-1
26. Forsyth, C.M., Andrews-Todd, J., Steinberg, J.: Are you really a team player? Profiles of collaborative problem solvers in an online environment. In: Rafferty, A.N., Whitehill, J., Cavalli-Sforza, V., Romero, C. (Eds.). Proceedings of the 13th International Conference on Educational Data Mining (EDM 2020), pp. 403–408 (2020)
27. Geden, M., Emerson, A., Carpenter, D., Rowe, J., Azevedo, R., Lester, J.: Predictive student modeling in game-based learning environments with word embedding representations of reflection. Int. J. Artif. Intell. Educ. (2020). https://doi.org/10.1007/s40593-020-00220-4
28. Gisolfi, A., Dattolo, A., Balzano, W.: A fuzzy approach to student modeling. Comput. Educ. **19**(4), 329–334 (1992)
29. Graesser, A.: Emotions are the experiential glue of learning environments in the 21st century. Learn. Instr. **70**, 101212 (2020)
30. Greer, J., McCalla, G. (eds.): Student Models: The Key to Individualized Educational Systems. Springer, New York (1994)
31. Grubišić, A., Stankov, S., Žitko, B.: Stereotype student model for an adaptive e-learning system. Int. J. Comput. Electr. Autom. Control Inf. Eng. **7**(4), 440–447 (2013)
32. Gunning, D.: "Explainable artificial intelligence (XAI)". *Defense Advanced Research Projects Agency* (DARPA) (2017)
33. Guzmán, E., Conejo, R.: Measuring misconceptions through item response theory. In: International Conference on Artificial Intelligence in Education, pp. 608–611 (2015)
34. Hambleton, R.K., Swaminathan, H., Rogers, H.J.: Measurement Methods for the Social Sciences Series, Vol. 2. Fundamentals of Item Response Theory. Sage Publications, Inc. (1991)
35. Johnson, W., Soloway, E.: Intention-based diagnosis of programming errors. Paper presented at the AAAI (1984)
36. Käser, T., Klingler, S., Schwing, A.G., Gross, M.: Dynamic Bayesian networks for student modeling. IEEE Trans. Learn. Technol. **10**(4), 450–462 (2017). https://doi.org/10.1109/TLT. 2017.2689017
37. Katz, I.R., LaMar, M.M., Spain, R., Zapata-Rivera, D., Baird, J., Greiff, S.: Validity issues and concerns for technology-based performance assessments. In: Sottilare, R., Graesser, A., Hu, X., Goodwin, G. (Eds.) Design Recommendations for Intelligent Tutoring Systems: vol. 5 - Assessment Methods. U.S. Army Research Laboratory, Orlando (2017). ISBN 978–0–9893923–9–6. 209–224
38. Kay, J.: Stereotypes, student models and scrutability. In: International Conference on Intelligent Tutoring Systems, pp. 19–30 (2000)
39. Kay, J., Zapata-Rivera, D., Conati, C.: The GIFT of scrutable learner models: why and how. In: Sinatra, R.A.M., Graesser, A.C., Hu, X., Goldberg, B., Hampton, A.J. (Eds.) Design Recommendations for Intelligent Tutoring Systems: vol. 8, pp. 25–40. – Data Visualization. U.S. Army CCDC - Soldier Center, Orlando (2020)
40. Kerr, D., Andrews, J.J., Mislevy, R.J.: The in-task assessment framework for behavioral data. Handbook of Cognition and Assessment, pp. 472–507 (2016)
41. Khajah, M., Lindsey, R.V., Mozer, M.C.: How deep is knowledge tracing? In: Proceedings of Educational Data Mining, pp. 94–101 (2016)
42. Koedinger, K.R., McLaughlin, E.A., Stamper, J.C.: Automated student model improvement. In: Yacef, K., Zaïane, O., Hershkovitz, H., Yudelson, M., Stamper, J. (Eds.) Proceedings of the 5th International Conference on Educational Data Mining, Chania, Greece, pp. 17–24 (2012)

43. Koedinger, K.R., Stamper, J.C., McLaughlin, E.A., Nixon, T.: Using data-driven discovery of better student models to improve student learning. In: Proceedings of the 16th International Conference on Artificial Intelligence in Education, pp. 421–430 (2013)
44. Lallé, S., Conati, C.: A data-driven student model to provide adaptive support during video watching across MOOCs. In: Bittencourt, I.I., Cukurova, M., Muldner, K., Luckin, R., Millán, E. (eds.) AIED 2020. LNCS (LNAI), vol. 12163, pp. 282–295. Springer, Cham (2020). https://doi.org/10.1007/978-3-030-52237-7_23
45. LaMar, M.M.: Markov decision process measurement model. Psychometrika **83**(1), 67–88 (2018)
46. Lee, M., Wagenmakers, E.: Bayesian Cognitive Modeling: A Practical Course. Cambridge University Press, Cambridge (2014). https://doi.org/10.1017/CBO9781139087759
47. Lehman, B., Zapata-Rivera, D.: Student emotions in conversation-based assessments. IEEE Trans. Learn. Technol. **11**(1), 1–13 (2018)
48. Levy, R., Mislevy, R.J.: Bayesian Psychometric Modeling. CRC Press, Boca Raton (2016)
49. Lin, C.F., Yeh, Y.C., Hung, Y.H., Chang, R.I.: Data mining for providing a personalized learning path in creativity: an application of decision trees. Comput. Educ. **68**, 199–210 (2013)
50. Lord, F.M., Novick, M.R.: Statistical Theories of Mental Test Scores. Addison-Welsley Publishing Company, Reading (1968)
51. Loukina, A., Madnani, N., Zechner, K.: The many dimensions of algorithmic fairness in educational applications. In: Proceedings of the Workshop on Innovative Use of NLP for Building Educational Applications, Florence, Italy, pp. 1–10 (2019)
52. MacLellan, C.J., Koedinger, K.R.: Domain-general tutor authoring with apprentice learner models. Int. J. Artif. Intell. Educ. (2020). https://doi.org/10.1007/s40593-020-00214-2
53. Min, W., et al.: DeepStealth: game-based learning stealth assessment with deep neural networks. IEEE Trans. Learn. Technol. **13**(2), 312–325 (2020)
54. Mitrovic, A., Martin, B., Suraweera, P.: Intelligent tutors for all: constraint-based modeling methodology, systems and authoring. IEEE Intell. Syst. **22**, 38–45 (2007)
55. Mislevy, R.J.: Four metaphors we need to understand assessment. Commissioned paper for The Gordon Commission on the Future of Assessment in Education (2012). Educational Testing Service, Princeton, NJ. www.ets.org/Media/Research/pdf/mislevy_four_metaphors_understand_assessment.pdf. Retrieved 28 Apr 2020
56. Mislevy, R.J., Almond, R.G., Lukas, J.F.: A brief introduction to evidence-centered design. ETS Res. Rep. Ser. **2003**(1), i-29 (2003)
57. Mislevy, R.J., et al.: Psychometric considerations in game-based assessment (2014). [white paper] Retrieved from Institute of Play website. https://web.archive.org/web/20160320151604/http://www.instituteofplay.org/wp-content/uploads/2014/02/GlassLab_GBA1_WhitePaperFull.pdf (2014)
58. Mislevy, R.J., Riconscente, M.M.: Evidence-centered assessment design. In: Handbook of Test Development, pp. 75–104. Routledge (2011)
59. Nabizadeh, A.H., Gonçalves, D., Gama, S., Jorge, J., Rafsanjani, H.N.: Adaptive learning path recommender approach using auxiliary learning objects. Comput. Educ. **147**, 103777 (2020)
60. Novick, M.R.: The axioms and principal results of classical test theory. J. Math. Psychol. **3**(1), 1–18 (1966)
61. Ohlsson, S.: Constraint-based student modeling. J. Artif. Intell. Educ. 3(4), 429–447 (1992)
62. Pardos, Z.A., Heffernan, N.T.: KT-IDEM: introducing item difficulty to the knowledge tracing model. In: Konstan, J.A., Conejo, R., Marzo, J.L. Oliver, N. (Eds.) Proceedings of the 19th International Conference User Modeling, Adaption and Personalization, pp. 243–254 (2011)
63. Reye, J.: Student modelling based on belief networks. Int. J. Artif. Intell. Educ. **14**, 63–96 (2004)

64. Ribeiro, M.T., Singh, S., Guestrin, C.: Why should I trust you? Explaining the predictions of any classifier. In: Proceedings of the 22nd SIGKDD International Conference on Knowledge Discovery and Data Mining, pp. 1135–1144 (2016)
65. Rich, E.: User modeling via stereotypes. Cognitive Sci. **3**(4), 329–354 (1979)
66. Rudin, C.: Stop explaining black box machine learning models for high stakes decisions and use interpretable models instead. Nat. Mach. Intell. **1**, 206–215 (2019)
67. Rudin, C., Radin, J.: Why are we using black box models in AI when we don't need to? A lesson from an explainable AI competition. Harvard Data Sci. Rev. **1**(2) (2019)
68. Rosé, C.P., McLaughlin, E.A., Liu, R., Koedinger, K.R.: Explanatory learner models: why machine learning (alone) is not the answer. Br. J. Educ. Technol. **50**(6), 2943–2958 (2019)
69. Seridi-Bouchelaghem, H., Sari, T., Sellami, M.: A neural network for generating adaptive lessons. J. Comput. Sci. **1**(2), 232–243 (2005)
70. Sison, R., Shimura, M.: Student modeling and machine learning. Int. J. Artif. Intell. Educ. **9**, 128–158 (1998)
71. Shute, V.J., Ventura, M., Bauer, M.I., Zapata-Rivera, D.: Melding the power of serious games and embedded assessment to monitor and foster learning: Flow and grow. In: Ritterfeld, U., Cody, M.J., Vorderer, P. (eds.) Serious Games: Mechanisms and Effects, pp. 295–321. Routledge, Philadelphia (2009)
72. Shute, V., Wang, L., Greiff, S., Zhao, W., Moore, G.: Measuring problem solving skills via stealth assessment in an engaging video game. Comput. Hum. Behav. **63**, 106–117 (2016)
73. Shute, V.J., Zapata-Rivera, D.: Adaptive educational systems. In: Durlach, P. (ed.) Adaptive Technologies for Training and Education, pp. 7–27. Cambridge University Press, New York (2012)
74. Stansfield, J.C., Carr, B., Goldstein, I.P.: Wumpus advisor I: a first implementation of a program that tutors logical and probabilistic reasoning skills. At Lab Memo 381, Massachusetts Institute of Technology, Cambridge, Massachusetts (1976)
75. Tenison, C., Arslan, B.: Characterizing pause behaviors in a science inquiry task. In: Stewart, T.C. (Ed.). Proceedings of the 18th International Conference on Cognitive Modeling, Applied Cognitive Science Lab, Penn State, University Park, PA, pp. 283–298 (2020)
76. Tatsuoka, K.K.: Rule space: an approach for dealing with misconceptions based on item response theory. J. Educ. Meas. **20**, 345–354 (1983)
77. Traub, R.: Classical test theory in historical perspective. Educ. Meas. Issues Pract. **16**(4), 8–14 (1997). https://doi.org/10.1111/j.1745-3992.1997.tb00603.x
78. Vassileva, J., Wasson, B.: Instructional planning approaches: From tutoring towards free learning. In: Proceedings of EuroAIED 1996, Lisbon, Portugal, 30 September–2 October 1996, pp. 1–8 (1996)
79. Vincent-Lancrin, S., van der Vlies, R.: Trustworthy artificial intelligence (AI) in education: Promises and challenges. OECD Education Working Papers, No. 218. OECD Publishing, Paris (2020). https://doi.org/10.1787/a6c90fa9-en
80. Webb, G.I., Pazzani, M.J., Billsus, D.: Machine learning for user modeling. User Model. User-Adap. Inter. **11**(1), 19–29 (2001)
81. Yudelson, M.V., Koedinger, K.R., Gordon, G.J.: Individualized Bayesian knowledge tracing models. In: International Conference on Artificial Intelligence in Education, 171–180 (2013)
82. Zadeh, L.A.: Fuzzysets. Information and Control, pp. 338–353 (1965)
83. Zakrzewska, D.: Cluster analysis in personalized e-learning systems. In: Nguyen, N.T., Szczerbicki, E. (Eds.) Intelligent Systems for Knowledge Management, 229–250 (2009)
84. Zhang, M.: Contrasting automated and human scoring of essays. R & D Connections **21**(2), 1–11 (2013)
85. Zhou, Y., Huang, C., Hu, Q., Zhu, J., Tang, Y.: Personalized learning full-path recommendation model based on LSTM neural networks. Inf. Sci. **444**, 135–152 (2018)

86. Zapata-Rivera, D.: Supporting human inspection of adaptive instructional systems. In: Sottilare, R.A., Schwarz, J. (eds.) HCII 2019. LNCS, vol. 11597, pp. 482–490. Springer, Cham (2019). https://doi.org/10.1007/978-3-030-22341-0_38

87. Zapata-Rivera, D.: Open student modeling research and its connections to educational assessment. Int. J. Artif. Intell. Educ. (2020). https://doi.org/10.1007/s40593-020-00206-2

88. Zapata-Rivera, D., Brawner, K., Jackson, G.T., Katz, I.R.: Reusing evidence in assessment and intelligent tutors. In: Sottilare, R., Graesser, A., Hu, X., Goodwin, G. (Eds.) Design Recommendations for Intelligent Tutoring Systems: Volume 5 - Assessment Methods. U.S. Army Research Laboratory, Orlando, FL (2017). ISBN 978–0–9893923–9–6. 125–136

89. Zapata-Rivera, D., Graesser, A., Kay, J., Hu, X., Ososky, S.: Visualization Implications for the Validity of ITS. In: Sinatra, R.A.M., Graesser, A.C., Hu, X., Goldberg, B., Hampton, A.J. (Eds.) Design Recommendations for Intelligent Tutoring Systems: Volume 8 – Data Visualization. U.S. Army CCDC - Soldier Center, Orlando, FL, pp. 61–68 (2020)

90. Zapata-Rivera, D., Greer, J.: Interacting with Bayesian student models. Int. J. Artif. Intell. Educ. **14**(2), 127–163 (2004)

91. Zapata-Rivera, D., Lehman, B., Sparks, J.R.: Learner modeling in the context of caring assessments. In: Sottilare, R.A., Schwarz, J. (eds.) HCII 2020. LNCS, vol. 12214, pp. 422–431. Springer, Cham (2020). https://doi.org/10.1007/978-3-030-50788-6_31

92. Zapata-Rivera, D., Liu, L., Chen, L., Hao, J., von Davier, A.A.: Assessing science inquiry skills in an immersive, conversation-based scenario. In: Kei Daniel, B. (ed.) Big Data and Learning Analytics in Higher Education, pp. 237–252. Springer, Cham (2017). https://doi.org/10.1007/978-3-319-06520-5_14

93. Zapata-Rivera, D., Vanwinkle, W., Shute, V., Underwood, J., Bauer, M.: English ABLE. In: Luckin, R., Koedinger, K., Greer, J. (Eds.) Artificial Intelligence in Education - Building Technology Rich Learning Contexts that Work, vol. 158, pp. 323–330 (2007)

Author Index

Printed in the United States
by Baker & Taylor Publisher Services